Governing Smart Specialisation

T0298944

In recent years, smart specialisation has been a key building block of regional economic and development policy across the European Union. Providing targeted support for innovation and research, it has helped identify those areas of greatest strategic potential, developing mechanisms to involve the fullest range of stakeholders, before setting strategic priorities and using smart specialisation to maximise the knowledge-based potential of a region or territory.

Governing Smart Specialisation contributes to the emerging debate about the role of the 'entrepreneurial discovery process' (EDP), which is at the heart of smart specialisation strategies for regional economic transformation. Particular focus is placed on what methods, procedures and institutional conditions are necessary in order to generate information that helps buttress policy decisions. It draws on existing literature that analyses the relevance of EDP within smart specialisation for regional policy. Chapters are complemented with case studies about regions with different geographical and socioeconomic characteristics in Europe: from Norwegian regions to the Greek region of Eastern Macedonia and Thrace.

As one of the first books to directly address the EDP, this is essential reading for students interested in regional economics, public policy, urban studies and technological innovation, as well as for policy makers in regional and national administrations.

Dimitrios Kyriakou is Senior Analyst of the Knowledge for Growth Unit at the Institute for Prospective Technological Studies Joint Research Centre, European Commission, Spain.

Manuel Palazuelos Martínez is Project leader of the Knowledge for Growth Unit at the Institute for Prospective Technological Studies Joint Research Centre, European Commission, Spain.

Inmaculada Periáñez-Forte is Scientific Officer of the Knowledge for Growth Unit at the Institute for Prospective Technological Studies Joint Research Centre, European Commission, Spain.

Alessandro Rainoldi is Head of the Knowledge for Growth Unit at the Institute for Prospective Technological Studies Joint Research Centre, European Commission, Spain.

THE GLOBAL FORUM FOR CITY
AND REGIONAL RESEARCH,
DEVELOPMENT AND POLICY

Regions and Cities

Series Editor in Chief
Susan M. Christopherson, *Cornell University, USA*

Editors
Maryann Feldman, *University of Georgia, USA*
Gernot Grabher, *HafenCity University Hamburg, Germany*
Ron Martin, *University of Cambridge, UK*
Martin Perry, *Massey University, New Zealand*
Kieran P. Donaghy, *Cornell University, USA*

In today's globalised, knowledge-driven and networked world, regions and cities have assumed heightened significance as the interconnected nodes of economic, social and cultural production, and as sites of new modes of economic and territorial governance and policy experimentation. This book series brings together incisive and critically engaged international and inter-disciplinary research on this resurgence of regions and cities, and should be of interest to geographers, economists, sociologists, political scientists and cultural scholars, as well as to policy-makers involved in regional and urban development.

For more information on the Regional Studies Association visit www.regionalstudies.org

There is a **30 per cent discount** available to RSA members on books in the *Regions and Cities* series, and other subject-related Taylor and Francis books and e-books including Routledge titles. To order just e-mail Cara.Trevor@tandf.co.uk, or phone on +44 (0) 20 7017 6924 and declare your RSA membership. You can also visit www.routledge.com and use the discount code: **RSA0901**

Governing Smart Specialisation

Edited by Dimitrios Kyriakou,
Manuel Palazuelos Martínez,
Inmaculada Periáñez-Forte and
Alessandro Rainoldi

Routledge
Taylor & Francis Group

LONDON AND NEW YORK

First published 2017
by Routledge

2 Park Square, Milton Park, Abingdon, Oxfordshire OX14 4RN
52 Vanderbilt Avenue, New York, NY 10017

Routledge is an imprint of the Taylor & Francis Group, an informa business

First issued in paperback 2019

British Library Cataloguing in Publication Data
A catalogue record for this book is available from the British Library

Library of Congress Cataloging in Publication Data
Names: Kyriakou, Dimitrios, 1964- editor.
Title: Governing smart specialisation / edited by Dimitrios Kyriakou, Manuel Palazuelos Martínez, Inmaculada Periáñez-Forte, and Alessandro Rainoldi.
Description: Abingdon, Oxon ; New York, NY : Routledge, 2017.
Identifiers: LCCN 2016014154| ISBN 9781138670877 (hardback) | ISBN 9781315617374 (ebook)
Subjects: LCSH: Regional economics. | Economic specialization. | Economic development. | Economic policy.
Classification: LCC HT388 .G68 2017 | DDC 330.9--dc23
LC record available at https://lccn.loc.gov/2016014154

ISBN: 978-1-138-67087-7 (hbk)
ISBN: 978-0-367-87626-5 (pbk)

Typeset in Times New Roman
by GreenGate Publishing Services, Tonbridge, Kent

Contents

Figures

Tables

Contributors

Mark Boden is a Project Leader within the Knowledge for Growth Unit at the IPTS, with particular responsibility for a European Parliament preparatory action on smart specialisation in the Region of Eastern Macedonia and Thrace. He has been at IPTS since 2002, and has led a number of projects on research and innovation policies and foresight. Prior to joining IPTS he was a Research Fellow at the University of Manchester, UK, where he worked on various aspects of the economics of technological change and science and technology policy. In 1988, he was awarded a PhD in the economics of technological change from the University of Manchester. He has also held visiting research fellowships in Japan and France.

David Charles is deputy head and professor of Innovation and Strategic Management of Lincoln Business School, University of Lincoln. He has previously held professorial appointments at Newcastle University, Curtin University and the University of Strathclyde and he is adjunct professor at the University of Tampere. His research interests include innovation management, innovation policy, regional development and university engagement with business and wider society. His work has been published in Research Policy, Regional Studies, Journal of Knowledge Management, Journal of Business Ethics, Cambridge Journal of Regions, Economy and Society, European Planning Studies and others. David has been involved in a number of high profile evaluations of European regional programmes over the last 25 years, most recently in the 'Evaluation of the main achievements of Cohesion Policy programmes and projects over the longer term in 15 selected regions', for DG Regio in 2011–2013. In the past he has particularly focused on the evaluation of innovation programmes, including the evaluation of the STRIDE community initiative and the RITTS programme.

Katerina Ciampi Stancova is a scientific officer at the Smart Specialisation Platform at the European Commission's Joint Research Centre – IPTS, Seville. Her research agenda includes smart specialisation, EU Research and Innovation Policy, EU Cohesion Policy, transnational and trans-regional cooperation, mutual learning, (global) value chains, less developed innovation systems (EU-13) and Digital Growth. In addition her research interests include human capital, international migration and regional dynamics on which she has published extensively. She received her PhD (2012) from Sant'Anna School of Advanced Studies in Pisa, her MA (2006) from the University of Pisa (International Relations and Politics) and her BA (2004) from Charles University in Prague (Political Science and International Relations). In the past, she was a visiting scholar at Georgetown University in Washington DC and Stockholm University. She also worked for Trento Rise, EIT ICT Labs and Create-Net in Trento developing educational programmes in the fields of businesses, entrepreneurship and innovation.

Dominique Foray is Full Professor at the École Polytechnique Fédérale de Lausanne (EPFL) and holds the Chair of Economics and Management of Innovation (CEMI). He is a member of the National Research Council (Switzerland); the Advisory Board of the Swiss Economic Institute (KOF); and a foreign member of the Center of Capitalism and Society (Columbia University, New York). He is also a new member of the Expert Commission for Research and Innovation (E-FI) of Germany. From 2008 to 2011, he served as chairman of the expert group 'Knowledge for Growth', a group of prominent economists created to advise the European Commission. During his service as a member of this group he developed the concept of smart specialisation (together with P.A. David and B. Hall) that is now a key policy mechanism of the EU (cohesion policy).

Carlo Gianelle is research fellow at the Institute for Prospective Technological Studies (IPTS) of the European Commission's Joint Research Centre (JRC). He holds a PhD in economics from the University of Siena, Italy, and studied at the University of California Berkeley, specialising in applied economics. His research interests encompass labour economics, innovation studies and regional studies. He has been involved in the implementation of the Smart Specialisation policy of the European Commission from its inception in 2011 and he has contributed in particular to the methodological development of the activities of the Smart Specialisation Platform.

Francesco Grillo is currently Associate to the Scuola Superiore Sant'Anna in Pisa and has been visiting Fellow at Oxford Internet Institute. He is managing director of Vision and Value, the management consulting firm. He is advisor to the European Commission (DG REGIO) on regional innovation strategies and personal advisor on Innovation to the Italian Ministry for Research, Universities and Education. He is a Philosophiae Doctor at the London School of Economics where he conducted a thesis on the effectiveness of public investments in R&D. He got a Laurea cum Laude in Economia from LUISS University in Rome and an MBA with High Honors from Boston University, MA where he studied as a Fulbright Scholar. He has written a number of peer-reviewed articles on methodologies for universities' evaluation and rankings, regional innovation strategies and smart specialisation, distributed information systems and monitoring of public policies, and application of ICT to public services. Previously at Bank of Tokyo – London as a Head of Italian Desk, he has been Associate with McKinsey. *The McKinsey Mind* introduces Francesco as a successful example of applying McKinsey problem-solving methodologies to public sector and political questions. He regularly writes a column on economics or politics for the front page of the Italian daily *Il Messaggero* and for the online edition of *The Guardian*. He is the author of three books on the impact of the Internet on transportation and the car industry, healthcare and the media.

Karel Haegeman is a scientific officer within the Knowledge for Growth Unit at the JRC-IPTS and is part of the team involved in the European Parliament preparatory action on smart specialisation in the Region of Eastern Macedonia and Thrace. He has Masters in business economics and in marketing, and has previously worked in innovation policy, general economic policy, project management and market research. At JRC-IPTS he has worked on the development of strategic and thematic foresight activities, and policy analysis in support of the European Research Area. He has also been part of several advisory boards of FP7 projects and of scientific committees of international conferences. For more details see https://es.linkedin.com/in/karelhaegeman.

Alexander Kleibrink, is a scientific officer at JRC-IPTS, Knowledge for Growth Unit at the European Commission's Joint Research Centre in Seville, and works for the Smart Specialisation Platform. He was previously a researcher in political science and research associate at the Freie Universität Berlin and the Hertie School of Governance. His research interests cover regional development, political economy of transition processes in the Balkans and policy reforms in Serbia and Croatia. He holds a MA in Public Administration and Policy from the London School of Economics. For more details see: www.linkedin.com/in/ alexander-kleibrink-8ab0b86.

Dimitrios Kyriakou has served as economic advisor to the Greek prime minister, serving with four Greek prime ministers, in 2011–2012. He has exercised the duties of vice-rector for research (director) in Salzburg Global. During that time he was selected to preside over AFS, an

American academic institution in Greece, including an undergraduate college. He has edited for more than ten years the technoeconomic refereed journal, *The IPTS Report*, and served as chief economist of the directorate for prospective studies (IPTS) of the Commission's Joint Research Centre. He has published extensively on technoeconomic matters, and has co-authored articles with Nobel-prize winner Bob Solow. He participated in the meetings (2005–2006) of Commissioner Potocnik's Knowledge for Growth expert group where the smart specialisation concept was born. He holds Bachelor's, Master's and PhD degrees, all from Princeton University.

Elisabetta Marinelli is a scientific officer at JRC-IPTS, Knowledge for Growth Unit. She is an economist by training and holds a PhD from the London School of Economics and Political Science in the field of Economic Geography. She has researched and worked in innovation, education and local development policies. She has experience in quantitative and qualitative research methods. She is part of the team involved in the European Parliament preparatory action on smart specialisation in the Region of Eastern Macedonia and Thrace. Previous to IPTS she worked at the London School of Economics, the University of Sussex, as well as for research consultancy companies and NGOs.

Inger Midtkandal is a Science and Technology Counsellor at the Royal Norwegian Embassy (Commercial section/Innovation Norway) in New Delhi, India. She has 15 years of experience working with different aspects of regional research and innovation from the Research Council of Norway and as a Seconded National Expert to DG-JRC, IPTS in Spain. She has also gained additional experience from private SME industry. Her educational background is in Economic and Political Geography from the University of Oslo, Norway, University of Pavia, Italy and Roskilde University Centre, Denmark.

Krzysztof Mieszkowski is the Seconded Nation Expert from the Polish Ministry of Science and Higher Education to work for the S3 Platform team (IPTS, Seville). Before joining IPTS for seven years he worked in the Ministry responsible for R&D policy in Poland. Following his previous professional interests he is particularly fascinated in the policy aspects related to smart specialisation, including strategy preparation but also its implementation, monitoring of results and evaluation. He took part in the official assessment of Polish and Lithuanian smart specialisation strategies. He has also participated in several events which dealt with the smart specialisation issues as a moderator, a speaker or an organiser. Currently he is also a PhD candidate.

Kevin Morgan is Professor of Governance and Development in the School of Planning and Geography at Cardiff University, where he is also the Dean of Engagement. He has published widely on the spatial dimensions of innovation and innovation policy and was one of the founders of regional innovation policy studies. He is currently the Project Coordinator of SmartSpec, a EU-funded FP7 project exploring the design and delivery of smart specialisation, the latest generation of regional innovation policies in the EU. In 2015 he was appointed Special Adviser to the EU Commissioner for Regional Policy.

Clemente J. Navarro is Professor at the Pablo de Olavide University (Spain) where he is Head of the Centre for Local Political Sociology and Policies. His research interests include public policy analysis and governance. He has been visiting professor in the Paul Harris School of Public Policies (University of Chicago), the University of Firenze and the Consiglio Nazionale della Ricerca. His most recent publications are in *Urban Geography*, *Political Studies*, *Public Administration Review*, *European Urban and Regional Research*, *Cities* and *Social Forces*.

Marja Nissinen is a postdoc research fellow at IPTS where, apart from RIS3, she is focusing on energy and KETs. Marja's present/previous professional interests encompass innovation studies – with recent emphasis on regional innovation policies – as well as business internationalisation and transition economies. With the exception of her early years at the University of Helsinki, she has mainly dealt with applied research: as Research Man-ager at HAMK and Senior Researcher at VTT. She has also worked as a Consultant and Senior Adviser in the fields of export and investment promotion in the Baltic Sea region. Accordingly, she used to be engaged in Baltic trade associations as a board member. Thanks to this expertise, she was contracted as a project specialist by the Finnish and Latvian Ministries of Foreign Affairs. Marja has lived in five European countries. Macmillan Press and St. Martin's Press are among her scientific publishers.

Manuel Palazuelos Martínez works for the European Commission, where he is currently Project Leader at the Smart Specialisation Platform for Energy (Unit Knowledge for Growth) of the DG Joint Research Centre. Previously, he developed a good part of his career at DG ECFIN, the Directorate General of Economic and Monetary Affairs of the European Commission in Brussels, where he held several positions. Prior to joining the Commission, Manuel taught in university for five years, at the Department of Economics of the London School of Economics (LSE), where he was awarded five annual prizes for excellence in teaching, including a national award. He also completed his postgraduate studies on European economics at the London School of Economics, as well as other Masters, postgraduate and university graduate degrees in both in Spain and the UK, mostly in subjects related international economics, obtaining many academic distinctions and awards. He has presented his research at numerous universities such as Columbia in NY,

Oxford, Cambridge, The London School of Economics or Georgetown in Washington DC, where he also received a best paper award.

Inmaculada Periáñez-Forte is a scientific officer at JRC-IPTS, Knowledge for Growth Unit at the European Commission's Joint Research Centre in Seville, and works for the Smart Specialisation Platform. Her research interests include regional development and governance related issues. Previously, Inma worked at the OECD in the Countries Studies Division at the Directorate for Science, Technology and Innovation and coordinated the OECD Smart Specialisation Project. Inma holds a law degree from the University of Seville, Spain, where she has also taught courses on EU law. She holds a LL.M in European Legal Studies from the University of Bristol, a MSc in Regulation from the London School of Economics and a Masters in Management, Evaluation and Planning of Innovation at the International University of Andalusia. She has participated in numerous regional, national and international events focused on smart specialisation and regional policy as a speaker, moderator and organiser. Currently, she is a PhD candidate at the University Pablo de Olavide (Seville). Her most recent publications are related to regional innovation policy, smart specialisation and higher education institutions.

Alessandro Rainoldi is Head of the "Knowledge for growth" Unit at the European Commission's Joint Research Centre, IPTS, Seville, working mainly on regional, R&I and taxation policies. In the same Unit he also specifically dealt with smart specialisation and regional modelling. He worked extensively for the Commission's Directorate-General for Regional and Urban Policy namely dealing with the negotiation and management of EU funding programmes in Italy, Malta and Romania and contributing to the policy agenda on issues related to governance, innovation, financial engineering and evaluation. He was part of the assessment committee of the European Energy Programme for Recovery. He previously worked at the study & research department of a leading Italian banking group and as a free-lance economic journalist. He teaches EU structural funds at the European College of Parma.

Andrés Rodríguez-Pose is a Professor of Economic Geography at the London School of Economics, where he was previously Head of the Department of Geography and Environment. He is the current holder of a European Research Council (ERC) Advanced Grant. He is President of the Regional Science Association International, where he served as Vice-President in 2014. He has also been Vice-President (2012–2013) and Secretary (2001–2005) of the European Regional Science Association. He is a regular advisor to numerous international organisations. He is the joint managing editor of *Environment and Planning C: Government and Policy*, an editor of *Economic Geography*, and sits on the editorial board of 29 other scholarly journals, including many of the leading international journals in economic geography, human geography, regional science, and management.

Jens Sörvik is post-doctoral researcher at the IPTS and is working in particular on topics related to ICT and RIS3, priority setting in Smart Specialisation, collaboration in RIS3 and has been part of projects on SMEs, Peripheral regions and KETs. He has also initiated and led the development of two online tools providing an overview of planned ICT investments under the structural funds, and an overview of smart specialisation priorities in EU regions and member states. Jens has a background in policy analysis, research and consultancy on topics related to research and innovation policy, with a particular focus on cluster policies. Jens has a PhD in Research Policy from Lund University, Sweden.

Callum Wilkie is a researcher in the Department of Geography and Environment at the London School of Economics and Political Science. Prior to undertaking this role, he completed an undergraduate honours degree in Geography at McGill University, and most recently, a Masters in Local Economic Development at the LSE. While he is well versed in a variety of topics associated with the study of economic geography, his primary areas of research relate to the geography of innovation; innovation policy; regional development policy; the geography of multinational firms; and urban economic growth.

Preface

Smart specialisation is indeed an example of fruitful interaction between science and policy. The concept was first developed in the context of a high-level expert group on 'Knowledge for Growth' created by the European Commission. It was subsequently incorporated in the 2010 'Innovation Union' EU flagship initiative under Europe 2020. At the same time, it was recast by the scientific community to foster regional economic transformation and incorporated as a key principle of investment in research and innovation in the framework of the EU regional policy.

The development of parallel tracks in science and policy, which constantly fed each other, has been made possible thanks to the collaborative work of scientists, policy officers, scholars and practitioners, involving, among others, some of the authors in this volume. Through its adoption and adaptation towards regional development, the smart specialisation concept has become a powerful instrument for place-based innovation-driven growth. Furthermore, evidence arising from regions and ongoing informal policy discussions signals that the smart specialisation approach may be evolving towards a methodology that goes beyond its application to the EU regional policy. In fact, smart specialisation is gaining interest in both scientific and policy-making communities linked for instance to urban and local development, but is also bridging the gap towards more thematic policy approaches such as industrial and energy policies. In this sense, these recent evolutions indicate that the applicability of the smart specialisation methodology is potentially wide.

This volume in particular tackles a core aspect of smart specialisation, namely the entrepreneurial discovery process (EDP). It promotes better implementation of the smart specialisation approach on the ground, making it a reality in the regions. It underlines that the EDP should not be taken for granted, nor treated as a black box into which information about regional capacities and characteristics are fed and out of which the identification of priorities and niche opportunities miraculously emerge. This volume does precisely that: it opens the black box, disentangling the relevant interactions and caveat emptors. Its goal is to help readers reach a better understanding of the EDP, escaping the proverbial image of a riddle, and to encourage policy-makers in translating EDP into practice in their regions and consolidating it in appropriate governance mechanisms. It marks another milestone in joining quality research and analysis with effective policy support and development, namely witnessed – inside the European Commission – by the long-standing collaboration between the Directorate-General for Regional and Urban Policy and the Joint Research Centre.

Vladimir Šucha
Director-General of the Joint Research Centre
of the European Commission

Acknowledgements

The success and final outcome of this book builds significantly on the discussions, input, feedback and positive criticisms received through the interaction of the authors with many regional and national authorities, academics, stakeholders and staff across EU institutions – especially colleagues from different services of the European Commission, in particular DG Regio and the Smart Specialisation Platform (S3P). Authors from the S3P would like to express their enormous gratitude to those policy-makers, academics and stakeholders who, in one way or another, have participated in the exploratory and discovery journey of what S3 has to offer. Though, evidently, any remaining errors are our responsibility, this book would not have been possible without the support and co-operation of those engaged in the development and implementation of the S3 concept.

> There is nothing permanent except change.
> Heraclitus

> To do all the talking and not be willing to listen is a form of greed.
> Democritus

Introduction

The 'entrepreneurial discovery process' (EDP) is the cornerstone of smart specialisation strategies (RIS3) and the smart specialisation (S3) approach, more generally. On the one hand, doing it right is a sine qua non condition for the success of S3. On the other hand, however, capturing its essence in implementation-friendly terms is so notoriously difficult that a famous dictum, and ultimate easy way out, comes to mind (even if it emerged in an entirely unrelated context): 'I cannot define it, but I know it when I see it' (US Supreme Court Justice Stewart is credited with it).

We will not take the easy way out; rather we aim at and strive after contributing to the debate on the role of the EDP, which is at the heart of smart specialisation strategies for regional economic transformation. Entrepreneurial discovery is a key process in the definition of RIS3 priorities and therefore essential to a successful design of a smart specialisation strategy. It is the first book which directly addresses the most controversial defining feature of smart specialisation: EDP, bringing together contributions by leading analysts in the field, both from the academic sphere as well as from the European Commission's JRC-IPTS S3 Platform, in order to clarify key aspects of the concept, and their policy implications.

Its point of departure is the need to dispel a common misunderstanding: simple surveys among triple or quadruple helix actors do not an EDP make. The essence of the entrepreneurial discovery process lies in its interactive nature, and in organising a fruitful, targeted dialogue that brings the different actors together in a participatory leadership process to carve out jointly the smart specialisation fields and develop a suitable policy mix to implement it.

The tall order behind it involves avoiding the Scylla of having specialists meet each other to repeat familiar notions within each area, as well as the Charybdis of huge groups producing soupy concoctions of notions. Instead the goal is to allow a wide array of sources of ideas to interact, producing cross-fertilisation (the eureka moment or less ceremoniously, the 'I hadn't thought of that' moment).

This, among other things, implies that the regional government no longer plays a role of omniscient planner but it will assess the potential of the new activities and empower those actors which are most capable of realising that potential.

This book examines the conditions for successfully capturing the concept and transposing it into policy, by operationalising the EDP. Particular focus is placed on what methods, procedures and institutional conditions are necessary to generate information that helps buttress policy decisions. It draws on existing literature that analyses the relevance of EDP within smart specialisation for regional policy. It follows this up with a detailed study on specific aspects related to the operationalisation of the concept, such as the need to recast/refurbish monitoring approaches and capabilities, the relevant role of local institutions or the state in the process of knowledge integration, or the new demands that EDP processes place on the local institutions. The objective is to contribute to the effective adoption and implementation of the EDP across diverse socioeconomic and institutional contexts.

We complement the analysis with case study reviews, drawing from regions from very different geographical and socioeconomic characteristics: from Norwegian regions to the Greek region of East Macedonia and Thrace. These EU experiences provide empirical evidence to illustrate the impact of smart specialisation and EDP on governance structures and innovation policies. The case studies present the different tools and programmes chosen to operationalise the concept and discuss the barriers they had to overcome and their achievements.

Chapter 1 addresses the methods and procedures of EDP. This chapter discusses why smart specialisation is an important principle and why the EDP is central in designing and implementing a smart specialisation strategy (RIS3).

Chapter 2, on exit and voice, discusses key pitfalls lurking in the background as EDP is implemented. They include the need to avoid entrenchment of incumbents, allowing voice to the voiceless firms/actors yet to emerge – which is another way of saying this arena should be kept contestable. They also include the need to protect the bottom-up emphasis of the process from top-down proclivities, and the importance of addressing the problems often plaguing collective action (such as free riding behaviour).

Chapter 3 addresses two prominent gaps in the collective understanding of the EDP: first, by identifying the actors who are responsible for the EDP, investigating their respective roles, and exploring how they should be engaged, and, second, by dissecting the relationship between the EDP and the institutional context within which it occurs recognising that institutions can exercise tremendous influence on the effectiveness and outcomes of the EDP.

Chapter 4 argues that RIS3 places enormous demands on the role of public institutions like regional governments and local universities in the EDP. The chapter revisits the state debate by assessing the perspectives of two rival economic thinkers, Friedrich Hayek and Dani Rodrik, both of whom have valuable (if very different) things to say about how the state should deal with knowledge, innovation and uncertainty. Furthermore, it explores the scope for/barriers to public sector innovation, drawing on the experience of the UK, where attempts are being made to reform a risk-averse public administration culture and counter state-centric forms of regional innovation policy.

Chapter 5 discusses the interaction of public and private sector entities in the EDP and the behavioural changes it may require on both sides, for instance regarding the role of lobbies, or more generally, bringing companies closer to policy, while avoiding/respecting conflicts of interests, and encouraging companies themselves to think more strategically and less short-term-driven. It suggests mechanisms aimed at systematically engaging entrepreneurs in a discovery process which is supposed to be at least initiated and coordinated by public administrations.

Chapter 6 examines the contribution of 'research and technology organisations' (RTOs) to EDP. How can RTOs discover new business opportunities and how can they inform public administration about them? How can RTOs be integrated in the EDP? The chapter suggests that RTOs are not only actors in continuous priority setting process but also essential partners to regional administration in the implementation of 'research and innovation' (R&I) strategies for smart specialisation, as well as partners to businesses and research actors in identification and exploitation of R&I opportunities.

Chapter 7 addresses monitoring and the related information feedback flow, representing a necessary element in order for the strategy to evolve and improve. This is particularly true in the design and implementation of innovation strategies for smart specialisation, which are aimed at generating sustainable and self-correcting processes of identification, development and evaluation of socioeconomic priorities, in a continuous EDP.

The second part of the book provides case studies, drawing from regions with very different geographical and socioeconomic characteristics. The studies, prepared by the team of S3 Platform, set out the pitfalls and barriers encountered, the solutions adopted, and the results obtained. The S3 Platform, established by the European Commission at its JRC-IPTS directorate (Joint Research Centre-Institute for Prospective Technological Studies) is a unique European Commission facilitator of the uptake and incorporation by regions and states of the smart specialisation concept and methodology in their research and innovation strategies (RIS3). The cases presented here build on and benefit from the experience gained by the S3 platform: the assessment of hundreds of strategies during the negotiations over the European Structural and Investment Funds (ESIF) Operational Programmes and the participation in numerous reviews/meetings focused on different aspects of smart specialisation all over Europe.

Authors' note

The views expressed in this book are purely those of the authors and may not in any circumstances be regarded as stating an official position of the European Commission.

1 The concept of the 'entrepreneurial discovery process'

Dominique Foray

1 Introduction

In this paper we will address the methods and procedures of entrepreneurial discovery (ED). As argued in the early literature on the topic, any smart specialisation strategy that did not include this principle would have an entirely different character. Why is it such an important principle? The aim of this chapter is to explain the centrality of ED in designing and implementing a smart specialisation strategy (RIS3). The arguments in this paper draw extensively on the insights addressed by a set of papers already published by Foray and co-authors on various aspects of this topic (Foray *et al.*, 2009; Foray and Goenega, 2013; Foray and Rainoldi, 2012; Foray, 2015), and the rest of the paper is organized as follows. Section 2 discusses the conceptual underpinnings of smart specialisation policy and why this approach is relevant for regional policy. Section 3 explains that the very logic of RIS3 – described as 'sector non-neutral' – requires governments to make choices and establish vertical priorities, which entails high risk. Section 4 then explains how ED is a unique concept to minimize such risks and provides a careful description of the 'anatomy' of an ED process. Section 5 is about translating the objectives and principles described in the previous sections at a certain level of abstraction into practical implementation: a set of tools and programmes that will provide a more operational content to the concept; and section 6 provides some final thoughts and conclusions.

2 In search of 'good' policies to stimulate structural changes in European regional economies: a primer on smart specialisation

During the last decades, horizontal policies were dominating the policy process at regional level in the European Union. Resources were mostly allocated in a horizontal manner – in order to avoid any preferential interventions and to act on general framework conditions and generic factors (such as public research infrastructure) which are important for the whole system. There were exceptions of course but horizontal policy was the main logic of resource allocation in the framework of regional and cohesion policy.

Horizontal policies are good policies! First they are likely to improve important components of the regional system of innovation. Second they minimize risks inherent in any policy which selects projects according to preferred fields. And, indeed, such policy has the potential to stimulate structural changes through various mechanisms such as diversification done by firms, spin-offs and start-ups, mobility of people and networking (Boschma and Frenken, 2011).

However if this policy is likely to work in the case of top regions, it did not in the case of transition and less advanced regions. (Percoco, 2013; Muscio *et al.*, 2013). Most of less developed regions and transition regions failed to improve the knowledge gap relative to the top regions. And when, in a few cases regions have managed to improve somewhat the knowledge gap, they had difficulties to translate it into real economic convergence. This is the case when improvement in the knowledge gap is mostly a public sector component, with very little effect of the policy in innovation capacities within the private sector (Veugelers and Mrak, 2009). There is no such thing as a quasi-magical effect of public research improvement notably in the form of knowledge spillovers.

Why can we observe such a differentiated impact of horizontal policies between regions of different levels of development?

Innovation requires not only general framework conditions – 'the basics have to be right' – but also specific capabilities and resources. In top regions, these capabilities are provided by industrial associations, large companies and universities (and public research organizations) through spillovers of research, training, diffusion of technologies to suppliers. These spillovers constitute the complementary capabilities that most SMEs can draw on even if they have not contributed to their provision (Berger, 2013). However, in the other regions, these sources of complementary capabilities have dried up or have never existed and large holes in the industrial ecosystems have appeared. To use the words of Suzan Berger: 'firms are home alone'. As she argues so well: 'even start ups with great innovation and generous funding cannot do it all in house. They need suppliers, qualified workers and engineers, expertise beyond their own'. In many cases, the ecosystem is too poor to provide all these capabilities.

In less advanced and transition regions, regional innovation policy needs therefore to address the whole set of capabilities required to innovate in specific sectors and emerging fields. In other words, a policy is needed to support the emergence of micro-systems of innovation: the network of companies, research institutions, specialized services and complementary capabilities that are mobilized to explore collectively a certain new domain of opportunities.

Historical cases of spontaneous emergence of micro-systems of innovation are numerous. For example:

1   In Finland, a few entrepreneurs in the pulp and paper industry viewed nanotechnology as a promising source of valuable applications and firms in this industry were taking steps to assess this potentiality. Some firms responded to these opportunities by increasing their R&D spending to explore recent advances in nanotechnology in order to develop applications for their own

sector. The emergence of a new R&D collaboration network – involving incumbents, research institutions, specialized suppliers and universities – was a critical step for the assessment of the usefulness and value of developing nanotechnology applications for pulp and paper processes. We see in that case an emerging micro-system of innovation at work that assembles different actors and leads to *the development of a new activity* (a smart specialisation) – at the crossroads between a new technology and a traditional sector.

2   As a result of a crisis situation faced by traditional markets in the silk industry, a dozen firms broke away from the Lyon factory to explore ways of orchestrating a fundamental transition from silk to technical fabrics. They were silk manufacturers who had discovered the potential of glass fibre to radically transform their products and these firms worked on the integration of these new materials into their processes. In the big Lyon chemical industry the silk firms found the specialists they needed to resolve complex knowledge integration problems. The nose of the Concorde supersonic airliner, the tailfin of the Airbus 330 and the sails of some of the boats participating in the America's Cup are products symbolising this successful transition. Here again a new micro-system of innovation boosted the development of a new activity and this dynamic led to the construction of very strong competitive advantages, realized by the creation of over 2,000 jobs between the early seventies and the end of the eighties.

3   The third case is that of the footwear industry in Northern Portugal, which has undergone profound renewal in a context of frantic global competition. The micro-system of innovation aiming at the development of new forms of flexible automation in the footwear industry has achieved the integration of engineering knowledge from the University of Porto (INESC), skills of companies specialized in industrial machinery, tools and software and the entrepreneurial vision of a few footwear manufacturing firms which understand very well the urgent need for revival via innovation. The integration of this knowledge facilitates the discovery and exploration of the potential of the automation associated with advanced cutting tools to increase the flexibility and quality of production. Economic experimentation with these technological developments determined a new business model. The latter is based on an increase in the variety of designs and the capacity to rapidly respond to small orders. This development has led the footwear industry to bypass global competition and become the second most important European producer in terms of exports and value added.

In these examples we see a new activity as complementing the existing structures and assets in order to form a micro-system of innovation to open and explore new opportunities. These micro-systems of innovation and new capabilities are related to existing industrial assets and have the goal to transform these assets (through modernization, diversification, transition processes).

By supporting such emerging micro-systems of innovation, as related to existing structures, the policy does not produce 'cathedrals in the desert' but stimulates knowledge-based activities embedded in and complementing existing structures in order to transform them.

These examples help us to understand also that a policy supporting emerging micro-systems of innovation (that is a RIS3) does not aim at narrowing down the development path of a region nor producing some sort of technological monoculture. Smart specialisation strategies reflect rather the capacity of an economic system (a region for example) to generate new areas of development and new options through the discovery of new domains of opportunity and the local concentration and agglomeration of resources and competences in these domains. As the three examples show, smart specialisation is about high technologies, but not high technologies only! In most cases, new high-tech projects are complementing existing assets and technologies to transform industries and economic structures.

3   A problem of choice: introduction to entrepreneurial discovery

But of course, a policy aiming at supporting the emergence of such micro-systems of innovation has a very different logic than the horizontal policy previously described. We can call it 'sector non-neutral' (or vertical). It is a very different policy just because different activities require different things. Supporting biotechnology development for fisheries will require the provision of capabilities in terms of research, suppliers, services which are very different from those required to support the development of advanced manufacturing technologies for the footwear industry or to support the development of ICT for tourism. Such a policy has to deal with the complexity and specificity of each activity and this has a cost. This is *haute couture* rather than *ready to wear*. An horizontal policy such as R&D tax credit is *ready to wear* (it has a cost but is relatively easy to implement). But providing the specific capabilities for a specific emerging activity is *haute couture* and therefore more costly.

It is therefore clear that a local government cannot address all potential specific capabilities and infrastructure needs for all new activities. This implies that choices need to be made between different emerging activities or different opportunities. As said forcefully by Hausmann and Rodrik (2006), 'it is not that choices are desirable, they are simply inevitable'.

The new policy logic raises, thus, a problem which is easy to perceive. This is the problem of choosing and selecting a few domains of priorities where the emergence of micro-systems of innovation will be strongly supported and large resources will be concentrated. Indeed, prioritizing certain technologies or domains always entails a risk because this implies predicting the future development of technologies and markets.

There is a long history of policies setting priorities and objectives in a top-down and central-planning mode and letting bureaucratic committees to decide what is better to left to the market. These policies generated a lot of inefficiencies and most often failed to stimulate dynamism and innovation. Such an old-fashioned mode of making choices and establishing priorities was fully used during the golden age of the so-called mission-oriented policies in the post-war period (from the 1960s to the 1990s). The government viewed itself as the omniscient planner with the *ex ante* knowledge about what to do and what to choose in terms of sectors and activities. One could argue that a lot of cluster policies – which clearly display some aspects of innovation systems – are very much top-down with governments dictating what technologies should be developed in what places (e.g. the French 'Pôles de Compétitivité').

There are many problems with this logic which can be the source of various inefficiencies, including picking winners, government failures, policy capture and anti-competitive effect. And the scepticism of many economists about such sector non-neutral policies is fully justified.

However the approach of RIS3 is not to take such potential risks of failures and distortions as a good case for abandoning any policy aiming at supporting the building of capabilities in specific domains. But rather the approach of smart specialisation is to care seriously about the design of the policy process so as to minimize all these risks. To summarize, RIS3 recognizes the need for government to be able to make strategic choices and targeted interventions so as to support the emergence of micro-systems of innovation in specific domains but recognizes also the need to avoid the usual mistakes frequently associated with top-down decisions and central-planning mode. As Sabel said so well: 'What if, as I and many others assume, there are no principals…with the robust and panoramic knowledge needed for this directive role?' (Sabel, 2004).

In the perspective of a sector non-neutral policy, three types of mistake need to be considered.

- *Mistake type 1* has been already mentioned: this is the mistake of the omniscient planner who knows what to do and what to choose and does not need any information from the grass roots. The temptation is high to buy consulting services which will write a nice report with any kind of figures and tables and produce thereby the illusion that the government has 'sufficient information and knowledge' to decide priorities in a top-down manner. Policy makers must guard against the intellectual logic imposed by the principal–agent model, according to which the principal (the government) knows from the start which specialisations should be developed and therefore confines itself to setting up the incentives for private industry to carry out the plan! (Rodrik, 2013). There is a potential mistake here because the logic of RIS3 is that the smart specialisations are not given *ex ante* through some kind of measurement of relative specialisation or critical mass. In RIS3, these specialisations will be discovered among several emerging activities.
- *Mistake type 2*: this is the mistake of sectoral prioritization. Sector prioritization generates distortions. There is no point supporting all firms in a given sector. The point is rather to support new activities and projects at a finer level of granularity.
- *Mistake type 3*: this is the mistake of choices made for ever. The profound logic of RIS3 is about generating new options for further diversification and transformation. This is not about deepening existing specialisation.

To avoid or minimize the likelihood of these mistakes, the design of the policy process needs to be carefully elaborated. In the rest of this paper we will limit our discussion to mistake type 1 because the central theme of the paper is the notion of ED. We have just argued that most traditional policies that were sector non-neutral involved central-planning modes and top-down decision processes and this generated many inefficiencies. The ED provision aims at breaking with such an inadequate tradition of policy intervention.

4 The anatomy of entrepreneurial discovery

The importance of ED is related to the recognition that the government does not have innate wisdom or the *ex-ante* knowledge about future priorities. They have not – even after having made highly sophisticated statistical presentations of the regional innovation system. The fundamental point here is the Hayekian argument that the knowledge about what to do is not obvious. It is a knowledge 'of time and place'; this is local knowledge which is dispersed, decentralized, divided. It is hidden and needs to be discovered. This is why the key concept is 'self-discovery' or ED. Putting it very candidly, the emphasis on entrepreneurial discovery as the main process for generating information to identify priorities means that the policy is not about telling people what to do, but rather about helping stakeholders to discover what to do and then implementing the necessary sequence of policies according to what has been discovered.

The box below presents many cases of ED. They are all real, coming from various regions and a few have been integrated in the RIS3 of particular regions. All these cases are about the first step of the process of the emergence of a micro-system of innovation and thereby of a smart specialisation dynamic.

Box 1.1 Cases of entrepreneurial discovery

- Exploring and developing biotech applications in the fishery and canning industries
- Exploring Internet potentials for e-commerce in the provision of tourism services
- Exploring nanotechnology potential to increase operational efficiency and quality in the pulp and paper industry
- Developing advanced manufacturing technology for the footwear industry
- Discovering the potential of integration between textile and chemistry
- Exploring the potential of animal genetics for the breeding sector
- Opening the domain of smart mobility within buildings
- Discovering the economic feasibility of producing Swiss caviar
- Discovering the potential of artificial underwater 'oases' for local diving tourism

---

What are the shared characteristics of all these cases?

4.1 ED precedes innovation

First, ED precedes the innovation stage and consists of the exploration and opening up of a new domain of opportunities (technological and market), potentially rich in numerous innovations that will subsequently occur. It is clear that the ED does not only amount to innovation – although it increases its probability – it does not just amount to a basic research phase either as it is essentially oriented towards the market and applications. It is the demonstration that a certain path of industrial or structural change is possible – for example developing from traditional silk manufacture to a production of technical fabrics; integrating nanotechnologies into the wood pulp production process; shifting from one potentially declining market to a new growing one. ED is the essential phase, the decisive link that allows the system to reorient and renew itself. It imparts to the economy potentialities for evolution. Indeed, the ED that drives the process of smart specialisation is not simply the advent of an innovation but the deployment and variation of innovative ideas in a specialized area that generate knowledge about the future economic value of a possible direction of change.

4.2 Structuring entrepreneurial knowledge and producing economic knowledge

Second, all cases of ED place the notion of entrepreneurial knowledge at the centre of the process. Entrepreneurial knowledge – composed of vision and integration between different bodies of knowledge – plays an essential role in the discovery of a new domain; it is the driver of the discovery process. Entrepreneurial knowledge involves much more than knowledge about science and techniques. Rather, it combines and relates such knowledge about science, technology and engineering with knowledge of market growth potential, potential competitors as well as the whole set of inputs and services required for launching a new activity. In many cases such entrepreneurial knowledge is fragmented and distributed over many sites and organizations, companies, universities, clients and users, specialized suppliers (some of these entities being located outside of the region). An important precondition for ED is therefore the integration of the knowledge through the building of connections and partnerships. The role of local (entrepreneurial) universities and regional agencies is likely to be critical in this process of knowledge integration. It would be a mistake to think that the ED process generates only technological knowledge – what works from a technological point of view. No! The discovery focuses especially on economic knowledge – the knowledge of what works (and does not work) economically, as elaborated by Hayek and which is central to the general theory of economic dynamism developed by Phelps (2013). The entrepreneurial discovery process is basically economic experimentation with new ideas, which, of course, will to a great extent emanate from scientific and technological inventions.

4.3 The locus of ED

Third, ED is not an extraordinary event; it is a normal search procedure to identify and realize new opportunities. In many cases ED is internalized within the large company since it is by definition capable of assembling very diversified knowledge and carrying out risky discovery projects by financing its projects with its own resources. Toshiba exploring the potential of 'clean factory farms' (converting old electronics plants to produce vegetables in a perfect germ environment) is a good case in point. But because the processes of entrepreneurial discovery and exploration of new domains of potential innovations usually require the integration of divided and dispersed knowledge, the organizational forms most appropriate for entrepreneurial discovery are the network-, association- or partnership-forms allowing the integration of knowledge originating from firms, research laboratories, specialized suppliers and clients. We also observe the presence of more horizontal associations, allowing for example the collaboration of small firms that share certain infrastructures and services for collective exploration of a new domain. Therefore, numerous organizational forms are possible for integrating divided and dispersed knowledge and managing the risks of entrepreneurial discovery projects, from the research laboratory-backed start-up to the large integrated firm, and all sorts of forms of networks in between.

4.4 The informational value of ED

Fourth, the recent work of Hausmann and Rodrik (2003) has brought the concept of 'discovery' to a wide audience but to the best of our knowledge, the earliest economic analysis of the concept of 'discovery' as distinct to innovation is provided by Hirshleifer (1971). In his work he developed a formal expression of discovery information as a compound event A which consists of the joint happenings: state a is true (something is possible) and this fact is successfully exploited (what is possible is created). The first event has a probability Πa while the second event has a probability ΠA with $\Pi a > \Pi A$. The discovery process provides information about Πa: something is possible that will happen with a probability ΠA. The discovery A may be about the potential of a general purpose technology application to transform processes in a traditional sector (cases of Finland and North Portugal above). Or it may be about the possibility of a diversification path based on the exploitation of potential economies of scope and internal spillovers. Or the discovery is about the possibility of a transition path from a low-productivity area to a higher one (case of Lyon above). We are talking of entrepreneurial *discovery*, not entrepreneurial *innovation*, and the distinction between 'innovation' and 'discovery' is central. Indeed, EDs are characterized by a strong learning dimension. The social value of the discovery is that it informs the whole system that a particular domain of

R&D and innovation is likely to create new opportunities for the regional economy. This is not the standard model, whereby an innovator excludes others from the use of the innovation in order to appropriate the largest fraction of the benefits. Discoveries have therefore a strong public nature.

4.5 ED, spillovers and entries: the dynamics of smart specialisation

Fifth, while entrepreneurial discovery signifies the opening up of exploitation opportunities, entry constitutes the confirmation that others see this discovery as meaningful. When the initial experiment and discovery are successful and diffused, other agents are induced to shift investments away from older domains with less growth potential to the new one. According to Hirshleifer (1971), public information about the discovery (about Πa) is socially valuable in redirecting productive decisions. Entry is a key ingredient of smart specialisation so that agglomeration externalities can be realized: the discovery of a potential domain in which a region could become a leader should very quickly result in multiple entrants to the new activity. This is the onset of the clustering phase of a smart specialisation process; i.e. the formation of a regional concentration of co-located activities and resources in related fields. Discoveries and subsequent emerging activities have thus the potential to provide learning spillovers to other agents in the regional economy. Thus, as Rodrik (2004) argues, the reward for entrepreneurial discoveries (if it is needed, i.e. in case of informational externality problems) has to be structured in such a way that it will maximize these spillovers.

4.6 Related variety

Sixth, we can see from many real cases that, in general, entrepreneurial discoveries relate to existing structures and local knowledge, and all of these cases involve the generation and exploitation of related variety opportunities (Frenken *et al.*, 2007) whereby 'regions diversify by branching into industries that are related to their current industries' (Neffke *et al.*, 2011; Boschma and Frenken, 2011). Most cases of ED exemplify the processes of transformation that link the existing productive structures to new domains of potential competitive advantages. However, ED may also involve a less frequent but important case of *the radical foundation* of a new domain. This case does not fall into the related diversification pattern and involves the opening up of exploitation opportunities unrelated to any existing productive assets.

4.7 ED and the level at which priorities should be set

Seventh, the centrality of the notion of discovery leads immediately to the understanding of what is the appropriate level of aggregation to set smart specialisation priorities. The level at which those priorities (new domains, new fields) are identified, assessed and supported is neither the sectoral level nor the individual/firm level. The relevant level is that of 'mid-grained' granularity. At this level:

- new activities/projects involve groups of firms and other (research) partners;
- the aim is to explore a new domain of (technological and market) opportunities;
- there is potentially a certain weight and a high significance in relation to the regional economy (in terms of the kind of structural changes it is likely to generate).

An example is the Finnish companies exploring the potentials of nanotech to improve the operational efficiency of the pulp and paper industry (above). In such a case, the priority is not the pulp and paper sector as a whole, but rather the activity involving the development of nanotech applications for the pulp and paper industry. What governments would support in this and the other cases is neither whole sectors nor single firms but the growth of new activities. The notion of a new activity is somewhat fuzzy. Of course economic activities take place at firm level, but the essence of smart specialisation – as well as of any kind of new industrial policy – is not to favour one particular firm but to support the development of collective action and experience aimed at exploring, experimenting with and discovering new opportunities.

The centrality of the notion of 'activity' as the relevant level of granularity is consistent with the need to avoid what has been described as mistake type 2 (sectoral prioritization).

4.8   *The structure of the process of entrepreneurial discovery in RIS3*

All cases described in Box 1.1 reflect a process that involves two main phases: the identification of priority areas; and the` development of action plans (projects, platforms, networks) within each of the selected areas. The first phase is useful but not enough. It is useful because the identification of priority areas may help to stimulate EDP in the right domains. It is not enough because learning and discovering where a region should strongly focus and concentrate resources requires concrete actions. EDP needs to be translated into real and concrete collaborative projects to explore a new domain and demonstrate feasibility.

The first phase of identification involves the following two steps.

- The starting point in this process deals with the analysis of the structures of the regional economy in order to identify potentials and opportunities. Such analysis is based on a mix of knowledge. On the one hand, there is a need to provide a sound analysis of regional assets – based on indicators such as sectoral productivity, capacity to compete, patent and industry specialisation, critical mass, extra-regional networks and partnerships. These are key statistics to identify potentials and opportunities in the regional economy. However, such formal analysis needs to be combined

with a more contextual knowledge and insider expertise about facts and issues that are less visible in the statistics. Is there a strong technical university and, if so, in what domains? In what domains are the large companies operating? What kinds of global value chains are positioned in the region? Finally, mega-trends (grand challenges) as well as the current development and propagation of the new GPTs need to be taken into consideration.
• This combination of different types of knowledge and analysis should form the basis for dialogue and interactions between the government and the stakeholders. From this process, priority areas will emerge – a certain number of potential domains of specialisation.

However, as already said, the process does not stop here. It also includes a second phase that involves the concretisation, the action plans that will put these priorities into practice. Such action plans include investments in exploratory projects, platforms and the empowerment of potential leaders who can stimulate collective actions in the priority areas.

Priority areas need to be quite narrow or at least not too broad. In too broad an area – called for example 'energy' – the 12 or 15 projects that are selected and supported are scattered or dispersed. Connections, synergies and spillovers will hardly happen and critical mass will not emerge. In a narrower priority area, the same number of projects will be more connected, providing potential scale, scope and spillover effects. Some platforms will be 'general-purpose' and the markets for specialised inputs (skills, services) will become thick.

There is, of course, a political rationale underlying the need for broad areas but this is not the right way to proceed because, at the end of the day, the region will not get what an RIS3 is supposed to deliver.

5 Entrepreneurial discovery policy

Thanks to the principle of ED, RIS3 exhibits a great policy potential: while addressing the issue of supporting the development of new areas of specialisation and activities through preferential interventions, it will try to promote and support the decentralized decisions of entrepreneurs concerning R&D, innovation and structural changes. In other words, this policy is an attempt to reconcile two logics of political action that are usually considered as being in potential conflict:

• The first logic involves setting priorities – not horizontal priorities such as improving human capital, developing good universities or building an effective intellectual property rights system – but vertical ones regarding particular fields and technologies as well as particular sets or networks of actors.

* The second logic is less controversial; it involves decentralized entrepreneurial initiatives, in other words the set of factors now recognized as the true engine for innovation and economic growth (Baumol, 2002; Phelps, 2013).

The only way to reconcile these two logics is for policy makers seeking vertical priorities to rely on an ED process. In other words the search for and identification of priorities will be carried out from the grass roots, not just from the top.

It should be clear, however, that the emphasis on entrepreneurial discovery as a decentralized and bottom-up process of producing information about potential priorities should not result in narrowing the scope of policy intervention. Emphasizing the role of entrepreneurial discovery is for us not a plea in favour of a laissez-faire policy and the constraints we have placed on the process should not result in some kind of shrinkage of policy scope to exclude all governmental actions as being too top-down! In many cases ED needs to be supported and facilitated and engendering and enhancing this discovery process provides a possible role for public policy in the smart specialisation arena.

5.1 Designing policy to encourage ED

Helping entrepreneurs and other actors to discover the next areas for specialisation involves complex policy actions. This is mainly about:

* supporting cross-sectoral and inter-institutional connections and collaborations in order to facilitate new knowledge combination and integration, as well as mobilizing potential ED leaders (a large firm, a local university, a public research organization, etc.) who can initiate and coordinate collective projects of ED;
* deploying ED infrastructures under the form of platforms of tools and services to support interdisciplinary and inter-sectoral explorations and exploitations of new opportunities;
* generating the proper incentives to encourage and support risky collaborative projects of exploring a new domain of opportunities and structuring these incentives in such a way that information spillovers (about the discovery) are maximized (recall that discovery has a strong learning dimension (above) and the ultimate goal of RIS3 is the generation of critical mass of diverse entities within a new domain of economic opportunity) and;
* identifying and assessing the most promising projects in order to prioritize them and support the early growth of the new activities.

A regional strategy that is characterized by the centrality of ED as a mechanism to generate the knowledge-input to set priorities provides great opportunities for regional government to develop and cultivate new governance capabilities such as embeddedness (ability to develop and maintain high intensity of interactions and communications with the private sector and other local stakeholders), an experimentalist culture and a dynamic and long-term vision (Rodrik, 2013; Morgan, 2013).

5.2 Operationalizing ED

In a highly developed region, entrepreneurial discoveries are likely to happen at a high rate: large firms, networks of SMEs, consortia including universities are strongly committed to opening and exploring new domains of technological and economic opportunities. In such cases, policies need to focus on observation and detection as well as selection of a few of them in order to support the early growth of the new activities and their development towards a cluster.

The situation is more difficult in less advanced regions in which there is a problem of capabilities and ability of local agents to connect and undertake collective exploration of new domains of opportunities. In regions that are poor in entrepreneurial capabilities, the main issue is therefore not insufficient incentives (informational externalities as a market failure) impeding the private effort of the *existing* entrepreneurs, but the lack of local entrepreneurial *supply* and in such a case policies need to be more pro-active to stimulate ED in specific domains and sectors. One policy challenge therefore appears to be to facilitate the building of inter-organizational connections and coordination of efforts in the sphere of experimentation and discovery. Platforms and networks, leaders and integrators, extra-regional resources are various options that need to be deployed in such case.

6 Conclusion

Smart specialisation as a policy concept has enjoyed a short but very exciting life! Elaborated by a group of innovation scholars in 2008 and 2009 (Foray *et al.*, 2009), it very quickly made a significant impact on the policy audience, particularly in Europe. The concept is now a key element of the EU 2020 innovation plan.

The growing popularity of smart specialisation in diverse circles (McCann and Ortega-Argilés, 2013), as well as the fact that its initial formulation left considerable latitude for policy makers to interpret the specific content and implications of its prescriptions in any particular set of circumstances, have generated a proliferation of ideas as to what 'smart specialisation' means for economic development and growth policies.

This is in principle good news since the generic approach has a strong potential to transform regional innovation policy making it more effective and efficient relative to the more traditional 'regional strategies'. However such fast growing popularity and high flexibility of the concept entail also great risks: the language of entrepreneurial discovery and smart specialisation becomes commonplace in the EU cohesion policy, but what we see being implemented in practice is often the rhetoric not the substance. The risk is that policy makers turn smart specialisation policy into another top-down planning procedure because they do not understand or neglect the principle of ED. This is why the message of ED centrality needs to be stressed again and better explained and the theoretical concept needs to be further operationalized. This is a necessary condition for the development of a new policy approach (RIS3) which can succeed in making compatible the possibility of regions to build a strategy based on a strategic vision served by clear priorities and the necessity to promote an economy of decentralized entrepreneurial initiatives.

Acknowledgements

The author gratefully thanks Inmaculada Periáñez-Forte as well as the other members of the RIS3 Platform for their careful comments and advice. The author is also very grateful to the participants of the Seminar 'S3 Governance: Entrepreneurial discovery process' (Pisa, 24–25 September 2014) who have provided many useful suggestions to a first draft of this paper.

References

Baumol, W. (2002), *The Free-Market Innovation Machine*, Princeton: Princeton University Press.

Berger, S. (2013), *Making in America*, Cambridge: MIT Press.

Boschma, R. and K. Frenken (2011), 'Technological Relatedness and Regional Branching', in H. Bathelt, M. Feldman and D. Kogler (*forthcoming*), (eds), *Dynamic Geographies of Knowledge Creation and Innovation*, Abingdon: Routledge.

Foray, D. (2015), *Smart Specialisation: Opportunities and Challenges for Regional Innovation Policy*, Abington: Routledge.

Foray, D. and X. Goenaga (2013), 'The Goals of Smart Specialisation', *JRC Scientific and Policy Reports, S3 Policy Brief Series, n°01*, IPTS.

Foray, D. and A. Rainoldi (2013), 'Smart Specialisation Programmes and Implementation', *JRC Scientific and Policy Reports, S3 Policy Brief Series, n°02*, IPTS.

Foray, D., P.A. David and B. Hall (2009), 'Smart Specialisation: the Concept', in *Knowledge for Growth: Prospects for Science, Technology and Innovation, Report, EUR 24047*, European Union.

Frenken, K., F. Van Oort and T. Verburg (2007), 'Related Variety, Unrelated Variety and Regional Economic Growth', *Regional Studies*, 41:5, 685–697.

Hausmann, R. and D. Rodrik (2003), 'Economic Development as Self-Discovery', *Journal of Development Economics*, 72:2, 603–633.

Hausmann, R. and D. Rodrik (2006), 'Doomed to choose', *Paper prepared for Blue Sky seminar organized by the Center for International Development at Harvard University* on 9 September 2006 (first draft).

Hirshleifer, J. (1971), 'The Private and Social Value of Information and the Reward to Inventive Activity', *American Economic Review*, 61:4, 561–574.

McCann, P. and R. Ortega-Argilés, (2013), 'Smart Specialisation, Regional Growth and Applications to EU Cohesion Policy', *Regional Studies*, 49:8, 1291–1302.

Morgan, K. (2013), *'The Regional State in the Era of Smart Specialisation'*, *Ekonomiaz*, 83:2, 102–125.

Muscio, A., L. Rivera Leon and A. Reid (2013), 'Can Smart Specialisation Help Overcome the Regional Innovation Paradox?', *Conference on Transition Economics meets New Structural Economics*, London: UCL-SSEES.

Neffke, F., M. Henning and R. Boschma (2011), 'How do Regions Diversify over Time? Industry Relatedness and the Development of new Growth Paths in Regions', *Economic Geography*, 87:3, 237–265.

Percoco, M. (2013), *'Strategies of Regional Development in European Regions: are they efficient?'*, *Cambridge Journal of Regions, Economy and Society*, 6:2, 303–318.

Phelps, E.S. (2013), *Mass Flourishing*, Princeton: Princeton University Press.

Rodrik, D. (2004), 'Industrial Policy for the Twenty-First Century', *CEPR Discussion Paper Series*, 4767.

Rodrik, D. (2013), *Green Industrial Policy*, School of Social Science, IAS Princeton (draft).

Sabel, C. (2004), *Beyond Principal–Agent Governance: Experimentalist Organizations, Learning and Accountability*, Amsterdam: WRR – Wetenschappelijke Raad Voor Het Regeringsbeleid.

Veugelers, R. and M. Mrak (2009), 'The Knowledge Economy and Catching-up Member States of the European Union', in *Knowledge for Growth: Prospects for Science, Technology and Innovation, Report, EUR 24047*, European Union.

2   Addressing EDP pitfalls
Exit, voice, and loyalty

Dimitrios Kyriakou

1 Introduction

'Happy families are all alike; every unhappy family is unhappy in its own way'– so reads Tolstoy's magnificent introduction to *Anna Karenina*, possibly the most breathtaking literary introduction ever written. Magnificent as it may be, and drawing its wisdom as far back as Aristotle, what came to be known as the *Anna Karenina* principle, does not however apply to other areas of human activity.

In fact, the obverse of it is true for what interests us here, the entrepreneurial discovery process (EDP): all successful EDPs are not alike – which is another way of saying one-size-fits-all approaches are not advisable. The case studies in the second part of this book attest to this.

Moreover, unfortunate EDPs share key traits, such as the inability to adapt to local conditions, or the reduction of EDP to surveys or consultation exercises. Entrepreneurial discovery (ED) is a key process in the definition of smart specialisation strategy (RIS3) priorities and therefore essential to a successful design of a RIS3, so let us begin with dispelling a common misunderstanding: simple surveys among triple or quadruple helix actors do not an ED process make.

The essence of the entrepreneurial discovery process lies in its interactive nature, and in organising a fruitful, targeted dialogue that brings the different actors together in a participatory leadership process to carve out jointly the smart specialisation fields and develop a suitable policy mix to implement it. The tall order behind it involves avoiding the Scylla of having specialists meet each other to repeat familiar notions within each area, as well as the Charybdis of huge groups producing soupy concoction of notions. Instead the goal is to allow a wide array of sources of ideas to interact, producing cross-fertilisation and 'eureka' moments. This implies discarding top-down omniscient dirigisme; facilitating interaction and building on its lessons; and underscoring the bottom-up character of the smart specialisation approach, in its role as a tool for regional development and economic transformation.

In what follows (and borrowing the terminology and metaphor of exit–voice–loyalty from celebrated development economist Albert Hirschman) we will address three of the important challenges/pitfalls that plague unsuccessful EDPs: countering the lure of top-down approaches/interpretations; mitigating collective action problems; and keeping the EDP arena open to and contestable by new entrants, which in exit vs. voice terms can be seen as giving voice to the voiceless.

2 Countering the lure of top-down approaches/interpretations

In the triangle used by Hirschman (exit, voice, and loyalty) in his treatise with the same title, and which we have used as an organising compass here, this issue of top-down approaches raises the issue of exit, for those regions/states that feel shunned, their economic transformation prospects stymied, by top-down decisions to concentrate research in specific regions, adulterating the EDP. In policy debates on specialisation there are those who argue in favour of top-down concentration of efforts across regions of a state, or even across states or regions in the EU.

The appeal and the arguments in favour of focusing on getting the most bang-for-the-buck are straightforward. They require however a certain set of assumptions in order to work, such as free and unfettered exchange, and the absence of powerful stochastic shocks against the activity in which one has specialised, or the ability to use financial instruments as insurance against such shocks. This in turn requires either the absence of individual sovereign states, or the impossibility of any sovereign risk (e.g. regarding impeding capital flows, expropriations, wars, etc.). Within individual countries specialisation among regions/communities is accompanied by strong central budgets which through tax-and-transfer schemes, targeted development assistance programmes, and infrastructural investment distribute benefits and smooth out the differential gains generated by the different activities in which different regions have specialised.

In the absence of the above re-distributional mechanisms the specialisation/concentration approach becomes hard to fathom; indeed most countries do not choose to specialise overwhelmingly in the activity in which they would get the most bang-for-the-buck. The few that have tried it (e.g. monocultivation agricultural economies focusing on coffee, cocoa in Africa) paid dearly for it, when the first strong negative stochastic shock hit them. Their counterparts in terms of regions within countries (e.g. mining areas in industrialised countries) have also suffered downturns when their 'mono-product' economy was hit; luckily for them, however, a strong central budget was usually there to help mitigate the extent of their income drop.

Observed sectoral and/or spatial specialisation patterns represent aggregates of individual choices made by (boundedly-) rational economic agents. These choices are not taken at random but are the reflections of persistent economic fundamentals contingent on history and geography. The empirical record at the country level is consistent with the view of pragmatic choices: as a rule, large countries tend to be technologically diverse and small countries focus on niches (Archibugi and Pianta, 1992). Malerba and Montobbio (2003, p. 428) find that international technological specialisation patterns persist over time and are the product of within-country, intersectoral knowledge spillovers.

There is also the scale argument – namely, that effective concentration allows a greater amount of resources to be devoted to specific research areas that were until then dissipated in numerous sub-critical areas. This is a strong argument. Many inventions are only possible when scale permits the deployment of capital-intensive hardware (e.g. expensive lab equipment) or the concurrent employment of scientists and engineers drawn from a wide spectrum of subject specialisms. With routinised innovation being primarily a social process, large agglomerations of knowledge workers can be expected to better facilitate the diffusion of past ideas, their recombination and consequent evolution into new-to-the-world innovations.

In addition to 'traditional' economies of scale, knowledge production is known to exhibit a quality known as 'indivisibility' (Arrow, 1962); that is, some scientific discoveries and technological inventions are only purposeful when they are achieved in their entirety (rather than in part) and in that sense are said to be 'indivisible'. At the same time though, as scale increases, the efficient organisation, control and administration of research projects becomes more difficult; for certain industrial sectors and above certain thresholds, demand saturation or exhaustion of technological opportunities may bring about diminishing returns to scale (Schmookler, 1954, 1966).

In other words, the productivity of research systems does not increase linearly with scale; the relationship follows a sigmoid pattern, with low (but increasing) returns for low levels of inputs, highest returns for medium levels of input and low (but decreasing) returns again for high levels of input. This is echoed in the empirical record: Dasgupta and Stiglitz (1980) find a positive association between concentration and innovation as long as the degree of concentration is not excessive and barriers to entry are not too strong.

However, at any given time only a subset of regions or scientific and technological specialisations find themselves at the point of increasing returns. When seen from an opportunity cost perspective, the relative returns to increased concentration for many regions may in fact be negative. Greater spatial concentration of spending on research and development and innovation (R&D) provides greater returns only in a select number of cases; in fact there are also indications that, in certain circumstances, concentration does not facilitate innovation. In their study of industrial growth in a large number of US cities during the second half of the twentieth century, Glaeser *et al.* (1992) find that urban sectoral clusters grow faster the less specialised is the rest of the urban economy.

2.1 Policy-induced specialisation

Almost by definition, a policy-induced specialisation drive is based on the assumption that the currently observed specialisation patterns (whether spontaneous or in part the result of past policy interventions) are somehow sub-optimal.

Top-down policies that dictate specialisation patterns to research agents would be difficult if not impossible to implement in the private sector. They would be largely applicable to public R&D. Even in this case though, the inducement of specialisation would be faced with significant implementation problems.

First of all a top-down approach would need an unimpeachable compass to choose where to focus. Revealed comparative advantage in one scientific field or a technological sector does not necessarily mean comparative advantage in all and stellar performance patterns are not necessarily stationary. It is possible to have a highly mobile population within a skewed distribution. In other words, those that perform at an average level at a certain point in time may develop excellent research in the future, and vice versa, i.e. excellent research groups may become complacent.

Determining ex cathedra in top-down fashion what may be the most promising thematic priorities for future growth is problematic. Despite concerted efforts, our ability to predict emerging fields of science and technology is still very limited (Pavitt, 1998).

Even if we knew in which areas to focus, a top-down 'optimal' degree of specialisation cannot be determined a priori. Concentration nurtures monopolies and/or generates oligopolistic behaviour. How and who decides what the competing entities should be? And where should those lucky few be located? Shutting the door to the first runner-up(s) is hard to justify and politically unpalatable.

As long as policymakers are convinced – and the innovation-studies community has been very persuasive on this over the years – that S/T is one of the very few levers they have to try to turn their country onto a higher standard-of-living path, they will want to be among those exploring the most promising science and technology (S/T) fields.

Within an EU context, political constraints are likely to be a big obstacle to interventions. In contrast to its counterparts in the usual comparisons (e.g. US, Japan), the EU is not a unitary state. National or regional authorities will be reluctant to do away with their aspirations of using R&D as a lever for switching gears towards higher growth paths and economic transformation, given the current lack of mechanisms to distribute any gains from increased specialisation within the EU.

Even if, despite the above implementation problems, a top-down inducement of specialisation were somehow feasible, its realisation would present considerable drawbacks, potentially severe enough to nullify any expected gains. To begin with, top-down induced concentration and loss of diversity increases susceptibility to stochastic shocks – as regions/countries with monoculture economies discovered a long time ago.

Top-down concentration and reduction in variety can constrain opportunities for new entrants and undermine the potential for new innovations to emerge. Variety and redundancy are important because they create openings for new entrants into the system. In science, these new entrants often sit on the margins of traditional disciplines and journals, and do not have stellar records that would be rewarded through a mere focus on 'excellence'. Although, mainstream scientists may poorly cite their publications, sometimes they work in new fields with exciting long-term research prospects. Software engineers, for instance, were often treated as low-grade technicians by traditional electrical engineering departments, and they had to locate their work at low-status universities. It was only through time and the rapid expansion of the software industry that their work was fully appreciated.

As mentioned above there is a large underlying concern about the existence of effective mechanisms (markets, fiscal schemes, smooth diffusion/absorption, etc.) for the distribution of any welfare gains emerging from R&D concentration, beyond the region/state which is the seat of such concentration.

Top-down concentrating research where the return on each euro spent is the highest may make short run sense for a profit-maximising firm (though it may well be inefficient in the medium to long run – portfolio theory applies here, too). However, it is quite likely politically infeasible and inefficient, not least because governments focus on welfare in their state/region, and welfare may depend on the ways benefits are distributed across states/regions, local externalities from R&D, stickiness of knowledge and researcher flows, and on overall human capital levels, which depend, in turn, on the distance from the technological frontier. Concentration expectedly generates reticence in a context where governments have been repeatedly told by experts that R&D and human capital development are key drivers of economic welfare, where knowledge diffusion/absorption is hard when R&D and human capital are weak, and where there is no distribution of welfare gains such as exists in a federal state.

2.2 Beyond distributional concerns: monopoly, monopsony, and other efficiency predators

Indeed, there are also arguments against overconcentration not simply based on distributional/cohesion issues, and the absence of the necessary accompanying institutions, but even in terms of pure efficiency: they relate to dealing with a dynamic setting in which what may seem optimal today may not be so tomorrow, as well as with the emergence of monopolies/monopsonies.

Monopsony must be avoided, just as much as monopoly. Research centres tend to have more autonomy when they do not depend on a single authority (similarly researchers in a research field are more autonomous when they do not depend on one funding source, or one mega-centre of research in that field). Concentration of power regarding funding decisions in an area of science in one centre subjects scientists to the exorbitant power of that single buyer/funder of their ideas/talents. The US system works as it does because of the multitude of funding sources at various different levels, giving proposals many different opportunities to be considered and funded (the art of creating productive chaos, which marks the US system).

On the other hand, in the US the government's role is important not only in terms of spreading the benefits from technical advances concentrated in Silicon Valley, or Rt. 128, or Rt. 1, or Raleigh–Durham, etc. It is coupled by a strong federal role in R&D funding. This, while not straitjacketing local or state funding, provides an important anchor and reference point.

Perhaps paradoxically, tensions regarding concentration are partly the result of the success of R&D and innovation studies in recent decades, identifying technology as a key discretionary ingredient of economic success. These arguments identified the role of technical progress as reflected in the residual in growth accounting, linking it with R&D, and through education and technology absorption with the ability to reap benefits from positive economic shocks, adjust to negative economic shocks, and to forge dynamic comparative advantage (such as Japan, or Finland did). These insights, coupled with persistent stickiness in knowledge diffusion/absorption, and with benefits accruing first (and more) to those in the vicinity of R&D strongholds (if for no other reason, because they attract dynamic firms near them) have made local policymakers very eager to build the next Silicon Valley – even if they have no long S/T tradition (neither did Silicon valley, nor Finland). It has also made them very reluctant to forego this goal/dream, in favour of well-established centres with long S/T traditions (i.e. seeing it as the equivalent of Silicon Valley not pursuing infotech in light of S/T tradition in the US northeast, or Finland not pursuing mobile telephony ceding the field to traditional telecoms powerhouses).

2.3 Flows of human capital

Potential growth and the ED process itself may depend on human capital availability, which in turn depends on research and on a region/state's distance from the technological frontier. Research plays different roles (including training); moreover, research and innovation interact in a variety of ways and the outputs of academic research go well beyond the generation of new knowledge as embodied in scientific papers. A key benefit of the research process is the development of trained problem-solvers. Research funding expands the pool of talent for firms to draw upon when developing new products and services. In many OECD countries considerable attention has been focused on ensuring a more 'inclusive' distribution of research. Given the characteristics of cumulative advantage in science, it has been found that left to itself research funding tends to be highly concentrated in a small number of regions. Policy measures have been designed to address this problem. In the US, for instance, the National Science Foundation EPSCoR programme has been set up to support proposals from less favoured US States. The SBIR programme also spreads research funding to many small firms, and has a counter-agglomeration impact.

Even regions that are currently at the technological frontier may benefit in the long run from an approach which avoids top-down geographic agglomeration. By not being monopolists of innovation and monopsonists of R&D talent in a research area, regions can gain not only through competition, i.e. by avoiding the complacency associated with not having tough competitors, but also through more complex bottom-up specialisation patterns, avoiding the single-crop, all-eggs-in-one-basket mega-specialisation in one area.

There is an analogous concern regarding the emergence/perpetuation of monopolies of S/T (and monopsonists of researcher talent) within smaller enclaves (at the level of region or state). This should not be taken lightly. Avoiding large-area monopolies does not mean condoning local ones. An antidote to local dinosaurs can be based on opening up competition in such local enclaves, while however taking care to have flows of human and other resources which the IIB scheme are bi-directional, and indeed multidirectional. After all, once a researcher has left his home in Bulgaria or Portugal to go to Germany or the UK, there is little to prevent the next logical step taking him where sirens sing loudest, and scientific/economic returns are portrayed as endless, i.e. the US.

While it is common to highlight the economic opportunities accruing from R&D that is close to the 'innovation frontier', economic benefits also accrue from R&D that is linked to regional and national concerns and which may not necessarily constitute new-to-the-world innovation. In fact, there is evidence that the social benefits stemming from the diffusion and assimilation of technology that is invented elsewhere are substantial (Eaton and Kortum, 1995). A more complete picture of the so-called 'untraded flows of knowledge' (Smith, 2000) will be key to devising effective ways of incentivising them.

3   Addressing collective action problems

We turn next to the issue of collective action in the context of the EDP by entities that have disparate or even competing interests (e.g. firms competing in a sector). In the triangle used by Hirschman (exit, voice, and loyalty) in his treatise with the same title, and which we have used as an organising compass here, this issue raises the issue of exit (e.g. for those firms choosing to free-ride) vs. loyalty (for those entities choosing to contribute).

The issue emerges more acutely in EDP instances in which technical bottlenecks are identified, whose removal with the help of promising (though often expensive) R&D would benefit all firms plagued by that bottleneck. These are often science and technology challenges that are neither basic enough to be distant from firms' concerns, nor applied enough to be easily appropriated by a single firm. To use the phrasing in Kyriakou (1997), they find themselves between R and D.

A large part of economic growth is explained by increases in total factor productivity. In simple terms, this means that the same inputs (i.e. labour and capital) can be combined more productively to generate output. The way this is achieved is through the innovations that allow us to combine the same basic inputs in ever more efficient forms. The direct role played by research in this simplified model is that it creates the knowledge on which such innovations increasingly often rely. Some of the knowledge produced by research may find its way into products after undergoing further refinements (and investment) in the development phase of the cycle. However, the creation of such knowledge may in practice be hindered by the fact that incentives have to be limited, so as to allow benefits from inventions or discoveries to accrue to society as a whole, after a reasonably short period of time, rather than to an individual inventor.

The results of basic science are usually sufficiently removed from immediately marketable results for it to be conducted in academic settings where ideas are exchanged freely and both the private sector and other researchers can benefit from them. At the other end of the spectrum, development work with obvious immediate market impact is usually undertaken or funded by individual firms. What has at times proved more difficult is funding efficiently intermediate types of research.

Turning ideas into concrete products is generally protected by patent and other intellectual property rules, which provide a mechanism whereby firms can recoup their investments through the unchallenged exploitation of their innovation thanks to temporary monopoly power over it in the market place. Obviously the balance between the interests of consumers and of producers has to be watched closely and is not always without friction.

However, there is potentially a grey area between basic research at one end of the scale and product development at the other encompassing problems that have an impact on an industry as a whole (and not merely individual firms).

These are often excellent candidates for targeting resources/research, identified through an ED process, as it concerns bottlenecks in translating ideas into marketable results.

However, it may not be forthcoming given the difficulty the firms investing in it have in securing the benefits of their investment to themselves. Indeed, although individual firms might in fact benefit from undertaking the research at their own expense (despite the possibility of 'free-riders' in the industry getting the benefit without the investment) they may be encouraged to wait to see if one of their competitors will take the first step, with the possible outcome (if all the firms apply the same reasoning) that the industry as a whole is held up.

3.1 The concept of public goods

To facilitate the discussion let us indicate in what sense public goods differ from other goods. Goods can be classified along an 'excludability' axis (corresponding to the ease with which others can be excluded from enjoying the good in question), as well as a 'rivalness' axis (corresponding to the degree to which my consumption of a good reduces everyone else's possibility to consume it). Public goods are both highly non-rival and non-excludable.

Growth models have identified the production of non-rival goods (technical progress leading to total factor productivity growth) as key to the growth process. Strong property rights give incentives to producers of such goods, but they may have quite unwelcome repercussions (imagine the effect of a non-expiring patent on the transistor, or on the do-loop in programming!) (Romer, 1993, pp. 354–358). The existence of non-rival goods, their importance for growth, and the need to balance the two sets of incentives (regarding production and distribution of non-rival goods) mentioned above, handicaps the application of the purely individualistic market-exchange laissez-faire models, and justifies institutions for collective action (one of the most important among them being the limited liability corporation) (Romer, 1993, p. 389).

There is then ample theoretical support for the importance of non-rival goods (and public goods as a subset of them). What about empirical evidence? With R&D used as a proxy, studies consistently compute large social rates of return on investments in non-rival goods (30 to 50 per cent). It is also much higher than the private rates of return accruing to those financing the investment in the first place. Based on Griliches' seminal survey (1992), total factor productivity growth at the national level can be explained as a result of measured spending on R&D. These results are consistent with cross-country studies by Lichtenberg (1992) and Coe and Helpman (1993) (reported in Romer 1993, pp. 354–358).

3.2 Research bottlenecks

Thus, the frontier of S/T may in certain cases be limited by the difficulty of organising collective action, when individual effort does not suffice to tackle problems. Although, by definition, these are areas which are not the preserve of basic research, there may be a case for policy intervention of a sort, to marshal efforts towards finding a solution to collective-action problems at the industry level. The goal is to organise effective collective action, where needed, in order to take advantage of mutually beneficial coordination, while using the pressure of competition and market tests to improve institutional arrangements.

A bottom-up approach (Kyriakou 1997) to deal with this in the context of the EDP could be for the firms in a certain industry to petition policymakers for the creation of investment agendas (IAs) to tackle specific industry-wide challenges when they had identified that such challenges had arisen and were creating an obstacle to the progress of their industry. Provided certain criteria are met, firms would then vote on whether to levy a small tax on the sales of the good they produce. If a (possibly qualified) majority votes in favour, the tax is imposed by the government on the entire industry. The proceeds, however, would not go to the government; rather they are used to fund the IAs outlined in the original petition by the firms, with one IA for each one of the issues to be tackled (e.g. one for a design-related bottleneck, another for a safety-testing procedure, another for training, etc.). Thus, the IAs would function by channeling tax obligations from the firms to R&D projects, in accordance with the specific mandate they are given by the industry funding them.

The crucial point is that although the amount each firm is obliged to contribute depends on its sales and the tax rate decided upon, the allocation of each firm's contribution to each of the various IAs set up in the sector is for it to determine – i.e. it would be able to decide what proportion to devote, for instance, to the design IA, safety IA, testing IA, etc.

Equally important is the fact that there can be an element of competition between IAs. If firms are not satisfied with the performance of a specific IA they can start a new one, either addressing the same issues or issues the firm(s) starting it consider more relevant. If disappointed, firms could vote to abolish any or all their IAs and rescind the tax.

3.3 Past examples of similar approaches

The proposal is not without precedents. One of the oldest forerunners exists in the US as a result of the enactment of the Agricultural Marketing Agreement Act of 1937. This act provided for setting up 'marketing orders', given a two-thirds majority approval and periodic 'referendums' to gauge continued support. Although marketing orders were also used as vehicles for output restrictions, about three quarters of them collect funds for R&D and market promotion. What they lack compared to the IA proposal is the provision for free entry of new IAs and the possibility of competition among them.

The most obvious and possibly most successful example of an idea of this kind is that of Bell Labs in the US, which was supported by payment of a small percentage of the revenues of operating companies to AT&T. To the extent that this 'support' was permitted by the regulators to be part of the rate base of operating companies, the government, in effect, sanctioned a tax to be used for industry-wide research. Since AT&T controlled the vast majority of the operators, free-riding behaviour was not a problem.

A more recent example comes from the US pharmaceutical industry. The US Food and Drug Administration was persuaded to raise the fees it levies when drugs are submitted for approval, so that more evaluators can be hired with the extra revenue, leading to a reduction in the 'approval-pending' time.

In Europe similar efforts have also been undertaken. These include cooperative research projects dedicated to industrial sectors, using a bottom-up approach and taking ideas for research projects which reflect the needs of the industry. Industry commonly finances cooperative research, in some cases with the help of public co-sponsorship. Research results are available for all participating companies, and they are supposed to be strictly pre-competitive. In some countries such as Germany, Belgium, France and the UK, there are established structures of cooperative research; in other countries efforts depend on more spontaneous actions. Institutional examples include, but are not limited to, the AiF in Germany (The National Body for Industrial Cooperative Research), FEICRO (The European Body for Industrial Cooperative Research), and the EU Commission's CRAFT (The European Programme for Industrial Cooperative Research).

The IA approach discussed here offers additionally the element of competition between the research entities set up this way, placing them within the context of a bottom-up ED process.

Most efforts to date (in Europe and elsewhere) have not included the competition element among such research entities set up by industries. In the examples described here, only one entity has usually been set up per industry, and it therefore exercises an effective monopoly. The multidimensional competition allowed by the proposal presented here is absent in these examples. It is also worth noting that contrary to the IA scheme presented here, in the above schemes the results are in general available only to participants in the scheme and not the entire industry.

3.4 Applicability and potential impact

The importance of the provision of public goods for growth is unquestionable. Public goods (such as the industry-wide public goods IAs are supposed to provide) are crucial in the growth process. The IA proposal, however, deals with goods that are neither purely public goods for which the government generally provides funding, nor among those which are best dealt with in the context of the private sector.

The intermediate zone between R and D covers what Nelson (1983) calls generic research, and he argues that it may offer large returns on investment in research. This area includes 'goods' such as programme design fundamentals, principles of computer interface design, and principles of chemical engineering. It may include in the future such projects as the setting-up of a biotechnical engineering school that would do for biotechnology what chemical engineering programmes at MIT did for the US petroleum and chemical industries, or the establishment of a separate software engineering discipline, training professionals for software production. It may include less fancy subfields such as single family home construction, an area which seems to have missed out on technological progress.

According to Nelson (1983) part of the problem in previous initiatives in this area was their top-down approach, which meant that they were not necessarily well matched to the needs perceived by participants within the industry (op. cit.).

Finally, the location of the R&D centres receiving funding from IAs is also an important issue. Governments are not likely to be indifferent to where Bell-labs look-alikes are situated. Furthermore, even if foreign firms participate in the IA approval and funding process, it is likely that spillovers will most readily benefit domestic research centres rather than foreign ones, giving incentives to countries to adopt this scheme early on. Thus, once started such a scheme is likely to spread quite quickly.

The IA proposal deals with goods that are neither purely public goods for which the government generally provides funding, nor among those which are best dealt with at the level of individual firms. It is one possible way for dealing with the hard issue of collective action in the EDP context. To continue with the Hirschman exit–voice–loyalty metaphor, the IA proposal can help address the issue, preventing 'exit' from collaborative arrangements, and safeguarding 'loyalty' to them.

4 Giving voice to the voiceless

The above brings us to the third issue, which involves the need to avoid further entrenchment of incumbents in the context of the EDP, allowing instead the entry of newcomers, and keeping the markets in question contestable – in the terms of the metaphor we are using, 'giving voice to the voiceless'.

To continue, by way of example, with the IA proposal discussed above, it is instructive to consider what effect the existence of an IA may have on potential future entrants to the market. Clearly, the benefits of the IA-funded research would need to be made available to them on the same terms as they are available to the incumbents, so as to avoid biasing the market in favour of the latter.

Keeping the corresponding markets contestable translates to making sure that newcomers can enter a market to compete with incumbents, in the sense of avoiding both legal and economic barriers. In practice, incumbents should not be able to impede entry of newcomers through legal obstacles, nor should they be able to deter new entrants by using their deep pockets to endure selling at a loss for a period long enough to drive new entrants out of the market and/or into bankruptcy. The interesting thing is that they may not even have to endure those losses, since a credible threat of such behaviour will deter new entrants, who will simply stay on the sidelines instead of suffering the costs of having to open and close shop.

In order to give voice to the voiceless, it is important that the EDP be open to incipient firms, and that potential (though not yet actual) start-up creators be involved in the process. Moreover, any programme/initiative adopted through this process should not have rules that implicitly, or explicitly deter the entry of newcomers, (e.g. by establishing criteria of longevity/turnover, etc. that are unreachable by newcomers). The EDP should avoid promoting a closed circle of entrenched incumbents by effectively guaranteeing access only to them, and giving them the power to shape objectives/criteria in their own image, and to their own circumscribed benefit; in short, a 'clubby' insiders vs. outsiders feeling should not hijack the ED process.

The reason for emphasising this third issue is not merely formalistic/legalistic; it is more importantly substantive. The point of departure of the S3 and the ED process within it is the desire to pursue at regional/national level an agenda of economic transformation. Almost by definition further entrenching incumbents (the paragons of the current state of affairs) would seem a counterproductive way to pursue such economic transformation.

5 Conclusions

The goal of EDP is to allow a wide array of sources of ideas to interact, producing cross-fertilisation and 'eureka' moments, i.e 'discoveries' of opportunities emerging out of this wedding of ongoing/potential R&D and existing/potential entrepreneurial drive. This implies discarding top-down omniscient dirigisme; facilitating interaction and building on its lessons; and underscoring the bottom-up character of the smart specialisation approach, in its role as a tool for regional development and economic transformation.

We have discussed three of the important challenges/pitfalls that plague unsuccessful EDPs: a) the lure of top-down approaches/interpretations, and how to counter them; b) the collective action problems (and a possible remedial) that inevitably emerge when entities (such as firms) with separate individual agendas must be mobilised and contribute their share towards a goal; c) the need to keep the EDP arena open to new entrants, and the corresponding markets 'contestable'. The latter, which can be a very challenging task, indeed, can be seen as giving voice to the voiceless in this process.

More generally, the way such challenges are handled reflects not only the EDP's chances for success, but also the way socioeconomic agents engage or disengage with/in the socioeconomic context that gave birth to them. This translates to whether they opt for (or are pushed to) exit, whether they are given (and exercise) voice in the shaping of outcomes, and at a deeper level, whether loyalty marks the relation of these socioeconomic agents and the institutions around them.

Bibliography

Archibugi, D. and Pianta, M. (1992), 'Specialization and size of technological activities in industrial countries: The analysis of patent data', *Research Policy*, Vol. 21, pp. 79–93.

Arrow, K. (1962), 'Economic welfare and the allocation of resources for invention' in R. Nelson (ed.) *The rate and direction of inventive activity*, Princeton University Press, Princeton.

CEC (2000), 'Towards a European Research Area', *COM* 6, January 1.

CEC (2007), 'The European Research Area: New Perspectives' (Green Paper). *SEC* 161–412, April 4.

Dasgupta, P. and Stiglitz, J. (1980), 'Industrial Structure and the Nature of Economic Activity', *The Economic Journal*, Vol. 90, No. 358 (June), pp. 256–293.

Eaton, J., and Kortum, S. (1995), 'Engines of growth: domestic and foreign sources of innovation', *NBER Working Paper, no. 5207*.

Georghiou, L. (2007), 'Interim policy options paper of the Expert Group, ERA rationales', in *The Future of Science and Technology in Europe, Discussion Papers for the Parallel Sessions*, Lisbon, Portugal.

Glaeser, E. L., H. D. Kallal, J. A. Scheinkman, and A. Shleifer (1992), 'Growth in cities', *Journal of Political Economy*, Vol. 100, No. 6, pp. 1126–1152.

Griliches, Z. (1992), 'The search for R&D spillovers'. *Scandinavian Journal of Economics*,Vol. 94 (Supplement), pp. 29–47.

Hirschman, A. (1970), *Exit, voice, and loyalty: Responses to decline in firms, organizations, and states*. Harvard University Press, Cambridge, MA.

Howells, J. (2005), 'Innovation and regional economic development: A matter of perspective?', *Research Policy*, Vol. 34, No. 8, pp. 1220–1234.

Kyriakou, D. (1997), 'Technology policy strategy: Between Research and Development', *The IPTS Report*, No. 12, March 1997, Seville, Spain, ISSN 1025-9384.

Malerba, F. and Montobbio, F. (2003), 'Exploring factors affecting international technological specialization: the role of knowledge flows and the structure of innovative activity', *Journal of Evolutionary Economics*, Vol. 13, No. 4, pp. 411–434.

Marimon, R. (2007), 'Governance and coordination of S&T policies in the European Research Area', *Provisional draft for the November 6, 2007 discussion of the Experts Group on Knowledge for Growth*.

Nelson, R. (1983), 'Government support of technical progress: Lessons from history'. *Journal of Policy Analysis and Management*, Vol. 2, No. 4, pages 499–514.

Pavitt, K. (1998), 'The inevitable limits of EU R&D funding', *Research Policy*, Vol. 27, No. 6, pp. 559–568.

Rodrik, D. (2004), 'Industrial Policy for the Twenty-first Century'. *Centre for Economic Policy Research, CEPR Discussion Paper No. 4767*, London, UK.

Romer, P. (1993), 'Implementing a National Technology Strategy with Self-Organizing Industry Investment Boards'. *Brookings Papers on Economic Activity, Microeconomics*, Vol. 2, pp. 345–399.

Schmookler, J. (1954), 'The level of inventive activity, *The Review of Economics and Statistics*, Vol. 36, pp. 183–190.

Schmookler, J. (1966), *Invention and Economic Growth*, Harvard University Press, Cambridge, MA.

Smith, K. (2000), 'Innovation as a systemic phenomenon: Rethinking the role of policy', *Enterprise and Innovation Management Studies*, Vol. 1, No. 1, pp. 73–102.

3 Institutions and the entrepreneurial discovery process for smart specialization

Andrés Rodríguez-Pose and Callum Wilkie

1 Introduction

Smart specialization approaches to regional innovation policies have attracted considerable attention since their conception (Foray *et al.*, 2009) and full-fledged endorsement by the European Commission (Foray *et al.*, 2012). With this attention has come significant interest in one of the approach's defining features: the 'entrepreneurial discovery process' (EDP). In the simplest sense, entrepreneurial discovery is an exercise that 'reveals what a country does best in terms of R&D and innovation' by enlisting those who best understand the strengths, capabilities, constraints and limitations of a territory in order to identify sectors, activities and technologies that could constitute the basis of a smart specialization strategy (Foray *et al.*, 2011: 7). According to Capello (2014: 7), EDP is a 'conceptual pillar' of smart specialization. Foray *et al.* (2011) and Coffano and Foray (2014) consider EDP *a*, if not *the*, feature that distinguishes smart specialization approaches from innovation strategies of the past and the one that lends these approaches their more 'bottom-up' character. Suffice to say the interest the entrepreneurial discovery process has garnered seems largely warranted. In spite of this attention, however, important questions remain open and much work is yet to be done in advancing our understanding of this critical exercise.

The following essay sets out to address two aspects of the entrepreneurial discovery process that have thus far, in our opinion, received insufficient attention. First, we explore 'who' is responsible for EDP. That is, we address the respective role of the actors that should be involved in EDP, as well as examine the way in which these actors should be engaged. Second, we delve into the relationship between institutional environment and EDP recognizing that institutions and the institutional context exercise considerable influence, both directly and indirectly, on the effectiveness and outcomes of the process. The exploration of the interaction between institutions and EDP culminates in a discussion of the implementation of the process across diverse institutional contexts and the geography of the entrepreneurial discovery process. In addressing these critical aspects, our aim is to further the collective understanding of EDP and ultimately assist in its operationalization as a fundamental part of smart specialization strategies.

2 The 'who' and the 'how' of the entrepreneurial discovery process

EDP is, by its very nature, an inclusive process. However, while the inclusivity of the process is generally accepted, critically important questions remain pertaining to who should be engaged and how this should be done.

2.1 The 'who'?

The first question related to EDP is that of 'who should be involved'. The logical answer to this question is that the process must be as inclusive as possible, involving a wide variety of stakeholders within local societies, as well as the vertical coordination of different tiers of government. Such a response, while relevant to the bottom-up nature of EDP, offers, however, little in the way of insight into the respective functions or roles of various types of actors nor does it provide any justification or reasoning for their inclusion.

Consequently, a clearer justification of the reasons behind the need to involve different types of actors in EDP is required. In the simplest sense, we may consider three types or classes of actors that must be involved in EDP, each of which serves a unique purpose and makes a substantive contribution to the process and the strategy more broadly: a) 'entrepreneurial agents' (Coffano and Foray, 2014); b) policy makers and the 'leaders' of the smart specialization strategy and c) the remainder of society.

Entrepreneurial agents assume the most privileged position in EDP as the sources of the 'entrepreneurial knowledge'[1] that is effectively the foundation upon which smart specialization strategies are developed (Foray *et al.*, 2011). Entrepreneurial agents assume any number of forms. The European Commission has, in fact, adopted a conceptualization that defines these actors in a distinctly different manner to what the term might connote – where entrepreneurs may be assumed to be firms, entrepreneurial actors are understood, in a triple-helix way, to include '*inter alia* firms, higher education institutions, public research institutes, independent innovators; whoever is best placed to discover the domains of R&D and innovation in which a region is likely to excel given its existing capabilities and productive assets' (Foray *et al.*, 2012: 12). This inclusive conceptualization seems particularly apt in light of the diversity of insights that are understood to constitute entrepreneurial knowledge. Firms do, however, assume a prominent role in the entrepreneurial discovery process (Coffano and Foray, 2014). Their engagement with the market enables them to provide a valuable understanding of the commercial viability of activities and opportunities as well as market dynamics (Cities Alliance, 2007) that effectively distinguish the entrepreneurial knowledge that the EDP seeks to elicit from simply 'knowledge about science and techniques' (Foray *et al.*, 2011: 7). This prominence of firms does not, however, imply that the insight provided by other entrepreneurial actors (higher education institutions or research institutes, for example) is 'second-best' to that provided by firms. Rather, entrepreneurial knowledge from *all* sources can be regarded as necessary and highly complementary (Coffano and Foray, 2014). That is, each actor inevitably possesses insights, perspectives and knowledge that are derived from their unique experiences and positioning relative to the market and other actors, all of which may be usefully combined and related to develop a comprehensive knowledge base used to inform the smart specialization strategy. This final point implies a central role for those tasked with processing the entrepreneurial knowledge from individual actors.

The second category of actor is policy makers. While entrepreneurial agents in some respects drive and may be the focus of the entrepreneurial discovery process, those tasked with leading the smart specialization effort assume a prominent role as well and, contrary to what might be assumed, are not 'passive' participants in the entrepreneurial discovery process. Their responsibilities are two-fold. First, the entrepreneurial knowledge embodied in and possessed by the various relevant actors must be aggregated.[2] Once this aggregation has commenced, the focus then must shift to its synthesis and processing. Entrepreneurial agents are, axiomatically, only capable of providing insight on the basis of their own experience (Iacobucci, 2014) and in that sense the entrepreneurial knowledge possessed by a single actor is narrow in scope. While there is inherent value in this knowledge in and of itself, its utility conceivably increases exponentially once it is positioned relative to entrepreneurial knowledge collected from other sources.[3] One could say then that the base of entrepreneurial knowledge is 'greater than the sum of its individual parts'. This discussion of the function of policy makers in the process must also make explicit that while policy makers are indeed active in the entrepreneurial discovery process and hold considerable responsibility, it is not their position to consciously 'pick-and-choose' stakeholders, as doing so would undermine the bottom-up, grassroots nature of the entrepreneurial discovery process and the smart specialization strategy more broadly (Iacobucci, 2014). In practice, there may be a need, arising from, for example, resource and temporal constraint, for policy makers to be somewhat selective in the engagement of stakeholders. The selection, however, must be *reactive* rather than *proactive*. That is, policy makers must, first, not have preconceived notions about which stakeholders should be consulted and, second and more importantly, choose stakeholders that are objectively the most capable of providing entrepreneurial knowledge as a result of *inter alia* their prominence in and interactions with the market and high-potential activities more specifically, as well as their participation in the critically important 'exploratory behaviour' (see Section 3.2).

The final class of actor involved involves members of society in general. EDP is not a standard process of stakeholder engagement – it is a process that is designed and implemented to elicit very specific information that is used to shape future policy decisions and the identification of certain activities that a region or economy could realistically be expected to capitalize upon. Hence, a premium is placed on the engagement of the aforementioned entrepreneurial agents (Foray *et al.* 2011). That said, this prioritization should not imply that actors who are not classified as entrepreneurial agents do not contribute or participate in EDP. EDP requires the active involvement of the broader society for two specific reasons. First, elaborating on a previous point, no actor is omniscient and the more inclusive the process of knowledge collection, the more comprehensive the knowledge base at the disposal of policy makers. Second, and more importantly, broad societal engagement contributes to the local ownership of the process and the strategy more broadly. This local ownership is critical for the smart specialization strategy as a whole as it provides a sense of involvement and empowerment and contributes to retain the place-based, contextually tailored bottom-up character of EDP.

2.2 The 'how'?

Once the roles of relevant actors in EDP are understood, the attention must shift to the collection of entrepreneurial knowledge itself and the interactions between contributing actors and policy makers. Interactions between actors and policy makers can assume any number of forms. These range, for example, from focus groups and workshops to broader community meetings or surveys (Cities Alliance, 2007).

There is likely no universal single best method for interacting with stakeholders and as such the selection of method must give ample consideration to financial, temporal or any other constraints that impinge upon the process (Cities Alliance, 2007) as well as the exact actors that the process seeks to engage and any factors that might influence their involvement. Moreover, what is of greater importance than the exact mechanism or method employed, as Section 3.3 will address, is that a sound relationship emerges and is sustained between policy makers and those contributing entrepreneurial knowledge and insight (Rodrik, 2004). The character of this relationship shapes the interaction and influences the utility of the exercise as a whole.[4] This means that while EDP is affected by local institutional conditions, EDP, in turn and if performed adequately, should be capacity or institution building.

3 Institutions and the entrepreneurial discovery process

The relationship between EDP and the institutional context within which it occurs has been, despite its importance, relatively unexplored. Institutions, however, are increasingly understood to be of tremendous relevance to innovation, growth and economic performance in general, and to the success of policies that take place at the local or subnational level in particular (Rodríguez-Pose, 2013). It would seem, then, that an investigation into the interaction between institutions and smart specialization strategies and EDP more specifically would not only be wise, but it is, in fact, necessary.

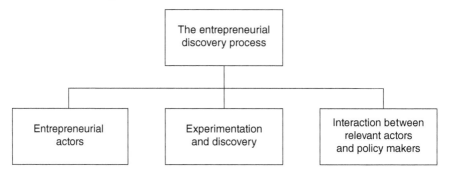

Figure 3.1 Fundamental components of the entrepreneurial discovery process

Assessing this relationship is not, however, a simple endeavour. The entrepreneurial discovery process is both inherently complex and multifaceted and, as the preceding section has highlighted, inclusive of a diverse set of actors. Institutions and the institutional context inevitably interact with the process in a variety of ways across a number of axes.

The most effective method for examining our relationship of interest involves decomposing EDP into what can be said to be its three fundamental 'components' or 'ingredients' and exploring the way in which institutions interact with each of them. The three fundamental components of the entrepreneurial discovery process for the purposes of this exercise are: a) entrepreneurial actors b) the generation of 'entrepreneurial knowledge' and c) interaction between policy makers and those in possession of 'entrepreneurial knowledge'. Each of these will be addressed in turn in the following sections.

3.1 Institutions and entrepreneurial actors

The first of the three aforementioned fundamental components are the entrepreneurial actors that constitute the sources of 'entrepreneurial knowledge' used to inform and guide the development of the broader smart specialization strategy. Quite simply, the entrepreneurial discovery process cannot occur in the absence of actors who, through their respective activities and experiences as well as interactions and engagements with other members of society, have developed a comprehensive knowledge of a given region's resources and assets as well as its strengths (and, conversely, weaknesses), capabilities, and, ultimately, its potential (Foray *et al.*, 2011). Implied by this centrality of entrepreneurial actors to the entrepreneurial discovery process is the importance of a context or environment that is conducive to both the survival and success of existing actors as well as, relatedly, to the emergence of new actors. This is the first axis along which institutions interact with the entrepreneurial discovery process. *Institutions effectively shape the context within which entrepreneurial actors exist, function, interact and ultimately generate entrepreneurial knowledge via the exploratory behaviours addressed in the proceeding section.*

The conduciveness of a region to supporting entrepreneurial actors and fostering the emergence of new ones is largely reflective of the region's conduciveness to economic activity. A region's capacity to host and foster economic activity is understood to be influenced by any number of factors. A particularly relevant and increasingly acknowledged one is the institutional context.

Institutions, formal and informal, condition the context within which economic activity occurs. Formal institutions, commonly understood as the 'rules of the game in a society' following the conceptualization of institutions forwarded by North (1990: 477), delineate a 'framework' within which economic activity occurs. Their codified nature lends them an element of immediacy and transparency (Rodríguez-Pose and Storper, 2006) that enables widespread understanding and acceptance. Informal institutions on the other hand, often recognized as 'individual habits, group routines and social norms and values' as per Amin (1999: 367), are less tangible. Nevertheless they are understood to serve a critically important function, promoting trust and facilitating cooperation and interaction among members of a society (Fukuyama, 2000). Taken together, formal and informal institutions work synergistically to 'reduce transaction costs and moral hazards' (Rodríguez-Pose and Storper, 2006: 6; see also Fukuyama, 2000) thereby promoting economic efficiency (North 1992; 2005) and ultimately fostering the emergence of a 'microeconomic environment that comes across to individual actors as a reason to have confidence in the economic process' (Rodríguez-Pose and Storper, 2006: 6) and one that is broadly conducive to economic activity and the viability of entrepreneurial actors (Jütting, 2003).

Not all institutional contexts are identical (Rodríguez-Pose and Storper, 2006) and as such, their suitability for hosting economic activity and, in turn, sustaining entrepreneurial actors varies as well. Sound institutional contexts characterized by, *inter alia*, well-functioning and appropriately monitored and enforced formal institutions and a high degree of 'institutional thickness' (Amin and Thrift, 1995) are associated with, above all else, efficiency and are effectively favourable for entrepreneurial actors. Sound institutional contexts afford them the opportunity to engage in the practices that generate valuable 'entrepreneurial knowledge'. Conversely, weaker institutional contexts characterized by either the complete absence of institutional constructs or, perhaps worse, poorly-functioning institutions impose unnecessary constraints on existing actors while also discouraging the emergence of new ones both of which inhibit the potential generation of entrepreneurial knowledge. Under these conditions, actors may use EDP for advancing private interests and capturing potential rents. Impacted information and insider–outsider problems will contribute to an elite capture of the EDP, effectively undermining its purpose, validity and effectiveness.

3.2 Institutions and the practices of experimentation and discovery

The second fundamental component of the entrepreneurial discovery process is the generation of 'entrepreneurial knowledge' through exploratory behaviour consisting of experimentation and the pursuit of new activities or opportunities. Such behaviour permits the identification of '[activities] and the domains of R&D and innovation in which a region is likely to excel given its existing capabilities and productive assets' (Foray *et al.*, 2011: 7) as well as 'new opportunities for commercially viable lines of business' (ibid.: 11). Simply put, entrepreneurial actors must actually be 'active' for the entrepreneurial discovery process to succeed. It is not, however, guaranteed that they will be.

The aforementioned exploratory behaviour is conceivably constrained by any number of 'impediments'. Some firms, for example – small and medium enterprises in particular – face profound, sometimes insurmountable, resource constraints, financial, human or otherwise, that preclude, or certainly restrict their capacity to engage in exploratory behaviour and, in turn, to contribute substantively to the entrepreneurial discovery process (Rothwell, 1989; Nooteboom, 1994). That said, the likelihood of entrepreneurial actors engaging in exploratory behaviour is widely understood to be inhibited by two more specific market failures: a) the 'incomplete appropriability problem' (Foray *et al.*, 2011: 12) and 'coordination externalities [or failures]' (Rodrik, 2004: 12). Rectifying, or at least addressing, these market failures is of utmost importance for the success of EDP and the smart specialization strategy more broadly.

The incomplete appropriability problem is something of a standard challenge associated with fostering innovative activity. It derives from the inability of entrepreneurial actors to realize a sufficient private benefit relative to potential public benefit from exploratory practices and innovation more generally to justify their pursuit (Rodrik, 2004; Foray *et al.*, 2011). It is, in the simplest sense, an issue of incentives and the misalignment of private and public benefit. Accordingly, efforts to mitigate the incomplete appropriability problem assume the form of the provision of incentives (Foray *et al.*, 2011) to high-potential activities to more closely align potential private benefit with potential public benefit (that would in the absence of policy, vastly outweigh potential private benefit) thus alleviating (or at least reducing) disincentives to exploratory behaviour.[5]

Coordination failures arise when the pursuit of a new activity or opportunity requires coordinated action involving more than one party (Rodrik, 2004). That is, if an activity will only be viable through a collective effort, an individual actor may be less inclined to pursue said activity out of concern that another actor (or actors) will not fulfil their prescribed or expected role compromising the viability of the activity for all parties involved.[6] Closely related to the notion of coordination failure is that of 'free-riding'. That is, in addition to concerns an individual actor may have about making an investment or pursuing a particular opportunity whose viability is conditional on the actions of one or more other actors, that same actor may also be wary of others benefitting from his or her investment to an extent that is disproportionate to the investments the others have made or the risk they have elected to bear. Rodrik (2004) proposes two solutions for the resolution of coordination failures. The first is, axiomatically, facilitating 'true coordination' (Rodrik, 2004: 14) amongst actors. The second is the provision of 'ex ante subsidies that do not need to be paid ex post' (ibid.).

The relevance of institutions to fostering exploratory practices, in addition to shaping the overall suitability and conduciveness of an environment to economic activity inclusive of exploratory behaviour (Section 3.1), is twofold.[7] *First, institutions influence the delivery and efficacy of, in this case, incentives.* Subsidization and financial support mechanisms assume a central role in the resolution of both types of market failures inhibiting exploratory practices, even more so in the case of the incomplete appropriability problem. The provision of incentives, however, is prone to hijacking that jeopardizes its effectiveness (Rodrik, 2004: 17). A well-functioning institutional context is perhaps less susceptible to the afflictions of corruption, rent-seeking and self-interested activity meaning that support or subsidization is more likely to be provided in a suitable manner – i.e. in a manner uninfluenced by favouritism, corruption or even hubris and unrealistic expectation, for example – in a sound institutional setting.

Second, institutions, both formal and informal, as addressed, foster trust and interaction, both of which conceivably contribute to the mitigation of the coordination problems. Rodrik (2004: 13), in this respect, asserts that '[the resolution of coordination failures does] not necessitate subsidization, and overcoming them need not be costly to the government budget' and suggests that simply facilitating coordination between parties may be sufficient. Sound institutions can, at least in part, contribute to achieving this coordination and can, where necessary, work synergistically with incentives to rectify the coordination problem hopefully impelling exploratory behaviour.

3.3 Institutions and the engagement of entrepreneurial actors

The third and final critical component of EDP is interaction between entrepreneurial actors and policy makers to facilitate the transmission of entrepreneurial knowledge. It is imperative that policy makers can communicate directly and efficiently with entrepreneurial actors so that that information EDP aims to elicit may be aggregated, processed and synthesized and ultimately used to direct future policy choices and the design of the smart specialization strategy (Foray *et al.*, 2011). While the exact character of the interactions between the two parties will inevitably vary, it is imperative, irrespective of context, that a sound 'ongoing' relationship exists between those capable of providing knowledge and those tasked with collecting it (Rodrik, 2004: 16).

Achieving such a relationship is, as Rodrik (2004: 17) observes, contingent on '[finding] an intermediate position between full autonomy and full embeddedness'. That is, entrepreneurial information is not effectively communicated through relatively 'distant' arms-length engagement between entrepreneurial actors and policy makers necessitating a more intimate relationship. The challenge that arises in pursuit of such proximity is that, to state it most directly, '[policy makers] end up in bed with (and in the pockets of) business interests' (Rodrik, 2004: 17).

The institutional environment is a prominent determinant of whether such a relationship can emerge and be sustained. Weak institutional contexts are susceptible to behaviour that would adversely affect the likelihood of a productive relationship flourishing. A lack of trust precludes the necessary openness and interaction and the absence of transparency and the associated potential for corruption undermine the overall functioning and effectiveness of the process. Conversely, the trust, openness and transparency facilitated by strong, well-functioning institutions permit the dialogue, interaction and overall 'closeness' that enables the effective communication of entrepreneurial knowledge.

3.4 Mixing it all together

Figure 3.2 provides a simplified illustration of the intricate and multidimensional relationship between EDP and the local institutional environment in each of the three dimensions covered in the previous sub-sections. What should emerge from the preceding discussion, above all else, is that the institutional context within which EDP occurs shapes the validity of the process at all stages and, even more importantly, can exercise tremendous influence on its effectiveness and outcomes. In that regard, being aware of, and acknowledging the institutional context in which EDP takes place are crucial for both the execution and success of the exercise.

4 Institutions and the geography of the entrepreneurial discovery process

The centrality of the institutional context to the execution of the EDP raises concerns about the 'geography' of the entrepreneurial discovery process and its viability across variable institutional environments. A sound institutional context seemingly provides the optimal setting for the entrepreneurial discovery process. Well-functioning institutions effectively support the emergence and success of entrepreneurial agents (Section 3.1), facilitate, both directly and indirectly, processes of experimentation and discovery (Section 3.2), and permit the internalization and subsequent application of entrepreneurial knowledge (Section 3.3). In this type of stronger institutional context it may be anticipated then that, once initiated, EDP should unfold more-or-less automatically.[8] In these environments, policy makers must remain vigilant

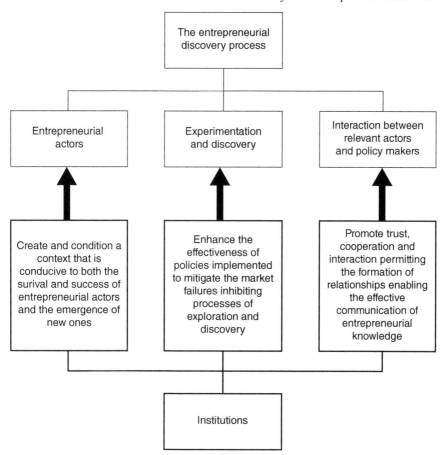

Figure 3.2 Institutions and the entrepreneurial discovery process

and active, but their overall role is greatly facilitated by the capacity of a system in which entrepreneurial agents are in a position to constantly 'discover' and 'reinvent' new entrepreneurial avenues on the basis of existing conditions and through related variety mechanisms.

Conversely, weak institutional contexts, at best, do not facilitate the entrepreneurial discovery process and, at worst, actually inhibit it. That is, environments are less conducive to economic activity and exploratory behaviour in the absence of well-functioning institutions that would otherwise reduce transitions costs, shape incentives and promote overall efficiency (Section 3.1). Additionally, an adverse institutional context hampers the emergence of a productive relationship between policy makers and entrepreneurial actors through which knowledge and insights may be communicated. This discrepancy between stronger or favourable institutional contexts and weak or adverse ones gives rise to a particularly important question: can

EDP, and by extension (given the fundamental nature of the process) smart specialization approaches, occur in weak institutional settings?

Certainly weak institutional contexts may inhibit and hinder the inception and constant renewal of EDP in those territories where a constant identification and (re)discovery of innovative potential is most needed. This does not imply that weaker institutions are an insuperable barrier for EDP in such environments. EDP will not, however, happen in them without a concerted effort and an awareness of the obstacles that inevitably must be addressed. Unlike in sound institutional settings, EDP will not occur automatically. Axiomatically, in these contexts more fundamental institutional reforms will have to occur. Such reforms, nevertheless, often require a longer time scale than is awarded to simple EDP in more amenable contexts. There is then a more immediate need for external intervention to aid regions and overcome the constraints imposed on the entrepreneurial discovery process by an unfavourable institutional context. Intervention would predominately assume two forms: technical support and financial incentives and support. Technical support, such as that offered through the 'S3 platform', can assist regions to develop the capacity to implement and execute the entrepreneurial discovery process and address the prominent institutional barriers (Foray *et al.*, 2011). Financial incentives and support, provided for example through the Cohesion and Structural and Investment Funds, can supplement this technical assistance and will also contribute to overcoming institutional deficiencies. External intervention, if performed adequately, can also limit the ever present risk of elite capture of EDP in weak institutional process and contribute to make EDP an institutional and capacity-building tool in and of itself.

It should be noted that external intervention, financial or technical, and capacity-building efforts more generally, will perhaps have the most immediate impact on formal (Section 3.1) institutional arrangements largely because of their tangibility, 'codifiability' and enforceability. Addressing informal (Section 3.1) institutions, whether that involves encouraging their development or 'correcting' adverse ones, presents a far more profound challenge for a host of reasons, the most notable of which are, first, the difficulty associated with intervening in an intangible entity (Rodríguez-Pose, 2013) and, second, the persistence and resilience of informal institutional arrangements (see, for example, Duranton *et al.*, 2009). Consequently, breeding broad-based trust, which is most readily associated with informal institutional arrangements, is remarkably difficult, yet, as discussed, is critically important for the entrepreneurial discovery process. The only recourse, at least initially, it would seem is targeting more formal institutional arrangements, be that through external intervention or otherwise, to effectively bolster the aforementioned 'institutional framework' (and in doing so, perhaps, correct existing corrupt, exclusive or generally adverse informal institutions), and then allow sound informal institutions, and, importantly, the trust they facilitate, to mature within a suitable formal institutional context over the longer period of time needed for this to occur.

Another critically important point that must be made explicit is that while external intervention can mitigate financial and technical capacity constraints, it is not a panacea. More specifically, the provision of support in itself cannot ensure that politicians and policy makers will be sufficiently committed to and engaged in the entrepreneurial discovery process and smart specialization strategies more broadly. In practice, there is likely no way to be absolutely certain that the requisite political willingness and motivation will exist. That said, there are perhaps steps that may be, and in fact, must be, taken to increase its likelihood. For example, a concerted effort could be made to minimize any ambiguities concerning the respective responsibilities and tasks of various actors and groups (Chayes and Chayes, 1993: 188). If all actors are, first, acutely aware of their obligations, and, second, capable of fulfilling those obligations (a result, perhaps, of external intervention), the likelihood of situations of 'non-compliance', that is where actors do not per-form their respective duties – which in this case would be committing entirely to the smart specialization strategy – is reduced (ibid.). Simply clarifying responsibility is, axiomatically, not sufficient in all contexts. That said, it is perhaps a suitable first step towards ensuring commitment and compliance.

Finally, it must be made explicit that while external assistance may very well play a particularly prominent role in the successful execution of the EDP in weaker institutional settings, it is absolutely imperative, however, that the ownership of and responsibility for the process remains local. The logic underpinning this assertion is that the novelty of smart specialization approaches to innovation is exactly that they are contextually tailored to a territory's unique capabilities and challenges through their local ownership and the leadership of the local actors who best comprehend the unique condi-tions of that territory. Overly involved external actors undermine this logic and the effort to move away from the top-down innovation policies of the past. An adequate balance between external assistance and local ownership must be achieved in regions where external involvement is necessary so that the region may overcome fundamental barriers but may still retain control over and shape the strategy in accordance with local conditions.

5 Concluding remarks

EDP is a critically important feature of smart specialization approaches. Its execution effectively establishes a base upon which policy makers can develop and implement strategies designed to foster the activities and tech-nologies that emerge as most viable from the process itself. Not surprisingly, increasing attention has been paid to the process and some progress has been made in developing a robust understanding of its many aspects and intrica-cies. That said, there is still a considerable way to go in order to make EDP an effective tool to maximise the innovation, entrepreneurial and growth poten-tial of every territory.

It was the intention of the paper to shed more light on EDP through an investigation into the actors who should assume a role within the process and then an examination of the complex relationship between the process and institutional context within which it occurs. Four central conclusions emerge from this exercise. First, entrepreneurial actors, policy makers and society more broadly all assume roles within the entrepreneurial discovery process and no single actor's role is more important than another's. Second, there are a range of methods through which policy makers may engage local stakeholders, but it is essential, irrespective of method, that a sound relationship is developed between the two parties to permit meaningful interaction and the sharing of insights and knowledge. Third, the institutional dimension of EDP cannot be overlooked as the institutional context influences the viability and outcomes of EDP. Fourth, and finally, EDP can, and in fact must, occur in both strong and weak institutional contexts, although external intervention will likely be necessary in adverse institutional environments to overcome the constraints and barriers that weaker institutions impose.

Notes

1 Entrepreneurial knowledge is commonly understood to 'combine related knowledge about science, technology and engineering with knowledge of market growth potential, potential competitors as well as the whole set of inputs and services required for launching a new activity (paraphrasing Foray *et al.*, 2011: 7).
2 Coffano and Foray (2014: 43), citing Bresnahan (2012), assert that entrepreneurial knowledge is 'fragmented and dispersed [and] is not available in compact form within one single entity'.
3 The definition of entrepreneurial knowledge proposed by Foray *et al.* (2011) emphasizes the notions of 'relating' and 'combining'.
4 The notion of a sound relationship between stakeholders and policy makers is addressed in more depth in Section 3.3.
5 Property rights and intellectual property protection would normally represent a viable option for addressing the incomplete appropriability problem. Foray *et al.*, (2011) among others, however, advocate against this approach because a central tenet of smart specialization is 'imitative entry' which would be inhibited by overly stringent intellectual property protection.
6 Rodrik (2004) addresses 'coordination externalities' in considerable detail.
7 Well-functioning institutions support the survival of existing entrepreneurial actors and encourage the emergence of new ones by providing an institutional context that is conducive to all forms of economic activity (Section 3.1). Exploratory practices, as a form of economic activity, are therefore facilitated by, or certainly garner some benefit from, a favourable institutional context.
8 'Automatically' is meant to connote without friction and unimpeded by institutional constraints, not that policy makers may act passively and assume that EDP will always occur spontaneously. There is still a need for the implementation of policies in the presence of market failures inhibiting exploratory behaviour, for example, and for concerted effort to aggregate and process entrepreneurial knowledge.

References

Cities Alliance. (2007), Organising the effort. In *Understanding Your Local Economy: A Resource Guide for Cities* (pp. 5–16). Washington, DC: Cities Alliance.

Amin, A. (1999), An Institutionalist Perspective on Regional Development. *International Journal of Urban and Regional Research*, 23(2), 365–378.

Amin, A. and Thrift, T. D. (1995), Globalization, Institutional Thickness and the Local Economy. In Healy, P., Cameron, S., Davoudi, S., Graham, S. and Madani-Pour, A. (eds) *Managing Cities: The New Urban Context* (pp. 92–108). Chichester: J. Wiley and Sons.

Bresnahan, T. F. (2012), Generality, Recombination and Reuse. In *The Rate and Direction of Inventive Activity Revisited* (pp. 611–656). Chicago: University of Chicago Press.

Capello, R. (2014), Smart Specialisation Strategy and the New EU Cohesion Policy Reform: Introductory Remarks. *Scienze Regionali*, 13(1), 5–14.

Chayes, A. and Chayes, A. H. (1993), On Compliance. *International Organization*, 47(2), 175–205.

Coffano, M. and Foray, D. (2014), The Centrality of Entrepreneurial Discovery in Building and Implementing a Smart Specialisation Strategy. *Scienze Regionali*, 13(1), 33–50.

Duranton, G., Rodríguez-Pose, A. and Sandall, R. (2009), Family Types and the Persistence of Regional Disparities in Europe. *Economic Geography*, 85(1), 23–47.

Foray, D., David, P. A. and Hall, B. (2009), Smart Specialisation: The Concept. In *Knowledge for Growth: Prospects for Science, Technology and Innovation*. Brussels: European Commission.

Foray, D., David, P. A. and Hall, B. (2011), Smart Specialisation: From Academic Idea to Political Instrument, the Surprising Career of a Concept and the Difficulties Involved in its Implementation. *MTEI Working Paper* No. 2011.001. Lausanne: École Polytechnique Fédérale de Lausanne.

Foray, D., Goddard, J., Beldarrain, X. G., Landabaso, M., McCann, P., Morgan, K., Nauwelaers, C. and Ortega-Argilés, R. (2012), *Guide to Research and Innovation Strategies for Smart Specialisations (RIS 3)*. Brussels: European Commission.

Fukuyama, F. (2000), Social Capital and Civil Society. *IMF Working Papers* No. WP/00/74. Washington, DC: International Monetary Fund.

Iacobucci, D. (2014), Designing and Implementing a Smart Specialisation Strategy at Regional Level: Some Open Questions. *Scienze Regionali*, 13(1), 107–126.

Jütting, J. (2003), Institutions and Development: A Critical Review. *OECD Development Centre Working Papers* No. 210. Paris: Organisation for Economic Cooperation and Development.

Nooteboom, B. (1994), Innovation and Diffusion in Small Firms: Theory and Evidence. *Small Business Economics, 6,* 327–347.

North, D. C. (1990), *Institutions, Institutional Change and Economic Performance*. New York, NY: Cambridge University Press.

North, D. C. (1992), Institutions, Ideology and Economic Performance. *Cato Journal*, 11(3), 477–496.

North, D. C. (2005), *Understanding the Process of Economic Change*. Princeton: Princeton University Press.

Rodríguez-Pose, A. (2013), Do Institutions Matter for Regional Development? *Regional Studies*, 47, 1034–1047.

Rodríguez-Pose, A. and Storper, M. (2006), Better Rules or Stronger Communities? On the Social Foundations of Institutional Change and its Economic Effects. *Economic Geography*, 82, 1–25.

Rodrik, D. (2004), Industrial Policy for the Twenty-first Century. *CEPR Discussion Paper* No. 4767. London: Centre for Economic Policy Research.

Rothwell, R. (1989), Small Firms, Innovation and Industrial Change. *Small Business Economics*, 1, 51–64.

4 Speaking truth to power

The political dynamics of public sector innovation

Kevin Morgan

1 Introduction

In some circles the notion of public sector innovation is considered an oxymoron. In neo-liberal narratives, for example, the public sector is invariably portrayed as a drag on innovation and economic development, in contrast to the private sector, which is assumed to be the quintessential source of creativity and value-adding activity. This stereotype has been challenged by more recent accounts, where the state is shown to have fostered rather than frustrated innovation and development (Mazzucato, 2013).

However, all sides agree that strategies for smart specialisation (S3) will place enormous demands on the public sector, especially on regional governments, and the key question is whether the state and its public agencies are up to the challenge. Our conceptions of the state are deeply imbued with the legacies of intellectual debates that have raged since the dawn of the 'great transformation' that spawned capitalism (Polanyi, 1944/1957). This chapter aims to address this challenge at a number of different levels.

Section 2 reprises the state debate by taking two radically different but highly influential economists to assess how their arguments can help us to understand the economic role of the state today. Section 3 explores two distinct but related dimensions of public sector innovation, namely innovation *in* the public sector and innovation *through* the public sector: the former examines the scope for/barriers to smart public administration, while the latter examines the role of the regional state in the process of entrepreneurial discovery, the process that lies at the heart of the S3 concept. The final section distils the arguments and assesses the implications for some of the most intractable problems in public sector governance – like failure, feedback and learning for example – problems that have not been adequately addressed by the theorists of the new industrial policy or by the policy-makers and theorists of smart specialisation.

2 Debating the state: from Hayek to Rodrik

No issue polarises political debate as much as the role of the state in economic life. The business community would be wrong to think that it is above such theoretical debates because, as Keynes famously said at the end of his magnum opus: 'Practical men, who believe themselves to be quite exempt from any intellectual influences, are usually the slaves of some defunct economist' (Keynes, 1936/1973). Two influential economists who are normally treated as polar opposites – Friedrich Hayek and Dani Rodrik – have much to contribute to our understanding of the state's role in economic affairs, albeit in very different ways.[1]

Drawing on a sophisticated theory of knowledge, Hayek offers a powerful critique of the limits of state intervention and his critique deserves to be treated seriously because it highlights the fallibility of the state. The key problem of a 'rational economic order' according to Hayek was the fact that 'the knowledge of the circumstances of which we must make use never exists in concentrated or integrated form but solely as the dispersed bits of incomplete and frequently contradictory knowledge which all the separate individuals possess'. In contrast to the neo-classical view that knowledge is readily accessible, Hayek underlined the significance of what we would now call tacit knowledge when he drew attention to that 'body of very important but unorganised knowledge which cannot possibly be called scientific in the sense of knowledge of general rules: the knowledge of the particular circumstances of time and place' (Hayek, 1945). The idea that knowledge is not given to any single agent in its totality, and the fact that the tacit element cannot be fully codified let alone centralised, fuelled his critique of state planning and his defence of the market, which he considered to be a form of 'decentralized planning by many separate persons' (Hayek, 1945).

Although neo-liberal critics of the state rarely refer to Hayek's seminal article on the use of knowledge in society, the latter informs two of their key propositions: first, that the state can never be a surrogate for the decentralised processing capacity of markets because it lacks the necessary knowledge; and, second, that the state should not seek to pick winners because it lacks the competence to do so and industrial policy will merely create perverse incentives by encouraging firms to engage in rent-seeking behaviour.

No one has done more to respond to this neo-liberal challenge than Dani Rodrik, who has sought to establish the design principles of an industrial policy for the twenty-first century (Rodrik, 2004). The principles (reproduced in Box 4.1) constitute a highly condensed set of policy recommendations for the design of a new industrial policy that is far more creative and capacious than what we normally associate with the term.

Although he accepts Hayek's criticism that the state has a knowledge deficit, Rodrik turns the critique on its head by arguing that firms suffer from the same problem, especially when they are exploring new technologies and emergent markets, where neither costs nor clients are known in advance. In Rodrik's conception, industrial policy is essentially a 'process of economic self-discovery', a process he describes as follows:

Box 4.1 Ten design principles for industrial policy

- Incentives should be provided only to 'new' activities
- There should be clear benchmarks/criteria for success/failure
- There must be a built-in sunset clause
- Public support must target activities not sectors
- Subsidised activities must have potential for spillover effects
- Industrial policy must be vested in agencies with demonstrated competence
- The implementing agencies must be monitored closely at the highest political level
- Policy-makers must have good channels of communication with the private sector
- Optimally, mistakes that result in 'picking losers' will occur
- Promotion activities need to have the capacity to renew themselves, so that the cycle of discovery becomes an ongoing one.

Source: Rodrik (2004).

The right image to carry in one's head is not of omniscient planners… but of an interactive process of strategic cooperation between the private and public sectors which, on the one hand, serves to elicit information on business opportunities and constraints and, on the other hand, generates policy initiatives in response. It is impossible to specify the results of such a process ex ante: the point is to discover where action is needed and what type of action can bring forth the greatest response. It is pointless to obsess, as is common in many discussions of industrial policy, about policy instruments and modalities of interventions. What is much more important is to have a process in place which helps reveal areas of desirable interventions. Governments that understand this will be constantly on the lookout for ways in which they can facilitate structural change and collaboration with the private sector. As such, industrial policy is a state of mind more than anything else.

(Rodrik, 2004:38)

Far from being a wholly autonomous agent, standing above and beyond the economic fray, the state becomes an *embedded state*.[2] That is to say the state is actually embedded in this interactive process of strategic cooperation and, by being a party to the self-discovery process, it is better able to appreciate the scope for/barriers to innovation and development. The idea of industrial policy as an iterative process of economic self-discovery is both compelling and challenging: compelling because it resonates with the realist conception of innovation as a collective endeavour in a highly uncertain world; challenging because the public sector is generally ill-equipped to deal with novelty and experimentation because they necessarily involve mistakes and failures (Morgan, 2013a). Because Rodrik's conception of industrial policy was such a seminal influence on the architects of smart specialisation (see Foray, 2015), it is important to address the challenge of public sector innovation.

3 Smart specialisation and the challenge of public sector innovation

Smart specialisation policy makes great demands on the public sector, not least because it comes at a time when many public sector bodies are being eviscerated by the 'age of austerity'. In other words, at a time when public sector innovation is more imperative than ever, the capacity of the public sector is being constrained like never before. Nevertheless, public sector innovation remains a critically important component in the S3 policy mix because, without it, the state and its public sector agencies are more likely to frustrate rather than foster the process of entrepreneurial discovery, the process that lies at the heart of smart specialisation.

Public sector innovation entails two distinct dimensions, namely: (i) innovation *in* the public sector and (ii) innovation *through* the public sector (European Commission, 2013). The first refers to the culture and practice of public administration, while the second refers to the policies and mechanisms through which public services and innovation support systems are designed and delivered. Far from being autonomous, these two dimensions are intimately connected because the public sector cannot be a competent interlocutor for its private and third sector partners if its administrative practices are slow, bureaucratic and impervious to feedback. In other words, the public sector's capacity for *external* engagement is predicated on its *internal* capacity for policy orchestration across multiple departments, which in turn determines the propensity for policy integration or policy fragmentation. To explore these generic issues at a more granular level, this section draws on the recent experience of the UK, where public sector innovation has emerged as a major theme of political debate. Securing innovation *in* the public sector is illustrated with reference to civil service reform, where the challenge has been defined as one of speaking truth to power. Promoting innovation *through* the public sector is illustrated with reference to the changing practice of regional innovation policy in an old industrial region, where the entrepreneurial discovery process is evolving from a state-centric process to a network-based process.

3.1 *Speaking truth to power: the challenge of smart public administration*

Public administrations are coming under pressure everywhere to be more agile, creative and responsive on account of the accelerating pace of socio-technical change on the one hand and burgeoning societal challenges on the other, challenges as varied as climate change, ageing societies, sustainable development, energy security, food poverty and the like. To rise to these challenges, governments need to render their public administrations fit for purpose and this inevitably entails reforming the civil service. One of the oldest in the world, the British civil service has been a beacon of good practice since the Northcote-Trevelyan settlement of 1854, which was described as

> the greatest single governing gift of the nineteenth century to the twentieth century: a politically disinterested and permanent Civil Service with core values of integrity, propriety, objectivity and appointment on merit, able to transfer its loyalty and expertise from one elected government to the next.
>
> (House of Commons, 2013:7)

Although these are the quintessential qualities of a conventional civil service – qualities that are far from being the norm around the world today – they are no longer deemed to be sufficient in a rapidly changing society. For example, the UK government minister in charge of the civil service has criticised it for being weighed down by its own stultifying culture, which he described as 'a culture that is overly bureaucratic, risk averse, hierarchical and focused on process rather than outcomes' (Maude, 2013). Even more significant than this ministerial criticism was the damning conclusion of an all-party parliamentary inquiry into the civil service, which was forced to conclude that:

> *the failure to learn from failure is a major obstacle to more effective government, arising from leadership that does not affirm the value of learning. This is something which the Civil Service has yet to learn from successful organisations. The present culture promotes the filtering of honest and complete assessments to ministers and is the antithesis of 'truth to power'. It is a denial of responsibility and accountability.*
>
> (House of Commons, 2013:26)

While many countries might once have aspired to the standards of the British civil service, the latter is now charged with a series of shortcomings that suggest that it is ill-equipped to manage rapid socio-technical change and other societal challenges. From a smart specialisation perspective, the most debilitating shortcomings of the British civil service would seem to be risk aversion (which means that it recoils from bold innovations); a culture that privileges process over outcomes (which means that policy design is valued over policy implementation); and the failure to learn from failure (which means that it has little or no capacity to reflect on and learn from past mistakes because time and space have not been afforded to monitoring and evaluation). A study of organisational learning across all central government departments found that the four biggest barriers were: silo structures, ineffective mechanisms to support learning, high staff turnover and the lack of time for learning (National Audit Office, 2009). While each of these shortcomings signals a serious governance problem, the combined effect amounts to a public administration culture that has a systemic bias towards inertia rather than innovation.

What compounds these problems is the fact that, despite political devolution, the UK remains one of the most centralised states in the European Union and this creates an enormous disconnect at the heart of the central civil service in Whitehall: to put it bluntly, the 'Whitehall machine' has a great deal of centralised power but very little local knowledge. This centralised civil service structure is deemed to be inimical to the public service reform agenda because, for innovation to flourish, the locus of control needs to shift to the frontline, where services are delivered and where user feedback can be easily monitored and acted upon. Public sector innovation requires the freedom to learn and experiment and the centralised 'Whitehall machine' is now widely regarded as a major impediment to public sector innovation (Seddon, 2014).

If the technical calibre of public administration in the UK has serious shortcomings, these problems pale into insignificance compared to the public sector corruption scandals in other parts of the EU. For example, the recent corruption scandals in Spain – involving kickbacks, illegal donations, tax fraud and embezzlement – straddle the entire political spectrum and cover large swaths of the country, from Catalonia in the north to Andalucia in the south. The scale of public corruption in Italy, Greece, Bulgaria and Romania is even worse, evidenced by the fact that they are all ranked at 69th out of 175 countries in the most recent *Corruption Perceptions Index*, the lowest score in the EU (Transparency International, 2014). Public corruption on this scale means that the values of the nineteenth century Northcote-Trevelyan settlement – the values of integrity, propriety and objectivity for example – need to be re-affirmed for the twenty-first century because the skill sets of smart public administration need to include a moral compass.

On a broader front the subject of public sector innovation is belatedly beginning to receive the attention it deserves. With notable exceptions (Borins, 2001; Rogers, 2003; Mulgan, 2007; Landabaso, 2012), it has not been treated seriously and this explains why the empirical evidence base is so poor (European Commission, 2013). In the past four years however we have witnessed a flurry of initiatives on public sector innovation. The *OECD Observatory of Public Sector Innovation* was launched in 2011 and it aims to map, assess and promote innovative practices across all member countries. The European Commission is now conducting public sector innovation surveys and the 2010 *Innobarometer* found that lack of sufficient human or financial resources was perceived as the most important barrier to innovation in the public administration (European Commission, 2011). More recently an Expert Group found that there were four types of barrier to public sector innovation: (i) weak enabling factors or unfavourable framework conditions (ii) lack of leadership at all levels (iii) limited knowledge of innovation processes and methods and (iv) poor measurement metrics and data (European Commission, 2013).

Although many of these reports confirm that the role of management is the most important driver of public sector innovation, and lack of funding the most important barrier, the fact remains that innovation in the public sector will always be difficult unless it deals more openly with the challenges of feedback, failure and learning that were highlighted in the reform of the British civil service.

3.2 Embedding the state: the institutional challenge of entrepreneurial discovery

Promoting innovation *through* the public sector is most challenging in less developed regions because, by definition, they have the weakest regional economies. Although regional innovation policy has been operating in the EU for some 25 years, it has been very state-centric throughout that period, enabling the regional state in less developed regions to dominate the agenda and allowing it a free hand to work with the 'usual suspects', that is to say the dominant firms and families who enjoy insider status. One of the notable aspects of smart specialisation is that it targets state-centricity and insiders for the first time because the *RIS3 Guide* specifically addresses the problem of rent-seeking agents and offers advice as to how robust governance arrangements can be designed to pre-empt such corrosive behaviour (Foray *et al.*, 2012). But a regional culture of state-centricity is not easy to eradicate because of the path dependent nature of public policy and the deeply embedded nature of regional conventions (Morgan, 2013a).

This section highlights the recent experience of regional innovation policy in Wales, where much of the country is classified as a 'less developed region' under the current EU classification. Wales offers salutary lessons for other less developed regions because it is trying to migrate from a state-centric to a network-based regional innovation policy repertoire. This migration is best illustrated by reference to the changing role of the Welsh Government in promoting innovation through the public sector in two radically different ways – from *controlling* the process in the case of the Technium programme to *curating* the process in the case of the Specific low carbon energy project. While the former is more likely to frustrate the entrepreneurial discovery process, the latter is more likely to foster it.

In the following analysis the *entrepreneurial discovery process* is conceived in a broader and more capacious way than the conception of Dominique Foray, who argues that entrepreneurial discovery 'precedes the innovation stage and consists of the exploration and establishment of a new domain of opportunities (technological and market), potentially rich in numerous innovations that will subsequently occur' (Foray, 2015:23). As we will see, the Specific project combines exploration *and* innovation in the development of a new domain that represents a novel activity for each member of the consortium.

The original rationale for the Technium Centres was twofold: (i) to commercialise near market academic research and (ii) to create high value jobs so as to retain graduates in Swansea, the second city of Wales (for a fuller account, see Morgan, 2013b). The idea of an incubator facility to support new technology businesses was originally mooted in the Regional Technology Plan (1996), the first regional innovation strategy ever produced in Wales. But the concept would not have been realised had it not met the emerging agenda of the property division of the Welsh Development Agency (WDA), which was at that time searching for a flagship project to spearhead the physical regeneration of Swansea Docks. This marriage of convenience spawned the concept of the Technium, which was presented to funders as an alliance between the university sector, which was reckoned to have expertise in *intellectual* property, and the WDA, which was responsible for *industrial* property. Having secured the backing of the Welsh Government, the concept was eventually funded for a two-year period through a £1 million ERDF grant. However, the most remarkable feature of the Technium story was the fact that a further nine centres were launched under a new regional innovation programme *before* the first centre in Swansea had been evaluated (DTZ, 2009).

Many of the Technium Centres had a strong sectoral focus, ostensibly to reflect local business clusters or academic expertise. But it was later discovered that this sectoral focus had actually been proposed by WEFO, the Welsh Government's EU programmes agency, which wanted to differentiate the centres to satisfy funding procedures. Given all these policy design defects, it was hardly surprising that the Welsh Government decided to close the majority of the centres in 2010, a decade after the Technium concept was originally conceived and after more than £100 million had been invested in the programme, most of it public money from Welsh Government and EU sources.

How are we to explain the extraordinary degree of central control exercised by the Welsh Government in the design and delivery of the Technium programme? Two factors – money and knowledge – help to explain this state-centric repertoire. First, the Welsh Government felt it had a right to exercise full control because the Technium Centres were largely funded by the public purse. Second, it felt no need to enlist the expertise of other partners because, as the Technium project morphed from its original purpose, a novel venture in intellectual property, into a conventional industrial property venture, it confidently believed it had all the requisite knowledge in-house to deal with it (Morgan, 2013b).

However, a radically different regional policy repertoire began to emerge in the context of the Specific low carbon energy project, where the Welsh Government assumed the role of *curator* rather than controller. The main aim of the Specific project is to develop functional coated glass and steel products that will transform the roofs and walls of buildings into surfaces that are able to generate, store and release energy – which in effect turns buildings into power stations (Worsley, 2012). Since the project embraces a fuzzy array of exploratory research, development and prototype production, it is broader than the conventional definition of entrepreneurial discovery, which is conceived as a pre-innovation process (Foray, 2015:23–27).

Specific was consciously designed to be an exemplar of open innovation and, thanks to a unique collaboration between government, academia and industry on a single site, it has made rapid progress, allowing the partners to move from R&D to pilot production in a remarkably short time. Although Swansea University and Tata Steel are the lead academic and industrial partners, as they were the initiators of the project, Specific is closer to an innovation ecosystem because the expertise of a host of other partners has also been mobilised, including world class companies like BASF and Pilkington on the industrial side and Imperial College and Cardiff University on the academic side. Though barely three years old, Specific is already widely regarded as one of the most successful regional innovation projects ever undertaken in Wales, a project that carries important lessons for the design of the entrepreneurial discovery process in other less developed regions.

Although they are local projects, Technium and Specific have a much wider resonance because, in their different ways, they embody two very different regional policy repertoires. Technium embodies the *state-centric* repertoire that has unfortunately dominated regional innovation policy for the past two decades, a repertoire that is strongly associated with the phenomenon of 'cathedrals in the desert' (i.e. projects that are a massive waste of money because they are under-utilised because they were not calibrated with the demand side of the regional economy). Specific, on the other hand, embodies a *network-based* repertoire in which innovation is conceived as a collective endeavour, where each partner recognises that what they can achieve by working in concert is so much greater than what they can achieve by acting alone. Specific is an example of what has been called 'collaborative creativity' (Isaacson, 2014), a quality that is now being recognised as the key to success in a wide array of knowledge-based innovations. This attribute of 'collaborative creativity' is akin to the values of collective entrepreneurship that will be necessary if the entrepreneurial discovery process is to be successful in less developed regions (Morgan and Price, 2011).

The crucial differences between the Specific and Technium projects are threefold: (i) the knowledge involved in the former was too tacit and specialised for the regional state to play a controlling role (ii) the bulk of the funding for Specific was spread across many partners and a smaller stake meant a smaller voice for the regional state and (iii) politicians and civil servants seem to have learned the key lesson of the Technium fiasco, which is that state-centric projects tend to fail if the skills of more knowledgeable partners in academia and industry are not acknowledged and harnessed (Morgan, 2013a).[3]

The role of the regional state may seem insignificant in the case of Specific, but nothing could be further from the truth. Indeed, when the history of the Specific project comes to be written it will be seen that the role of the Welsh Government was highly significant on two counts. First, its initial financial investment of £2 million may seem modest compared to the enormous sum it committed to the Technium Centres, but the *timing* of its investment was crucial because, by acting as an early stage investor, the Welsh Government demonstrated its confidence in the project and this persuaded other investors to come forward. Second, the Welsh Government assumed the role of *curating* the Specific project, a role that is more akin to the embedded state that we discussed earlier, where the state is content to be an equal partner in a network of innovators rather than a controller of others on account of its status in the hierarchy.

4 Conclusions and implications

Although the public sector is today facing unprecedented pressures, not least from the 'age of austerity', it has a major role to play in the S3 era of regional innovation policy. In fact it is not too much to say that the promise of smart specialisation will not be fulfilled without the public sector playing its full part in *all* stages of the process. Even in the entrepreneurial discovery process, the very heart of the S3 exercise, public sector bodies have important contributions to make alongside the firms that are at the forefront of the process by dint of their technological and commercial knowledge. Among these public sector bodies the regional state and local universities will loom large, especially in less developed regions, where such public institutions will be obliged to take the initiative. However, in regions where the state and its public agencies need to play a leading role, it is imperative that they do so in the light of the insights that we distilled from the work of Hayek and Rodrik.

For all their differences, both Hayek and Rodrik have important things to say about the role of the state. Highlighting the significance of unorganised knowledge, 'the knowledge of the particular circumstances of time and place', Hayek said it was a fatal conceit for state planners to think they could capture such dispersed knowledge and therefore he argued that the state would always suffer from a knowledge deficit, the implication being that it should resist the urge to intervene. However, Rodrik turned this anti-state argument on its head by extending it to the private sector, where he argued that firms suffer the same plight. His argument in favour of an enlightened industrial policy is robust and compelling and it also makes the intellectual case for the kind of pro-active (but embedded) state that is needed in the S3 process.

But Rodrik's argument is also very challenging because it assumes a public sector that can routinely absorb mistakes and failures. As he says, perhaps half-jokingly, if governments make no mistakes, 'it only means that they are not trying hard enough' (Rodrik, 2004:25). The embedded state that he advocates is first and foremost an experimental state, a state that is well-disposed to experiment, to explore and to engage in a process of self-discovery with its industrial partners. Again, this is the kind of state that is needed to make a success of the S3 exercise. However, the political culture of the public sector is becoming increasingly schizophrenic: while it extols public sector experimentation when it leads to successful innovation, it berates public sector managers if they make a mistake. In other words the public sector is enjoined to innovate, so long as it does not lead to mistakes or failures, outcomes that tend to trigger public sector crises and political scandals. To redress this schizophrenic culture, national governments will need to deal frankly with three taboo issues that have stymied public sector innovation – namely feedback, failure and learning.

Although the significance of robust and honest *feedback* is impossible to overestimate, especially in evolutionary theories of change, we tend to assume that such feedback is readily available. The truth of the matter is that robust and honest feedback is like gold dust – and seemingly just as difficult to get. In almost every sphere of life – but especially in the protean worlds of business and politics – feedback is filtered and tempered by a whole series of things, like power, status, hierarchy, fear, and ambition. That 'whistleblower' laws have been introduced in many countries to help public sector workers find their 'voice' clearly speaks volumes for the fact that feedback faces formidable obstacles and on no account should it be assumed to be easily forthcoming.

If feedback is hard to manage, *failure* is even more difficult, especially in the public sector where taxpayers' money is at stake. In contrast, in some parts of the private sector failure is now something of a badge of honour because it is assumed to be synonymous with learning. Among organisations that take 'error management' seriously – in the airline and healthcare sectors for example – the evidence suggests that when people talk openly about their mistakes, morale and performance improve (Clegg, 2014). Far from being a badge of honour, failure in the public sector can spell disaster for managers and their political superiors. Rodrik is surely right to argue that we need to have a higher tolerance of failure because it is part and parcel of experimentation and innovation and therefore the aim should be not to try to outlaw mistakes but to reduce the costs of mistakes by learning from them and by learning to fail faster so to speak. To have a more enlightened understanding of failure in the public sector, the S3 policy community will need to mobilise a wider constituency so as to include such groups as public auditors, legal advisers and of course politicians, the very people that are responsible for fuelling the risk-averse culture that is the kiss of death for innovation in the public sector.

Finally, the public sector will need to allocate more space, time and resources to *learning* about what works where and why because monitoring and evaluation are still seen as Cinderella activities. The barriers to organisational learning in the British civil service – silo structures, staff turnover, ineffective mechanisms to support the acquisition and dissemination of good practice and the lack of time devoted to learning – are common to the public sector throughout Europe. As well as needing more time and space for learning, the public sector also needs 'a menu of methods for trying things out, including pilots and pathfinders, incubators and laboratories (and a flexible approach so that sometimes pilots can be ended early and half-formed ideas can be tried out in safe environments)' (Mulgan, 2007: 26).

If the deep cultural barriers to public sector innovation can be tackled in a more open and honest fashion – and feedback, failure and learning are simply three of the most egregious examples – then public bodies will be better equipped to promote innovation in and through the public sector.

The stakes could not be higher because the S3 vision will stand or fall on the competence of the public sector and its capacity to be more creative, more experimental and more tolerant of failure.

Notes

1 Critics of the state are to be found on both sides of the political spectrum. For a left-of-centre critique see James C. Scott's *Seeing Like a State*. Although widely assumed to be an anarchist critique of the state per se, it is in fact a critique of certain kinds of state, particularly those that are 'driven by utopian plans and an authoritarian disregard for the values, desires and objections of their subjects' (Scott, 1998:7).
2 The concept of the embedded state draws on Peter Evans' concept of 'embedded autonomy' which highlights the need for industrial policy-making to be embedded in a network of linkages with private enterprises as opposed to the arm's length relationship extolled by the neo-liberal state repertoire (Evans, 1995; Cooke and Morgan, 1998).
3 The danger of state-centricity looms larger, and is therefore more difficult to counter, when the state is the largest or the only funder of a project, which underlines the importance of multiple funding streams.

References

Borins, S. (2001), Public Management Innovation in Economically Advanced and Developing Countries, *International Review of Administrative Sciences*, 67, pp. 715–731.

Clegg, A. (2014), Lessons in Failure from the Error Management Gurus, *Financial Times*, 16 September.

Cooke, P. and K. Morgan (1998), *The Associational Economy: Firms, Regions and Innovation*, Oxford University Press, Oxford.

DTZ (2009), *Evaluation of the Technium Programme*, DTZ, Cardiff.

European Commission (2011), *Innobarometer 2010: Analytical Report on Innovation in Public Administration*, DG Enterprise, Brussels.

European Commission (2013), *Powering European Public Sector Innovation: Report of the Expert Group on Public Sector Innovation*, DG Research and Innovation, Brussels.

Evans. P. (1995), *Embedded Autonomy: States and Industrial Transformation*, Princeton University Press, Princeton NJ.

Foray, D. (2015), *Smart Specialisation: Challenges and Opportunities for Regional Innovation Policies*, Routledge, London.

Foray, D., Goddard, J., Beldarrain, X.G., Landabaso, M., McCann, P., Morgan, K., Nauwelaers, C. and Ortega-Argilés, R. (2012), *Guide to Research and Innovation Strategies for Smart Specialisations (RIS3)*, European Commission, Luxembourg.

Hayek, F. (1945), The Use of Knowledge in Society, *American Economic Review*, XXXV(4), pp. 519–530.

House of Commons (2013), *Truth to Power: How Civil Service Reform can Succeed*, Public Administration Select Committee, HC 74, London.

Isaacson, W. (2014), *The Innovators*, Simon & Shuster, New York.

Keynes, J.M. (1936/1973), *The General Theory of Employment, Income and Money*, Macmillan Press, London.

Landabaso, M. (2012), What Public Policies Can and Cannot Do for Regional Development, in P. Cooke, M.D. Parrilli and J.L. Curbelo (eds), *Innovation, Global Change and Territorial Resilience*, Edward Elgar, Cheltenham.

Maude, F. (2013), *Ministers and Mandarins: Speaking Truth unto Power*, Speech to Policy Exchange, London, 5 June.

Mazzucato, M. (2013), *The Entrepreneurial State: Debunking Private versus Public Sector Myths*, Anthem Press, London.

Morgan, K. (2013a), Path Dependence and the State: The Politics of Novelty in Old Industrial Regions, in P. Cooke (ed.), *Re-framing Regional Development: Evolution, Innovation, Transition*, Routledge, London.

Morgan, K. (2013b), The Regional State in the Era of Smart Specialisation, *Economiaz*, 83(2), pp. 103–125.

Morgan, K. and A. Price (2011), *The Collective Entrepreneur: Social Enterprise and the Smart State*, The Charity Bank, Tonbridge, Kent.

Mulgan, G. (2007), Ready or Not? Taking innovation in the public sector seriously, *Provocation*, 3, NESTA, London.

National Audit Office (2009), *Helping Government Learn*, HC 129, London.

Polanyi, K. (1944/1957), *The Great Transformation: The Political and Economic Origins of Our Time*, Beacon Press, Boston, Mass.

Rodrik, D. (2004), *Industrial Policy for the Twenty-First Century*, John F. Kennedy School of Government, Harvard University.

Rogers, E.M. (2003), *Diffusions of Innovations*, Free Press, New York.

Scott, J.C. (1998), *Seeing Like a State: How Certain Schemes to Improve the Human Condition Have Failed*, Yale University Press, New Haven and London.

Seddon, J. (2014), *The Whitehall Effect*, Triarchy Press, London.

Transparency International (2014), Corruption Perceptions Index 2014 (www.transparency.org, accessed 8 August).

Worsley, D. (2012), How to turn a building into a power station, *Western Mail*, 27 December.

5 Structuring the entrepreneurial discovery process to promote private–public sector engagement

Francesco Grillo

1 Introduction

How can we make the entrepreneurial discovery process (EDP) part of the ordinary life of an institution (or at least of those institutions whose responsibility it is to design and implement regional and urban policies)? Is it possible to overcome the paradox of having civil servants, whose job description does not entail making choices, taking risks and enduring failures, managing processes which are in fact defined by choices, risks and failures? How can we make bureaucrats and innovators work together? Is the above feasible without engaging in the question of more profound change in the very nature of public administrations? Are there institutional conditions, which can make institutions more capable of initiating and sustaining innovation? Does not an effective EDP imply also a transformation in the approach of lobbies to policy making? How can we make companies be part of the decision-making process so avoiding policies getting captured by (conflict of) interests? And how can we use this opportunity to make companies themselves to think more strategically and longer term than they normally do?

More specifically this chapter will define some mechanisms that will allow for systematically engaging entrepreneurs in a discovery process which is supposed to be at least initiated and coordinated by public administrations. For the sake of this chapter we will focus on a specific typology of entrepreneurs: private, for profit companies, whereas entrepreneurs can also be non profit organizations (this category tends to be normally associated with 'social innovators'), single public administrations or research centres/universities (especially when they generate spin offs).

A dialogue between the two worlds is not completely novel. The literature on 'districts' which flourished in the eighties and nineties (Becattini, 1990; Porter, 1998) found many examples of it and, actually, this interaction between companies and government was found to be one of the reasons for their success.

More recently, the paradigm of 'smart specialization' that the European Commission has embraced as a prerequisite to the development of regional development programs, has led most of the European regions to experiment with such a dialogue even beyond the formalized structure of the so-called 'partnership principle' which has been central to regional policies since their inception.

Even though most programs have been approved by now, the question has become 'how can we sustain this interaction so that EDP becomes a permanent and even more pervasive feature of the implementation of regional and urban policies?'

The issue of the institutionalization of the entrepreneurial discovery process can be addressed at different levels.

At the highest possible one we may see consequences on the next generation of structural funds regulations, as well as on the review of the so-called Europe 2020 strategy which was supposed to provide a framework for the quest for the EU's smart, sustainable and inclusive growth. This will have obvious consequences even for the organization that the European Commission (and its agencies) will use to sustain smart specialization and cohesion policies.

At the level of the implementation of the specific structural funds programs, single regions may, instead, experiment with new processes to monitor the implementation of the programs, new templates to review programs on the basis of systematic feedback from knowledge holders, even twinning with other regions who share similar smart specializations.

We, however, also need to solve a problem of institutional capabilities, as well as capabilities from the private sector side to conceive a strategy for a system whose interests go beyond the normal perspective of a firm. Innovation strategies tend to have wider scope than innovation programs within firms, both in terms of time (often business have got shorter term needs) and space (spill-overs are more normal for policies whereas companies are more concerned with the ownership of their know-how).

We will first try to recap what an EDP is and why it is important and essential that companies and government work together so that an EDP takes place. In the following sections, we will then try to pinpoint the problems with making private and public sector engage with each other and identify solutions. In the last section we will elaborate on the innovations at an institutional plane which would buy time and political endorsement to the change management process we are describing.

2 The entrepreneurial discovery process as a new paradigm for successful regional innovation strategies and efficient regional development programs: who should we involve in an EDP and what do we actually mean by 'government' and 'business'?

The concept of entrepreneurial discovery process is considered a core element of any Smart Specialization Strategy (S3), whereas the existence of such a strategy is a conditionality ex-ante for regions and member states to access structural funds within the 2014–2020 programming period. More broadly

EDP is a prerequisite for successful regional innovation strategies (Grillo and Landabaso, 2011) and, therefore, it applies even in non European contexts (OECD, 2011 and 2015).

Even more widely one can assume that most innovation is by now happening outside single (private or public) organizations and, in fact, it is taking place in 'open' environments (a region, a city but even a 'virtual community' not bound to any place) where innovators are not bound by hierarchical relationships and yet join a common discovery process.

With this specification the EDP becomes not only essential to regional and urban governments in order to generate smart, sustainable and inclusive growth but also an undertaking which can unfold value to business. Companies can, theoretically, gain a lot by being part of the process through which regional innovation strategies get developed because:

- they can increase their capability to understand the environment they belong to and to anticipate how their constituency (consumers, regulators, civil society) will react to changes in their offering;
- they can use diffused knowledge to speed up their own innovation processes;
- more importantly, they will be more likely to lift the (infrastructural or regulatory) constraints that may make them more capable to grow;[1]
- some challenges that the public sector is facing nowadays, such as increasing demands from citizens for higher quality and more personalized public services against greater budgetary constraints, also provide an opportunity for the business sector (Social Innovation Exchange and Young Foundation, 2010).

But what is after all an entrepreneurial discovery process?

> Smart specialisation fundamentally is based on a process of entrepreneurial discovery. Entrepreneurs in a broad sense (firms, higher education institutions, independent inventors and innovators) are in the best position to discover the domains of R&D and innovation in which a region is likely to excel given its existing capabilities and productive assets.
>
> (Foray *et al.*, 2009, p.7)

They (the entrepreneurs) do so by joining a common process through which opportunities are identified and common problems preventing entrepreneurial potential to unfold.

At the centre of the entrepreneurial discovery there are, then, entrepreneurs coming from different areas and innovation is seen as something that connects those areas, uses knowledge and, actually, combines such knowledge in a collective problem solving exercise with the intention to create value for a certain community.[2] Smart specialization areas themselves tend to combine public, profit, non profit and research stakeholders and to, ultimately, transfer knowledge from one industry to another.

Within a smart specialization-based policy, the government no longer plays a role of supreme planner working in isolation. And yet it has got an even more difficult job. It is the government, in fact, which will:

- initiate the entrepreneurial process;
- convince innovators to join by ensuring participants that it is a fair game and nobody is taking a free ride;
- be responsible for writing strategies, programming documents and tenders out of the discovery process so that innovators get empowered also in the implementation phase;
- make sure that partnerships amongst innovators become a continuous process so that strategies are evaluated and reviewed constantly.

This view of EDP does, however, imply a paradox.

EDP is recognised as the only method, which is capable of yielding a large enough number of sustainable smart specializations providing each region, each city, with the possibility to develop its own distinctiveness and excellence. Yet the EDP as we just defined it implies people with different semantics, objectives, and approaches to innovation to be dependent on each other for innovation to happen.

Normally public administrations are considered the weak ring of the innovation circle (Halvorsen *et al.*, 2005).

However, problems exist also on the private companies front. The case where companies do really engage themselves in conceiving and implementing strategies together with institutions is very rare.

Nevertheless, something which is normally underestimated is that we do not have 'government' or 'companies' as some sort of monolithic world with unified behaviours vis-à-vis innovation and each other. Within the two typologies of stakeholders we have organizations and people with very different attitudes and, as we will elaborate later, it is essential that both public administrations needing to develop smart strategies and companies willing to collaborate carefully select each other so that dialogue is more effective. This, in fact, will also apply to the other worlds (research and groups of 'civil society') of the four blades of the quadruple helix whose interaction is necessary for innovation to happen (Lundvall *et al.*, 2007; Wilson, 2004): to ask for simultaneous 'collaboration' of all 'stakeholders' appears way too generic and segmentation is necessary for making partnerships an opportunity for collective problem solving.

So the question is also: who are really the actors to be involved in carrying out an effective EDP? How can we define a taxonomy of stakeholders so that different instruments can be developed for engaging each of them? We will come back to this point in the next section where we will try to make explicit the differences between public and private sectors in their approach to innovation so that we can then identify solutions for each of these problems.

3 The problem setting: why is it difficult for public and private sectors to engage with each other in an entrepreneurial discovery process?

The reason why EDP is difficult is normally associated with problems that public administration may have when it comes to producing innovation (Halvorsen *et al.*, 2005).

We think that a more effective way to approach the problem solving is to recognize that innovation is difficult for each of the worlds that EDP expects to get together. Whereas it is not difficult to enumerate the fundamental reasons why a bureaucracy tends to have a hard time when it comes to managing change, we cannot underestimate the fact that even companies tend to be much more risk adverse and conservative than it is normally acknowledged (and the same applies to the other two typologies of innovators – universities and civil society – which EDP normally involves).

Moreover, innovation is not alien to public administrations and large innovative processes have taken place especially in the last couple of decades in the public sector (UN, 2014). In fact, some of the most ambitious, countrywide innovation programs have taken place in the rather wide arena of the so-called e-government.

The problem, however, is that government and public administration have two rather different approaches and they even give two different meanings to what innovation is. The identification of the problems and, therefore, of specific ideas which could solve each of them can, therefore, be facilitated by referring to a number of differences that mean innovation is approached differently in the two worlds.

There are ten problems or ten gaps to be filled.

3.1 A different approach to knowledge

In the private sector innovation is about acquiring a 'competitive advantage and this tends to restrict the sharing' (Hartley, 2005) of new knowledge. 'By contrast, the drivers in the public sector are to achieve widespread improvements in order to increase public value' (Moore, 1995) and as such knowledge tends to be born as a good which is intended to be common.

3.2 A different vision of failure

Failure is an intrinsically fundamental part of any innovative process. If you do not fail, if you do not allow yourself to fail, you cannot have innovation because innovation has – by definition – uncertain outcomes and thus if you do not accept the idea that some of the experimentations will not succeed, you cannot simply launch them (Green *et al.*, 2001). Public administrators are not legally allowed to fail unless they are engaged in something which is explicitly tagged as research (or less frequently as experimentation) (Koch, 2006). They, for instance, cannot allow for differences in the quality of services provided to two different areas of experimentation for two different organization models, neither are they allowed to have a temporary interruption of delivery of services due to a failure of some new technology (Nicholls, 2003). Companies, instead, accept – in their day-by-day activity – the possibility of different performances across different segments and geographical areas: this may be due to either differences in performances or, indeed, novel ways to do things or novel products to be marketed.

3.3 A different propensity towards taking decisions

More or less smart specialization means, by definition, that resources get allocated to specific industries (or even better phases of the value chain within industries) or niches within them or locations (as one may expect from a strategy for tourism) or segments of populations (for instance, certain innovators whose contribution is crucial for innovation to happen) (Foray *et al.*, 2011). The process by which entrepreneurial opportunities get identified requires, then, at a certain point, a decision in terms of (scarce) resources allocation.

It is once again a widespread feature of civil services that makes public administrations feel – at least in principle – not completely comfortable with EDP, because the very objective of a bureaucrat (in the eighteenth century tradition of the 'modern state') is to ensure that all citizens, all constituencies, get equal treatment. Unequal distribution of resources, albeit only temporary and based on evidence and efficiency reasons, is not normally accepted. Companies, instead, create (or destroy) value through decisions (Nutt, 2005).

3.4 The skills gap and the danger of picking the winner and/or the dinosaur

Public administrations are normally said to be equipped with a set of (mostly legal and administrative) skills, which are not aligned with the technological and managerial expertise that EDP requires. In fact, the skills gap may even be more profound.

In order to smartly specialize yourself, you need to position yourself vis-à-vis the rest of the world. You cannot identify your unique position, your distinctiveness if you do not know what other regions are doing: this is, in turn, very useful also in order to identify your partners and competitors, investors and innovators you want to attract, and the potential trajectories of development and differentiation. This requires a global or international knowledge of market and technology dynamics. The vast majority of public administrators (a remarkable exception are the international organizations) are – again by definition – linked to a certain place and are – almost invariably – not as outward looking as the guidelines on smart specialization would like (Rainey *et al.*, 1976).

Companies, and more precisely that specific breed of companies made up of multinationals with value chains spanning around the globe, have by definition a knowledge advantage (Grillo *et al.*, 2015, Buchanan, 1975).

The skills gap would, however, not even be filled by a mere transposition of global know-how to public administrations. Once we have completed the necessary diagnosis of the international position of a certain region's possible areas of smart specialization, the choices to be applied to public investments are, in fact, different from the ones which would apply to a portfolio policy of a conglomerate.

A firm would select the so-called 'stars' as areas where to invest more resources; for a country, instead, it may not make sense to select firms or sectors which are already winning in growing sectors, where this would imply pouring money where money is already piling up. Likewise, it would not make sense for a region to simply select industries just because of their size (and importance to employment level).

Smart specialization will correspond to areas where there is a 'potential' competitive advantage, which is prevented from being used because of a constraint (it can be the lack of an infrastructure or, even, of a technology) that the market is failing to remove.

3.5 The organization gap

Public administrations tend to be organised horizontally by typology of administrative tasks to execute (Scott, 1992). Companies, instead, organize themselves by business units (although this is combined by functions into a more complex matrix). The latter organization chart is more consistent with smart specialization that still tends to be associated (even though this does not need to be the case) with industries.

This is equally true for the management of regional development programs where you have units responsible for administrative tasks (for instance drafting programming documents; managing public procurement; auditing expenses; evaluating activities) which are not differentiated by 'smart specializations'.

3.6 The paradox of experience

Attempting to remedy the gaps in terms of skills and organization can even make the situation worse. In an unstable environment, public administrations tend to call experts whose function is to endorse the decisions which will have to be ultimately made. The contradiction between 'smart specialization' and 'experts' is precisely that the former require an innovation, which mostly comes by combining knowledge coming from different domains.

A similar mistake is made when public administration paradoxically reacts to innovation by relying through public procurement on continuity even more than in ordinary contexts.

The third risk of overshooting vis-à-vis the skills gap is wrong partnerships: public administrations are captured by organizations which have a knowledge that is necessary and that the administrations do not possess.

3.7 The intellectual challenge of the metrics and the managerial one of accountability

Public value is much more difficult to assess than value created for the shareholders. The consequence of this is that in the public sector it is less easy than in the private one to convince people about the convenience of good policies versus bad ones.

Moreover indicators are crucial to hold managers responsible for the outcome that they produce. This problem of metrics seems to be even greater when it comes to innovation whose benefits are supposed to unfold over a relatively long period of time (Halvorsen *et al.*, 2005).

3.8 The short termism of managers and the problem of the political cycle

The problems, however, are not only about the public sector. As we said before managers tend to be suspicious with projects whose spill-over is too wide and may benefit competitors. Also, they are often too much bound to the need to get results in the current quarter (Brochet *et al.*, 2015).

Policy makers tend to be even more short term oriented than executives. Their time span may be even shorter than a quarter: when their success is measured by daily polls, they lose interest in something like R&D programs, which will have their impact in a few years.

3.9 The obstacle of pre-defined agendas

In order for EDP to really happen, problem-solving exercises need to take place amongst individual knowledge holders who are ready to change their mind. Collaboration amongst actors who are supposed to represent other actors are, by definition, slow and not very effective (Ibid.). People joining a process which is supposed to generate innovation should feel free to change their mind and to consider themselves as part of a learning exercise.

3.10 Power versus knowledge

Last but not least, all the above problems refer to a much wider cultural and institutional question.

The difference between companies and governments is that, within the former, 'power' should (in theory) be allocated where skills are, whereas, within the latter, skills are (in theory) moved to the institution where 'power' (to spend money, for instance) is assigned by the law.

This conception of power is simply opposite to the one which is suggested by a context (the so-called 'information society') where knowledge circulates with no respect any longer of the hierarchical lines which have defined the concept of the 'modern state' for about two centuries.

Our proposal is an attempt to enumerate specific differences in approach to innovation between the public and the private sector, so that it, then, becomes possible to draft a number of possible solutions. However as we mentioned above, these differences may have to be qualified. We cannot think of government as a monolith, and the same is true within companies.

Propensity to innovation may vary according to factors like the size of the company (where it is not always true that the bigger, the better), the industry dynamics, and the internationalization of the firm (percentage of exports on turnover, participation in global value chain etc.).

Similarly governments are very different according to different institutional levels, geography, and thickness of social capital around them. For instance, the author found that stability of governments as well as selective openness of policy-making processes (Grillo and Nanetti, 2016) is necessary for engaging in innovation policies the knowledge holders whose contribution is indispensable for their success.

More importantly, one should look at the people who matter. Amongst other things, owners and managers have different objectives within a firm; and similarly agendas of policy makers can diverge from the one of civil servants.

A smart regional innovation strategy becomes so if stakeholders choose the right stakeholders for kicking off the EDP and, then, gradually involve others once early wins have been achieved.

4 The problem solving: a tool kit for improving the engagement of government and business with each other

This chapter hopes to better operationalize the problems of making public administration and private companies work together so that we can then identify some specific actions.

4.1 Do not overstretch the entrepreneurial discovery process and focus it on those 'common' issues, which are typically outside the proprietary domain of the organizations involved where knowledge can be combined

As we mentioned before a different approach to the very ownership of knowledge can make government and companies diverge (Albury and Mulgan, 2003). The trick here would be not to be too wide or ambitious when it comes to defining the agenda of the knowledge exchange.

Contents which relate to proprietary knowledge and industrial competitive advantages would not be part of the regional innovation process. The EDP would, instead, focus on those portions of the value chain where (nearly) all participants are failing and where the common good would be to combine ideas on how to overcome the common problem.

This would, for instance, apply to hotels, restaurants and other firms engaged in tourism in a certain area that misses the knowledge of who are their actual and potential clients, what are the buying and fidelization factors, how is the region doing on these factors, and who are the main competitors.

Here common knowledge can be created by pooling together partial and much less useful information possessed by individual firms.

4.2 Give value to failure through a proper knowledge management system

Allowing for failure is essential but failure will not be allowed until we find a way to make sense of it (Koch, 2006). If one observes the world of venture capital (especially in areas like biotech and pharmaceutical), he/she would realize that the real (economic) value of failure can be the knowledge which it can produce. This is, by the way, also the method by which highly innovative public administrations (an example would be NASA) have bought the right to fail even on very expensive programs.[3]

This would lead to a completely different approach to drafting strategies and programs (Mulgan, 2007).

For instance, digital agenda should – under this new prospective – be conceived as a number of groups of experimentations. Each of them – to be carried out in a place willing to test it – would aim to solve one specific problem (for instance: to convince people to accept some form of congestion charge as a tool to diminish traffic and raise money for public transportation; or to increase the elderly's use of e-government applications). With this approach possible solutions would be tested; some of them would legitimately fail; the applications which won would, then, be reused in the rest of the country (or region or city).

This entire approach will, of course, imply that innovations like the Pre Commercial Procurement will be further developed and become mainstream at least for some portion of the programs where failure and experimentations will become explicit tools to further innovation.

4.3 Integrate choices of 'smart specializations' with the formalization of spill-over mechanisms that can make choices acceptable to a large enough part of the constituencies and engage policy makers

Like for failure, choices create a challenge to what civil servants can do according to the law, their corporate culture and the social norm (Ibid.).

In order for choices to be accepted we believe two things need to happen:

- smart specializations need to be integrated by explicit spill-over mechanisms so that it is clear how value created in a specific territory or industry or research area or public service, can be spread at a later stage to the rest of economy/ society; for instance a research advancement in a certain industry can become an enabling technology in another;
- policy makers need to be engaged in making choices on the basis of a number of evidence-based options that the strategy would have identified.

4.4 Internationalization of civil services workforce, cross-border partnerships with other regions and further sharing of methodologies on how to identify potential competitive advantages which are linked to market failure

The skills gap can be covered by introducing, in your staff, people who are capable of developing a knowledge of the global value chain and thus helping the region to identify its distinctiveness. The same result can be achieved by developing cross-border partnerships with regions sharing the same broad smart specializations.

It will also be necessary to embark on a further research effort to develop and share methodologies, which can operationalize ideas on how to really select smart specializations (a new generation of guidelines should probably be encouraged on this). The issue here is to minimize the investments on either shining stars (because they would invest in innovation even without the public aid) or on big dogs (characterized by decreasing market share in mature industries) where the return on the investment may be too small and far away in time. However, the identification of potential and not actual competitive advantage whose deployment is linked to the removal of a market failure poses a number of methodological challenges, which need to be more properly tackled.

4.5 Reorganize the organization meant to implement operational programs by smart specialization

This would create teams who will progressively accumulate knowledge and relationships by smart specialization and whose accountability will be on achieving S3 targets.

This may imply a wider reform of public administrations of which the implementation of smart-specializations strategy may be an ice-breaker and experimentation territory.

4.6 Recruit networkers instead of experts, target public procurement to innovators so that skills gaps are efficiently covered and select the partners who are readier to be engaged

Individuals who know experts and yet can have a comprehensive enough vision of the overall innovation process may be preferred to proper experts who may be resistant, for the reasons we have mentioned, to change.

A profound change in public procurement procedures would be necessary if we agree that the EDP needs skills which are not amongst the ones that make up the 'technical assistance' that normally serves public administrations in charge of development programs.

4.7 Develop metrics for smart specializations in order to detect, in shorter periods of time, performance of innovation policies and create incentives for achieving results

The idea that the results of innovation are unavoidably measured over a long time period is relatively untrue: the capability of public investment programs to raise further private investments should be one of the signs which detects the credibility of an innovation strategy and the quality of partnership upon which it is based.

These indicators may also proxy performance and incentives for program managers should be linked to it.

4.8 Engage public opinion on results of new metrics[4] and target innovation friendly, less short-term oriented companies

Communication of smart specialization results will create benchmarking, cooperation and, sometimes, virtuous competition amongst institutions. More importantly it will make clear the value to the economy and society of a regional innovation strategy.

Multinational companies, which do not belong – per definition – to a specific territory, may not always be the best possible partners. Small and yet growing young companies or even start-ups which are involved in international trade and whose founders or executives have an international background and yet have strong ties with a certain area are certainly an interesting partner. However even larger, more consolidated firms could be worthwhile engaging in the process. It is nevertheless important to understand what the advantages and the costs of involving different kind of firms are so that institutions can differentiate the approach.

4.9 Create **fora** where knowledge holders represent nobody but themselves (using techniques like Chatham House Rule[5])

It should be clarified that the problem-solving phase of drafting innovation strategies is for individuals bearing knowledge and not for representatives of organizations, so that real interaction may take place. Specific instruments (like Chatham House Rules whereby opinions expressed at the meeting will not be referred to specific individuals) may facilitate the brainstorming.

4.10 Encourage institutional flexibility so that resources are moved (through reserve performances) from more performing to less performing regions

The idea that resources are allocated to specific institutions regardless of their capabilities should be overcome. Mechanisms should be in place so that subsidiarity is applied: money will be reallocated across institutional levels at different levels so that results are maximized.

As mentioned before, the solutions mentioned above will become part of an ambitious change management process, which public administrations will have to go through. Such a change will be even more profound than a more traditional plan for strengthening institutional capabilities: it will require not only some training, but also wider organization turn-arounds, new accountability methods and, sometimes, new people. This will need time and institutional endorsement to the transformation. In the next section, we will review some of the innovations at a high institutional level, which may provide energy to such an ambitious change management process.

5 The institutionalization of the EDP

We just tried to enumerate the specific challenges to public administrations as well as companies to better engage with each other in an entrepreneurial discovery process. These challenges can be seen as part of a wider transformation, which has got the potential to even question the organization of governments and the nature of civil servant jobs. As such the entrepreneurial discovery becomes a change management, learning process which provides the opportunity not only to strengthen the regional innovation strategy, but also to reform public administrations around concrete objectives of smart growth. Such a challenge can, thus, only be won if there is a strong commitment to smart specialization at various institutional levels so that an expectation is created that the EDP is here to stay and that Public Administrations are better to embark on the organizational transformation that smart specialization requires.

At the highest possible institutional level, one may envisage that smart specialization becomes part of the revised version of the EUROPE 2020 strategy which is the strategic framework under which different policies for promoting smart, sustainable and inclusive growth are coordinated. The review of such a strategy will most likely be radical because the current Europe 2020 strategy is not working (due to the economic crisis but also, according to many, to some of its own characteristics) (European Commission, 2012).

The chapter proposes the following ideas:

*   Include the smart specialization paradigm in Europe 2020 strategy as one of the characteristics of a growth which is supposed to be 'smart'.
*   Make regions (and cities) actors alongside states in Europe 2020; this will also mean having them be accountable for results, having indicators at regional (and urban) levels and issuing region (and city) specific recommendations, alongside current country specific recommendations.
*   Change the main indicators of success. Here we see at least two novelties:
    *   the expenditure on R&D/GDP target should be replaced by the ratio between expenditure on R&D from business/GDP (leaving room for some further sophistication of this indicator to allow for the relative inadequacy of R&D to capture the entire concept of 'innovation'): this would arguably create the incentive to measure the performance

of public investments in innovation by more precisely measuring how much public investments were successful in stimulating investments from business through an improvement of expectations, place related factors and expected return on investments, as well as better engagement of companies which is a prerequisite to all the above;
- the openness of regions (their capability to export, to export in highly globalized industries, attract investments, but also students/ researchers etc.) should also more systematically be an objective.
• Extend the smart specialization paradigm to policies other than 'regional policies' and then clarify that even the European Social fund, the European Digital Agenda and HORIZON 2020 should support or promote smart specialization.

Similarly, making smart specialization a more central feature of programs may have an impact on the very structural funds regulation and we then see that they:

• Transform the ex-ante conditionality to an itinere one; the evaluation and the review of the Regional Innovation Strategy (RIS) would be an on-going process to be finalized each year with the changes needed so that operating programs continue to be consistent with the RIS.
• Extend the conditionality of regional innovation strategies beyond the European Regional Development Fund to the European Social Fund (ESF); this would also require that the two programs are much more closely coordinated.
• Redefine the ear-marking mechanism so that the minimum threshold (80 per cent for advanced regions and 50 per cent for less advanced ones) applies not to certain (four) typologies of expenditures but to the percentage of the money which will be spent on companies, research centres and NGOs and other beneficiaries belonging to a certain specialization area.
• Clarify that part of technical assistance is to assist the transition towards smart specialization-based programs and that part of the ESF resources are for growing the institutional capabilities needed for initiating and sustaining EDP.
• Encourage the creation of incentives and of reserve funds which are specifically dedicated to reward project managers who engage business in strategy development and the co-finance programs; performance-based rewards are, in fact, very useful in that it becomes clear that, alongside partnerships amongst administrations, there is also competition so that differences in performances are appreciated and risk taking becomes acceptable vis-à-vis results-based accountability;
• Encourage the adoption of financial innovations so that the state (or regions) create close end funds together with international investment bankers which specialize themselves per area of smart specialization.

This would also lead to the need to:

- Reinforce European level capabilities (the Seville platform could be the place) to develop a knowledge management system capable of mapping 'smart specializations' across regions[6] so to encourage collaboration, avoid duplication, and share knowledge.
- Promote (again around the Seville platform) the growth of a cross-border community of 'discovery entrepreneurs' which will increasingly aggregate by smart specializations workgroups; this could also take place by encouraging the selection of some 'Mr. Innovation' for each of the national and regional institutions involved, where she or he may not necessarily be part of the leading public administration (and may even come from business, or universities or 'civil society').

Last but not least, changes may also be needed at the level of the programs and more specifically:

- One of the most radical changes is to move from an articulation of the objectives of the program for typologies of investments (research, digital technologies, business promotion, energy, environment, etc.) to a structure of the programs by smart specialization, where resources will either be allocated progressively to specializations or moved on the basis of results and reviews of RIS.
- This would greatly make the programs easier to be understood by people, entrepreneurs, actors we want to involve. The actions to be realized will, in fact, be conceived not as a generic support but as an initiative meant to produce economic value.
- The changes would bring about also a modification in the way indicators are conceived: they won't be understood any longer as generic targets which are often too macro and, therefore, too exogenous to the programs to be really capable of motivating people. This, in turn, will lead to modifying the mechanisms through which performances of programs are monitored and evaluated, as well as the processes through which performance-based rewards are established and distributed.

Not all the above mentioned modifications may be feasible and not all of the suggestions (for instance the one referring to structural funds regulation or the structure of programs) may be envisaged in the next months or years. However, most of them will require a challenge to institutional capabilities and experimentations with new approaches to developing programs. A realistic, synchronized, constantly increasing commitment to EDP is essential: in fact, the name of the game is that either the EDP becomes more pervasive or it will be reversed.

6 Conclusions

The chapter has been an attempt to suggest an original problem setting and problem solving of the paradoxes linked to the entrepreneurial discovery process. It does so by focusing on the specific issue of how two specific categories of innovators – government and companies – can engage with each other in EDP.

We started by recapitulating why EDP is important to territories, but also as an opportunity to generate value to companies. We, then, enumerated ten different reasons, which make the approach to innovation different between public administrations and companies and, thus, difficult to exchange knowledge between the two. We, however, also stressed why it is not useful to talk about 'the government' and 'the private sector' as such, and why it is therefore important that EDP engage first the administrations and then the private entrepreneurs who are readier to collaborate.

We, then, proposed one action for each of above ten problems, which can transform these differences from an obstacle to a factor which can make EDP more effective.

Last but not least, we attempted to identify some institutionalizations of EDP that would buy time and political endorsement to the learning process entailed by those actions.

The chapter should be seen as an attempt to raise further debate both amongst academicians and practitioners on a question which is crucial to the success of the next generations of regional policies, as well as the European strategy for smart, sustainable and inclusive growth.

Notes

1 For more motivations for innovation in the private sector see Halvorsen *et al.*, 2005.
2 The involvement of private and/or voluntary sectors is also underlined as a tool for innovation in the public sector by IDEA Literature review (2005, p.19) and Borins, 2006. The involvement of the private sector: 1. Opens the public sector to private sector competition, 2. Develops partnership between sectors, 3. Involves volunteers and voluntary sector organizations in services.
3 This would be, in fact, true up to a point: the withdrawal of federal funds from the Shuttle programs is an example of the fact that even for failure there is a limited budget.
4 The engagement of citizens and public opinion in general in social innovation (both in the development of Horizon 2020 and in the Europe 2020 Specialization Strategy) is the goal set by 'Voices for Innovation'. For more information see www.voicesforinnovation.eu.
5 When a meeting, or part thereof, is held under the Chatham House Rule, participants are free to use the information received, but neither the identity nor the affiliation of the speaker(s), nor that of any other participant, may be revealed (www.chathamhouse.org/about/chatham-house-rule).
6 A map already exists and is available at the website of the platform (http://s3platform.jrc.ec.europa.eu/map, accessed 3rd March 2015). However, the definition of the smart specializations is still too 'large' to allow focus on the EDP.

References

Albury, D. and Mulgan, G. J. (2003), *Innovation in the Public Sector*, Cabinet Office, London.

Becattini, G. (1990), *The Marshallian Industrial District as a Socio-Economic Notion*, in Pyke, F., Becattini, G. and Sengenberger, W. (eds), *Industrial Districts and Interfirm Cooperation in Italy*, International Institute for Labor Studies.

Borins, S. (2006), *The Challenge of Innovating in Government*, Innovation series, IBM Center for The Business of Government.

Brochet, F., Loumioti, M. and Serafeim, G. (2015), *Speaking of the Short-Term: Disclosure Horizon and Managerial Myopia*, Harvard Business School Accounting and Management Unit Working Paper No. 12-072. Available at SSRN: http://ssrn.com/abstract=1999484 orhttp://dx.doi.org/10.2139/ssrn.1999484, accessed 10 November 2014.

Buchanan, B. II (1975), 'Red-Tape and the Service Ethic: Some Unexpected Differences Between Public and Private Managers', *Administration & Society* 6: 423–444.

European Commission (2012), *Guide to Research and Innovation Strategies for Smart Specialisations* (RIS3). Available at: http://s3platform.jrc.ec.europa.eu/documents/20182/84453/RIS3+Guide.pdf, accessed 4 October 2014.

Foray, D., David, P. A. and Hall, B. (2011), *Smart Specialisation – From Academic Idea to Political Instrument, the Surprising Career of a Concept and the Difficulties Involved in its Implementation*, EPFL, Lausanne.

Green, L., Howells, J. and Miles, I. (2001), *Services and Innovation: Dynamics of Service Innovation in the European Union*, Final Report PREST and CRIC, University of Manchester.

Grillo, F. and Nanetti, R. (2016), *Innovation, Democracy and Efficiency*, Palgrave Macmillan, Basingstoke.

Grillo, F., Dutton, W. H. and Cobo, C. (2015), 'Economic Geography in the Internet Age', *Symphonya: Emerging Issues in Management*, 1.

Grillo, F. and Landabaso, M. (2011), 'Merits, Problems and Paradoxes of Regional Innovation Policies', *Local Economy*, 26(6–7): 544–561.

Halvorsen, T., Hauknes, J., Miles, I. and Røste, R. (2005), *On the Differences between Public and Private Sector Innovation*, PUBLIN Project, report D9, Oslo: STEP; available at: http://unpan1.un.org/intradoc/groups/public/documents/apcity/unpan046809.pdf, accessed 5 November 2014.

Hartley, J. (2005), Innovation in Governance and Public Services: Past and Present. *Public Money & Management*, 25(1): 27–34.

IDEA (2005), *Innovation in Public Services: Literature Review* Available at www.idea.gov.uk/idk/aio/1118552, accessed 20 November 2014.

Koch, P. M. (2006), *Interact: Innovation in The Public Sector and Public–Private Interaction*, Norden, Oslo.

Moore, M. H. (1995), *Creating Public Value: Strategic Management in Government*. Harvard University Press, Cambridge MA.

Lundvall, B. A., Jensen, M. B., Johnson, B. and Lorenz, E. (2007), 'Forms of Knowledge and Modes of Innovation'. *Research Policy*, 36(5): 680–693.

Mulgan, G. (2007), *Ready or not? Taking Innovation in the Public Sector Seriously*. Nesta.

Nicholls, R. (2003), *Notes on Governance*, Serco Government Services.

Nutt, P. C. (2005), 'Comparing Public and Private Sector Decision-Making Practices'. *Journal of Public Administration Research and Theory*. 16: 289–318 Available at: www.michaeldavidson.biz/images/uploads/Comparing_Public_and_Private_D-M.pdf, accessed 25 November 2014.

OECD (2011), 'Regions and Innovation Policy', *OECD Reviews of Regional Innovation*, OECD Publishing.

OECD (2014), *All on Board. Making Inclusive Growth Happen*, OECD Publishing.

Porter, M.E. (1998), *On Competition*, Harvard Business School Press, Boston.

Rainey Hal, G., Backoff, R. W. and Levine, C. H. (1976), 'Comparing Public and Private Organizations', *Public Administration Review*, 36(2): 233–244. Available at www.jstor.org/stable/975145, accessed 15 October 2015.

Scott, R. W. (1992), *Organizations: Rational, Natural and Open Systems*, Englewood Cliffs, NJ: Prentice Hall.

Social Innovation Exchange and Young Foundation (2010), *Study on Social Innovation*. Bureau of European Policy Advisors.

United Nations (2014), 'E-Government for the Future We Want', *United Nations E-Government Surveys*, United Nations.

Wilson, E. J. (2004), '*The Information Revolution and Developing Countries*', MIT Press, Cambridge, MA.

6 Entrepreneurial discovery process and research and technology organisations

David Charles and Katerina Ciampi Stancova

1 Introduction

Research and Technology Organisations (RTOs) are key innovation infrastructures, and sites of knowledge and technology creation. In addition, they play a crucial role in human capital accumulation, technology transfer and international cooperation in Research and Innovation (R&I). RTOs can represent the interests of local research and technology communities and advocate for them locally and nationally.

RTOs have developed in many European countries at both national and regional levels to assist in the support of local industry, often around specific industrial technologies or sectors (Arnold *et al.*, 2010). With a core responsibility for technological upgrading they play a key role in regional and national innovation systems (Rush *et al.*, 1996), and thus are expected to make an important contribution to regional smart specialisation strategies. Their potential role in smart specialisation is multiple, but a key contribution is likely to be to support the entrepreneurial discovery process together with connecting firms and other actors at local and international scales, and building research and technology capacities.

Many RTOs have a policy role and have capabilities to identify industry needs and technological opportunities (Attané, 2015). Also, RTOs have considerable experience in analysing firms' needs and technology forecasting and provide policy advice services to their regional governments. Such expertise could be used by regional governments to help identify opportunities and assist in developing and continuing entrepreneurial discovery processes, especially where governments have limited experience of collaboration with industry. RTOs, as increasingly international organisations, can also facilitate access to global knowledge for regional government and regional firms through their networks and research collaborations.

2 Research and Technology Organisations

RTOs tend to be public or private non-profit organisations that provide a range of research, development and technology services, principally to business and governments. Although the definitions of RTOs vary, reflecting RTOs' institutional statutes, governance, business models, funding models and resources, the public missions and industrial support objectives of RTOs seem to be aligned.

The European Association for RTOs (EARTO) defines RTOs as

> regional and national actors whose core mission is to harness science and technology in the service of innovation or public bodies and industry, to improve the quality of life and build economic competitiveness in Europe. RTOs are generally non-profit organisations and their revenues are re-employed to fund new innovation cycles.
>
> (www.earto.eu)

Although not so frequently identified in studies of the innovation ecosystem as universities, they are significant elements in innovation systems at regional and national level. It has been estimated that RTOs across Europe have revenues of €18.5 to €23 billion with a wider economic impact of up to €40 billion (Arnold *et al.*, 2010).

RTOs come in a diversity of forms, size and governance, and hence can be classified on a number of dimensions which helps to explain their varied relationships with smart specialisation strategies. One important dimension is their geographical spread. Some RTOs are very regionally focused and were created to support industry in a particular region, so even if they have small offices outside the region, the bulk of their activity is focused in the region and their mission is primarily to support the region. A number of examples of these exist across Europe. In Spain many regions have established RTOs with support from the EU Structural Funds to assist the technological development of local industry. The Basque Country for example had a number of such technology centres dating back well before the Structural Funds, but with the network having been developed further since the 1990s and now consolidated into two groupings, Tecnalia and IK4. Together these comprise 17 centres and over 2,700 employees. Elsewhere a region might only have one or two RTOs – the Trento region of Italy has one, EURAC, which has 377 staff.

Another common form is a national RTO which may be at a single location but addressing the whole of a country's needs, or distributed across the regions of a country. In Finland, VTT is a national RTO with its main location in Espoo near Helsinki but with branches in other cities, mainly Oulu, Tampere and Jyväskylä. It sits within the responsibility of the Ministry of Employment and the Economy which provides partial funding of 35 per cent of a total income of €251 million. The 2,351 staff are spread across a wide range of technology areas, as VTT provides a national service across industry as a whole. In Germany the Fraunhofer Society is also an example of a networked RTO, as well as Europe's largest RTO. With 66 centres and 24,000 employees, Fraunhofer centres are located in all regions of Germany and provide support for almost every possible technology field. Most of Fraunhofer's €2bn income comes from industry and research contracts, but 30 per cent comes from government base funding split 90:10 between the Federal Ministry of Education and Research and the regional Land governments.

Finally there are some RTOs which are increasingly international, oper-ating across borders both in terms of their market and the location of their offices and labs. In the UK TWI, formerly The Welding Institute, was origi-nally a research association part-funded by national government to support welding and joining technologies. However it now has no core government funding and is a non-profit organisation based on industrial contracts. In order to seek out new sources of funding it has established additional offices internationally (in Australia, Bahrain, Canada, China, India, Indonesia, Malaysia, Pakistan, Thailand, Turkey, UAE and USA) in order to service its main clients. Some of these overseas offices are now very large with 80 people in India and 120 in Kuala Lumpur, emphasising the global nature of their work, and the total group employment is over 1,000 staff.

The geographical scale of operation is partly shaped by the governance and mission of the RTO: those funded by regional governments tend to focus on their home region, although seeking research partnerships internationally to ensure access to new knowledge. National RTOs have a responsibility to cover the whole national territory, whilst those without government funding will tend to be more market driven, to the extent of focusing on international markets as in the case of TWI. Most RTOs now have some form of internationalisation strategy, and many nationally funded RTOs are establishing international offices and labs. The more RTOs are asked to seek private sector funding the less likely they are to be purely regionally focused, and hence independent RTOs without core govern-ment funding are more likely to seek out international markets, with a greater reliance on large multinational companies as a core client base (Table 6.1).

Table 6.1 Geography of RTOs

	Governance or key funders			
Geographical scale of facilities and main client base	Regional government	Regional-national collaboration	National Government	Independent
Mainly region	Tecnalia*, Basque County; EURAC, Bolzano			CIRCE, Spain
National network across regions		Fraunhofer Institutes*, Germany	VTT*, Finland; RISE*, Sweden	
Single national location	IMEC*, Belgium			C-Tech Innovation, UK
Significant international presence				TWI

*Also have international offices.

Source: Developed by the authors.

RTOs typically occupy a space between the public and private sectors, and between the development of basic science and the commercial application of technology. On the latter the Technology Readiness Level (TRL) 9-point scale can be used as indicative of RTO activities. Typically RTOs have limited engagement in levels 1 and 2 which relate to basic science principles and the development of technology concepts. However, TRL 3 which relates to analytical studies around the proof of concept is where the RTO role is more prominent, running through to level 7 which covers a system prototype in an operational environment. The subsequent levels 8 and 9 relate to the implementation of actual systems in demonstration and operational environments and these activities are driven by private firms. However RTOs can be found here as well. Different RTOs will operate in different spaces along the TRL scale depending on the capacities of firms and the willingness of firms to subcontract near-market work to the RTO.

Some RTOs play an important role in the development of new products which then may be commercialised by firms but examples exist of significant innovations developed in RTOs such as the MP3 compression system developed by the Fraunhofer Institute (Smith, 2015). However the primary role of RTOs is more focused around the support for innovation in companies than being the source of new innovations. On the public–private scale there are again a variety of positions, some RTOs operating in a strong public sector role as policy advisors on research and innovation, perhaps helping regions in the design of innovation strategies. More frequently RTOs undertake projects for the public sector to develop innovation solutions to societal challenges. This might include both local projects as well as participating in Horizon 2020 projects such as on assistive technology for the elderly or sustainability (see for example Tecnalia, 2012). RTOs often bring back some regional components in the EU-funded projects by offering partnership with their regions as 'test beds' for the new technology being developed (e.g. many examples in smart cities initiatives and in transport). Finally they play core roles in directly supporting industry through collective activities such as technology watch and awareness raising as well as direct subcontract research for individual firms. These activities are mapped out in Figure 6.1.

2.1 RTOs in innovation-based regional development

RTOs have been identified as key agents in regional innovation systems, and particularly as key elements of regional innovation strategies in many parts of Europe over the past 20 to 30 years. Even earlier though RTOs were established as national initiatives to promote innovation (Rush *et al.*, 1996), in some cases with some form of regional delivery.

The conceptualisation of regional innovation systems identifies a regional knowledge generation subsystem and an exploitation subsystem, the latter consisting largely of firms. Research organisations both public and private constitute important elements in the knowledge generation subsystem,

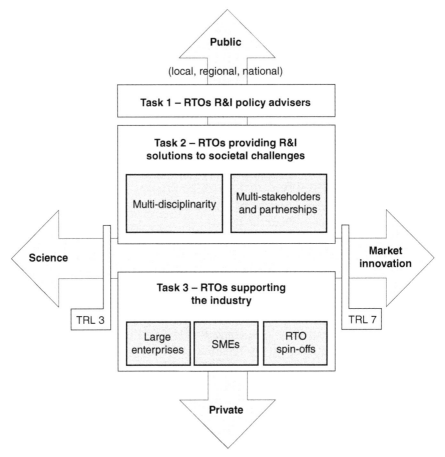

Figure 6.1 Place of RTOs on the Technology Readiness Level scale and their
orientation to policy

alongside universities and various forms of training and knowledge dissemination bodies (Cooke, 2004). However, until now, much of the theory of
regional innovation systems (RIS) tends to focus on universities as perhaps
the more ubiquitous and larger element of the knowledge generation infrastructure. RTOs though have typically been much more closely linked with
the needs of business, as they do not have the additional roles of education
and basic research that the universities have.

Asheim *et al.* (2007) have stressed the importance of proactively creating
regional advantage through the engineering of regional innovation systems.
The sectors or clusters in such systems will require particular knowledge bases,
defined by Asheim *et al.* as analytical, synthetic or symbolic. The first two of
these benefit greatly from the involvement of RTOs. Analytical knowledge

bases are rooted in scientific knowledge and innovation depends on formal research and development, with knowledge often being exchanged via codified formats such as patents and publications. This is a core role for RTOs. However RTOs also engage in synthetic knowledge bases which are focused more around engineering type knowledge and the application and combination of existing knowledge. Here knowledge exchange has a stronger tacit component requiring closer collaboration between an RTO and its clients, often a core feature of the way RTOs work: direct contracts for R&D activities from industrial clients is a significant component of RTOs' revenues and a core element of knowledge transfer. Symbolic knowledge bases are perhaps less significant for RTOs as this form of knowledge tends to be more closely associated with the creative industries and creative skills.

Accordingly many regions have invested in the development of RTOs as part of regional innovation strategies. Since the early 1990s and the introduction of innovation into the European Regional Development Fund (ERDF), a large number of regions have identified a need to develop industry or cluster orientated research organisations to promote innovation and its diffusion to industry groups as part of those strategies. The Basque Country is a good example of this with the regional government supporting additional RTOs in their region around specific technology areas, and building on some pre-existing RTOs. One of the early examples of an RTO in the Basque region was the Ikerlan centre, developed in 1974 to support the cooperative companies of the Mondragon Group. The primary objective of this centre was to support innovation for a local cluster of firms. Subsequently many other regions have developed such regional centres, drawing on the experience of those regions which have benefitted from national investments in industrial research centres – the experience of Grenoble with major investments in CEA, CNET and CNRS labs being an example well recognised in the academic and policy literature (see for example Lawton Smith, 2003).

An important issue in the establishment of new RTOs, as with other forms of public research labs, is the question of how they fit in their regional context. There is a danger that without local networks and clusters that can absorb the knowledge generated and circulated by new labs they end up as cathedrals in the desert (Cooke, 2001). So consequently, the development in recent years of regionally focused RTOs, often linked closely with regional cluster strategies, has been aimed at directly linking into regional needs. These developments in some cases have formed the basis of 'pre-S3' good practice cases. Walendowski (2011) for example identifies the five centres of excellence developed in North East England in the 2000s as a distinctive regional strategy in which the research base was used to underpin the core growth pillars of the regional economy. Two of these centres in particular developed into mature RTOs which subsequently attracted national funding and a role beyond the immediate regional needs, yet still form crucial parts of the regional innovation system.

2.2 RTOs and the smart specialisation concept

The roles that RTOs play in smart specialisation strategies (S3) build on the idea of stakeholder involvement in S3 that originates in the quadruple helix concept (Carayannis *et al.*, 2015), which refers to government, universities and research organisations, industry and civil society being active in the regional innovation systems. The RTOs play multiple roles in smart specialisation: they contribute to the entrepreneurial discovery process; they play an important role in connecting actors; and they build research and technology capacities and contribute to technology transfer.

First, in the phase of development of the RIS3, RTOs can provide the analysis of needs and opportunities. RTOs already provide analysis of the national and regional context and potential for innovation, develop shared visions about the future of their regions, contribute to the selection of a limited number of priorities for national and regional development, establish suitable policy mixes, as well as contributing to monitoring and reporting.

Second, RTOs connect stakeholders geographically (in the region, country and internationally) and across sectors. They also interact continuously with industry and public administration in the region, search for good national and international partners for regional clients, connect with the local population and make research and technologies popular across generations, as well as carrying out forward-looking activities, consultancy and advisory services for other regions.

RTOs seek to develop international networks especially through their participation in Horizon 2020 projects, and hence can be a vehicle for internationalising regional strategies through supporting inter-regional collaboration. In addition, the internationalisation of regional smart specialisation strategies can take place through collaboration between RTOs and those regions lacking RTOs. For example, the countries that joined the EU after 2004 and are often lacking RTOs, might want to outsource specific research infrastructure, knowledge and services in order to meet their smart specialisation objectives. RTOs are ideal partners for these regions due to their specific expertise, infrastructure and skill base. Financial resources are available for the collaboration including European Structural and Investment Funds (ESIF) and EU instruments to support twinning and teaming.

Internationalisation is both an opportunity and challenge. Internationalisation is essential for RTOs to increase their competitiveness, growth and profit. On the other hand public authorities may be afraid that internationalisation can divert the benefits of public investments and the 'expatriation' of an RTO's research and innovation results.

A particular strength of RTOs is their involvement in European and international networks and value chains, and whilst this brings potential challenges where governments fund them to support domestic businesses, the RTO may be in an ideal position to identify cross-border linkages and to source knowledge from other regions. The RTO can help bring a more global perspective, especially where the RTO has considerable international experience.

Many RTOs are currently pursuing internationalisation strategies, driven by a need to seek out new sources of knowledge and revenue, especially from global companies, and a desire to participate in international collaborative research projects such as Horizon 2020 as this brings access to state of the art technologies. National and regional governments in some cases set targets for Horizon 2020 projects as an indicator of excellence and success as well as a means of increasing resources without needing further investment by the home sponsor. Such access to international knowledge is a great opportunity for the support of local companies, although direct participation of local small and medium-sized enterprises (SMEs) in such international partnerships may be limited by the need to balance the membership of EU research consortia across several countries.

The challenge of internationalisation though is that RTOs will seek contracts with international firms which may be in competition with firms in the home region. For RTOs with a strong degree of regional governance and funding the region can seek to influence the RTO strategy to avoid such competition as the prime function is to support local industry. Elsewhere though the international focus may be more significant especially as governments cut core funding, and there may be little power to prevent the RTO from undertaking projects for firms that compete with domestic firms.

Third, RTOs transfer knowledge to SME clusters and help SMEs articulate demand for research and technology. They also support emerging activities and enhance capacity building close to the market, helping to create new business opportunities by developing accelerator incubators involving disruptive technologies, entrepreneurs, capital, etc. Also, they contribute to the improvement of technological capabilities aligned with RIS3 priorities, and help public administrations innovate by means of independent competitive policies (consultancies, demonstrations, eservices, eGovernment, etc.). Finally, they raise awareness and promote ongoing constant and effective discussions among stakeholders.

Indeed, it is the core role of RTOs to provide technology and innovation support to companies and this is often focused around specialist areas of technology and hence particular industry clusters. So RTOs often act as central resources for industry clusters and hence would be key delivery elements of a smart specialisation strategy aimed at upgrading the technological capabilities of such a cluster.

Many RTOs are central to particular clusters where they have a long history of supporting innovation. Often it is the presence of a particular regional cluster or industry that stimulated the development of the RTO in the first instance, as policymakers sought to enhance the prospects of a cluster through investment in a collective research capacity. In some cases the RTO has a national remit but the obvious location was to place it at the centre of a regional cluster. Thus the German Fraunhofer centres are often based in regions with a critical mass of potential client firms, and Spanish regions have established research institutes related with local clusters or areas of expertise.

The RTO therefore provides a central innovation resource for the cluster as a 'club good' which firms in the cluster can access and benefit from. In this sense the availability of expertise from the RTO helps to raise the level of knowledge exchange within the cluster, and enhances the competitiveness of the cluster as a whole.

In establishing new cluster initiatives, the RTOs could play a core role in providing practical support to the cluster organisation in mapping out firms and technologies, as well as taking on an active role in the facilitation of cluster interactions amongst firms. A particular advantage of the RTO is that they build close working relationships with many firms through their knowledge exchange activities and membership schemes and hence become trusted partners. This is a great advantage in facilitating collective cluster activities, where one of the challenges is to win the trust of firms to commit time to cluster meetings and initiatives.

2.3   RTOs and EDP

There is a risk that the EDP remains a 'paper' process, unless it is supported by implementation strategy, policy and tools, and it has a real impact on the distribution of public funds. In considering the role of the RTOs, it is assumed that the EDP has two main dimensions. First the region has to develop a process for identifying priorities for funding (Foray and Goenaga, 2013). This will require the assessment of a range of opportunities that may emerge and the aligning of public support with those opportunities or projects that promise good results. For this there will need to be a policy process involving strategy development, project selection, and subsequent monitoring and evaluation (Charles *et al.*, 2012). In parallel though there will need to be an EDP involving the private sector working with other institutions such as universities and RTOs in the identification and shaping of opportunities, developing proposals and making applications for funding (Foray and Goenaga, 2013). Both of these processes require consideration of the principles of the EDP.

RTOs may take an essential role in the EDP and their contribution would include:

- providing for evidence-based input;
- involving different regional stakeholders;
- evaluating regional strengths and weaknesses;
- providing expertise on implementation of regional/national research and innovation strategies;
- participating in RIS3 monitoring – gathering and organising information relevant to RIS3 implementation; and
- providing advice on revising and updating the RIS3.

Because RTOs are often closer to the businesses in a region, and engaged in monitoring and informing firms about technological and market opportunities, then they have a crucial role to play in ensuring that regions recognise real business opportunities. The RTO experience in analysing firms' needs and technology forecasting and providing policy advice services to their regional governments, implies that they can assist regional governments in the implementation of the EDP. Such expertise may be used by regional governments to help identify market and technological opportunities and assessing the outcomes of entrepreneurial discovery processes, especially where governments have limited experience of collaboration with industry.

A key part of the RTOs' mission is to assess the needs of their clients and member companies and many RTOs have developed processes and tools to support this role. PERA Technology, for example, in the UK and Estonia, has a range of services including horizon scanning and concept generation, through to commercial and business planning. Swerea in Sweden have a method called MAKExperience which improves innovation capacity and helps firms to create technological offers based on companies' needs. RTOs are also heavily involved in identifying future opportunities and forecasting the future directions of particular technologies, and often provide such services to their industrial clients. These services lie at the heart of the EDP – identifying the technological opportunities being pursued by the entrepreneurs within a region and how these combine with regional expertise and assets to form the basis of new clusters. RTOs then can be important players in the development of smart specialisation strategies, although in some cases there will be a risk that an RTO will promote its own area of expertise as a result of being more aware of the opportunities in that area.

So a region seeking to implement a strategy based on the EDP may draw on the support of the RTO in identifying strengths and weaknesses within the region, deciding where to encourage firms to collaborate in developing an EDP leading to new cluster proposals, and advising on the allocation of funding to particular groups of firms or priorities. In this role the RTO is part of the strategy development and policymaking team, and this may be particularly important where the RTO is heavily funded by the relevant level of government and has typically been involved in the support for policy. At a later stage the RTO could also be involved in the monitoring of progress in S3 projects and in the eventual review and revision of the strategies.

On the other hand an RTO may play a different role as part of the EDP, working with firms and other knowledge actors in developing the new opportunities. This role may not be precluded by the involvement of the RTO in the selection of priorities, but the potential for conflict of interest would need to be managed carefully. However where the RTO is relatively independent of government then its main role would potentially be an entrepreneurial one, identifying opportunities and working with firms to develop proposals for funding. Here the RTO operates more like a firm than a policy organisation and its value is to its collaborating partners as a source of new innovations or technological and market knowledge in creating new opportunities. In some cases RTOs play the role of a strategic contract research organisation for a group of companies, helping them to develop new products and working closely with them on their new product strategy. In this role then the assessment of smart specialisation projects could be a clear conflict of interest as the RTO would be submitting projects itself as part of a collaboration, and could not be expected to give judgement on competing bids.

2.4 RTOs and implementation

While carrying out activities related to the implementation of RIS3 strategies, RTOs have been facing a number of challenges. The most common challenges are: insufficient and short-term financial support, unsupportive policy instruments, inadequate timescales and in some cases a dilemma of internationalisation.

The problem of insufficient and short-term financial support is linked to the issue of decreasing availability of public resources for R&I activities and thus reduction of public funding devoted to RTOs. Generally, public resources are used for the establishment, maintenance and management of RTOs. In the past the public core funding accounted for one third of all RTOs resources; now it is approximately between 12 per cent and 20 per cent. The current situation requires RTOs to diversify their sources of funding and search for more competitive and industry funding. This can create some difficulties for RTOs in terms of delivering results that have an impact on the territory and population. Additionally, the need for funding diversification can hamper alignment between the research and technology focus of RTOs and regional smart specialisation priorities.

This is linked to the issue of policy instruments that are put in place by public authorities to implement RIS3. Public authorities are currently operationalising the RIS3 strategy and RTOs are useful partners in the process, e.g. advising with the financial instruments or available facilities and resources. Their role, however, can differ depending on an RTO's status, size and activities.

The issue of timescales is linked to different business and industry production timescales and the operational time of public administration. For example, business and industry timescales are very short and requires private actors to take quick decisions, move quickly from the development to demonstration and use all possible resources to achieve their business objectives. They have at their disposal private financial resources that allow them to shorten the R&D and production timescale and deliver results in the shortest time possible. This is the case with i.e. disruptive technologies that emerge very quickly and thus pose high requirements on the market leaders. On the other hand, timescales within which public institutions operate are much longer given their institutional and political nature. Public financial resources are not available immediately because they are subject to approval based on political consensus. Also, public institutions have to apply transparent selection, distribution, monitoring and reporting procedures. Policy and financial instruments and transparent procedures need to be thus defined well before public money is distributed. These discrepancies in timescales can create problems to RTOs in responding to industry and public needs while depending on diversified funding sources.

Finally, internationalisation is both an opportunity and a challenge for RTOs. Internationalisation is essential to increase RTOs' competitiveness, growth and profit. On the other hand public authorities are afraid that internationalisation can cause ineffective employment of public investments and 'expatriation' of RTOs' R&I results. Internationalisation can thus generate conflicts and misunderstandings between RTOs and public authorities.

3 Conclusions for policy

RTOs offer a core set of skills and competences needed by regions to successfully develop smart specialisation strategies. These skills sit in a number of areas from support for policymaking to longer term opportunity recognition and direct support to firms within the S3 clusters. Specific opportunities for RTOs to engage with regions in S3 plans have been identified to include support for the entrepreneurial discovery process, support for internationalisation and the development of cluster groupings.

Yet there are a number of challenges to be faced by regions and RTOs in maximising the contribution that can be made by the RTOs to S3s. RTOs are distributed unevenly across Europe, some regions having a wide range of RTOs and others having few or none. Some are more industrially focused and more likely to fit with the areas of specialisation selected by the region. They are perhaps more important industrial sectors and less well developed around social innovation areas which may be more important in regions lacking a strong industrial tradition.

Specific policy recommendations can be summarised as follows:

• Public agencies involved in the development of smart specialisation strategies should seek to better involve RTOs in the design and implementation of RIS3s. Representatives of the RTOs should be included in working groups established to draw up strategies, and to advise on how to draw out the implications of EDP. RTOs are well placed to assess the opportunities that are available around particular technologies and sectors and therefore review proposals made by industry for support programmes. RTO representatives may also have a role to play in the monitoring and evaluation of RIS3s.

• RIS3s may support interventions to encourage collaboration between RTOs and SMEs for knowledge exchange and innovation support. Many regions have encouraged the development of RTOs and their links with SMEs in recent years through projects to support collaborative research projects or through knowledge exchange projects. Such projects, aimed at target clusters within RIS3s, should be developed to facilitate collaborative innovation. RTOs may be supported in developing technological competences in RIS3 priority areas through targeted grants. RTO collaboration with SMEs may also be promoted inter-regionally through Horizon 2020 projects and through complementary projects to connect SMEs with the results of EU-wide collaborative research. So RTOs working in a RIS3 priority area could be encouraged to strengthen their capability around that theme with a regional research grant, encouraged to build on this through a Horizon 2020 project and then additional research or knowledge transfer support may be offered to ensure the wider uptake of the outputs of the research investments within the region.

- Internationalisation activities of RTOs may generate tensions and conflicts between public authorities and RTOs, mainly in the regions where RTOs are strongly rooted in the local innovation systems. How can this tension be managed? Public authorities and RTOs need to get together and discuss the threats and opportunities related to internationalisation including the return on public investments in the region as well as the need of RTOs to grow and compete internationally. Both partners need to understand each other's needs and find a good balance between internationalisation and keeping the RTOs' activities in the regions. Specifically, regional authorities might apply specific co-financing rules in case of international projects, e.g. provide financing only for the part of the project that is relevant for the region and where impact on the territory can be proved. Yet this rule is not easy to apply because regional authorities need to develop impact evaluation procedure, parametexrs (short-term, medium-term and long-term) and indicators (e.g. quality and quantity of jobs created) and these criteria are difficult to define. RTOs might be useful partners in the process. They can for example provide information on the results of their international projects, participation in Horizon 2020 together with other regional stakeholders (directly or indirectly) or estimated impact of their international activities on other regional stakeholders including SMEs, industry, universities, civil society, etc.

- Many regions plan to use their RIS3 to help develop competitive clusters, drawing on existing strengths. Often these will include the RTOs as they have previously been developed to support significant local industries within the region. The precise role of the RTO in a cluster initiative may vary depending on the needs of the cluster and the strengths of the RTO, but will usually involve technical support to SMEs, collective training activities and networking. A particular role for the RTO may be support for cluster coordination as an organisation trusted by the business community. The RTO could thus help to bring firms together at networking events, identify future opportunities and market trends and facilitate the identification of shared needs within the cluster. The RTO's international partnerships may also help in making links with similar clusters in other regions to facilitate collaboration and benchmarking.

- An identified difficulty for some RTOs is the integration of ERDF support into their financial model. ERDF support is not available in all regions. Some regions provide project funding for RTOs which can be matched with ERDF support to enable the RIS3 roles identified above. In other cases where RTOs are more dependent on private sector funding it may be more difficult to find matched funding for an ERDF project, and the RTO may consider that ERDF part funding for a project represents an opportunity cost. Regions may therefore consider how best to support RTO involvement through different funding models. If matching funding is not available from the regional government then RTOs should be assisted in developing interventions in which private sector contributions from industry users can be used for matched funding. In addition care should be taken on the specification of required outputs or results so that RTOs can have a high degree of certainty about their ability to meet output targets for what might be speculative research projects where the outcomes are not always knowable in advance. A special challenge is that even if there were willingness to use RTO competence from another region, the funding rules may in practice prevent the use of this kind of competence as, in the case of knowledge work, the work would be carried out outside the borders of the region.

References

Arnold, E., Clark, J. and Jávorka, S. (2010), *Impacts of European RTOs: A Study of Social and Economic Impacts of Research and Technology Organisations*, a report to EARTO. Technopolis, Brighton.

Asheim, B., Coenen, L., Vang, J. and Moodysson, J. (2007), Constructing Knowledge-Based Regional Advantage: Implications for Regional Innovation Policy, *International Journal of Entrepreneurship and Innovation Management*, 7: 140–155.

Attané, M. (2015), Setting the Scene: Presentation by EARTO Secretariat to EARTO-JRC Joint Workshop, Seville, 28 May 2015.

Carayannis, E. G., Grigoroudis, E. and Pirounakis, D. (2015), Quadruple Innovation Helix and Smart Specialization Knowledge Production and National Competitiveness, *Tech Monitor*, July–September, pp.19–27.

Charles, D., Gross, F. and Bachtler, J. (2012), 'Smart Specialisation' and Cohesion Policy: A Strategy for all Regions? *IQ-Net Thematic Paper* No. 30(2), EPRC, Glasgow.

Cooke, P. (2001), Regional Innovation Systems, Clusters and the Knowledge Economy, *Industrial and Corporate Change*, 10: 945–974.

Cooke, P. (2004), Evolution of Regional Innovation Systems: Emergence, Theory, Challenge for Action, in P. Cooke *et al.* (eds). *Regional Innovation Systems*, Routledge, London, pp.1–18.

Eurostat (2014), GDP Per Capita in the EU in 2011: Seven Capital Regions Among the Ten Most Prosperous, *Eurostat News release*, STAT/14/29, 27 February 2014.

Foray, D. and Goenaga, X. (2013), The Goals of Smart Specialsiation. *S3 Policy Brief Series*, No. 1/2013, European Commission, Joint Research Centre, Institute for prospective Technological Studies, Spain.

Lawton Smith, H. (2003), Knowledge Organizations and Local Economic Development: The Cases of Oxford and Grenoble, *Regional Studies*, 37: 899–909.

Rush, H., Hobday, M., Bessant, J., Arnold, E. and Murray, R. (1996), *Technology Institutes: Strategies for Best Practice*, International Thompson Business Press, London.

Smith, K. (2015), *Research and Innovation Organisations in the UK: Innovation Functions and Policy Issues*, Department for Business Innovation and Skills, UK Government, London.

Tecnalia (2012), *Annual Report*, Tecnalia, Derio, Bizkaia.

Walendowski, J. (2011), Policies and Process of Smart Specialisation: Realising New Opportunities. *Regional Innovation Monitor, Thematic Paper 2*, Technopolis Group, Brussels.

7 Monitoring innovation and development strategies

Stakeholder involvement, learning, and sustainable policy cycles

Carlo Gianelle and Alexander Kleibrink

1 Introduction

Monitoring policies and policy strategies refers to an organized set of activities encompassing (i) the iterative collection and elaboration of information on the direction and evolution of socio-economic phenomena and the delivery of policy measures, and (ii) its use in the decision-making process for adjusting the course of policy actions. The presence and correct functioning of a monitoring mechanism represents a necessary element in order to create 'sustainable policy cycles' and to guarantee the improvement and 'evolvability' – the ability to produce more appropriate responses to challenges than any yet existing, borrowing from evolutionary science (Altenberg, 1994, p. 47) – of policy strategies, public programmes and projects through experimentation, learning and self-correction (Sabel and Zeitlin, 2008; 2012).

This is particularly true in the design and implementation of innovation strategies for smart specialisation aimed at generating sustainable processes of selection, nurturing, evaluation and eventually re-definition of economic and social priorities for territorial development (European Commission, 2012; European Parliament and Council, 2013). Such processes ought to feature the interplay between policy authorities and stakeholders in a non-hierarchical way, through what is called an *entrepreneurial discovery process* (Foray, 2015). In this context, monitoring is crucial for providing the information base and signals for policy action and it can act as a support and inducement mechanism for stakeholder and citizens' engagement, also making the decision-making process more transparent and accountable.

In this chapter, we introduce and discuss the fundamental notions of policy, strategy, and monitoring in the context of democratic, real-world human societies. We illustrate these normative considerations in the more specific context of innovation strategies for smart specialisation. Our conceptual discussion is informed by original data from a survey on the structure and content of monitoring mechanisms for smart specialisation strategies across European regions and countries (Kleibrink *et al.*, 2016). The evidence available on the first experience with the design and implementation of such strategies indeed reveals that linking monitoring to the strategy's intervention logic constitutes a significant challenge for policy makers and public programme officers.

Legitimacy is a central element of public policies in democratic societies. How concerned citizens and organisations perceive their involvement in the making and execution of policies (input) and the results they produce (output) are key to justifying public interventions. Both input and output legitimacy provide the normative framework for public policies in modern democracies. We discuss the role of stakeholders in policy strategies and highlight how their involvement in the design and operation of monitoring activities is crucial to the notion of sustainable policy cycles. According to this logic, strategy monitoring goes far beyond auditing and the fundamental tenets of new public management.

We describe in great detail how the policy cycle unfolds and how it relates to monitoring. At this point, it suffices to define policy cycles as processes that cover agenda-setting, policy formulation, decision-making, policy implementation and policy monitoring and evaluation (Howlett and Ramesh, 2003). While this neat stage-wise definition suggests a linear sequential model, in real policy practice the different stages very often overlap and may occur in a different order. Importantly, the relationship between designing a policy and implementing it is often characterized by an 'implementation gap'; that is, for many different reasons those individuals and organisations implementing policies defect from originally adopted objectives and instruments (Bardach, 1977).

In this chapter, we show how monitoring can contribute to closing this gap and creating what we call sustainable policy cycles. At the very least, such cycles organize 'deliberate, comparative evaluation of collaboration in design and production' among public and private agents (Sabel, 1995, p. 20). An institutionalized monitoring framework can provide both the necessary information to apply tacit knowledge as well as the arena in which agents interact and collaborate.

2 The nature and role of monitoring in strategic policy making

Monitoring territorial strategies for innovation and development has two main functions: an *analytical* function which is primarily internal to the strategy designing and managing, and an *advocacy* function which concerns the relationship between the strategy and the broader economy and society and can thus be regarded as mostly external to the strategy development process (Rip, 1997; Romer, 1993; Saltelli, 2007).

The analytical function involves the identification and codification of information in order to support policy action during the implementation of projects and programmes. It also ensures policy learning and ownership in the community of policy makers and stakeholders that are closely connected to the strategy design and management (Magro and Wilson, 2015; Nauwelaers and Wintjes, 2008). The advocacy function involves the generation and communication of information about the aims, achievements and progress of the strategy to the broader economy and society.[1] It is meant to convey a narrative able to engage a broader set of actors in the strategy's transformational agenda within and outside the territory and to facilitate consensus on its rationale and the need for it.

To illustrate these two functions, let us briefly turn to real world examples. The regional government of Lower Austria collects and organizes relevant data on regional economic and innovation policy in a comprehensive yet concise balanced scorecard that allows for a detailed and timely analytical monitoring.[2] For assessing its position in comparison to other German and European regions, the government of Baden Württemberg resorts to its own tailor-made innovation index which supports a robust narrative on innovation leadership in Europe, together with a sound analysis of innovation performance dynamics.[3]

In terms of advocacy, the Silicon Valley region in California has long been at the forefront of innovation communities worldwide. The multi-stakeholder organisation Silicon Valley Joint Venture has been publishing an index of the broader socio-economic developments in the region since 1995. This index aggregates 26 indicators of trends in Silicon Valley's economy and quality of life reported on an annual basis (Saxenian and Dabby, 2004).[4] Over time, this index has been increasingly tailored to stakeholder needs and has contributed to a feeling of joint ownership in a region that is otherwise very much characterized by competition and individual achievements. In fact, it supported a narrative that framed policy and business debates by pinpointing gaps where action was required. This example clearly shows how monitoring information contributes to the creation of advocacy coalitions entailing various public and private agents with shared belief systems and the capability for sustained coordinated action in sustainable policy cycles (Sabatier and Jenkins-Smith, 1993).

To better understand the functions of monitoring, we start by (re)considering the concepts of policy and policy strategy in modern democracies. Public policy is a coherent set of rules, instructions, and actions aimed at influencing the evolution of a human society by means of setting incentives for individual behaviour. To have a policy therefore primarily means to guide the evolution of a society, or to plan for change and innovation. The opposite to this would be a condition in which change to and innovation in the status quo occur without an overarching strategy, that is, by the sole virtue of unco-ordinated, unplanned actions and interactions of the members of a society (Kauffman, 1993; Minelli, 2009).

For simplicity, but without loss of generality for the aim of the present work, let us think of a human society as a system of agents, individuals or organizations that can be described in terms of its state or the type and level of interactions between its members and the associated outcomes. Policy can influence individual behaviour in such a system in two main ways.

The first is 'limiting the possible' by means of tightening or loosening the constraints of the system, i.e. the rules that govern the relationships between the agents, set limits to their autonomy, and ultimately determine the set of possible states the system can reach. Which specific state actually materializes would then depend on the effect of the individual decisions taken within the boundaries of admissible behaviours, either in response to changing pressure and conditions of the external environment or simply following an idiosyncratic logic. The second is 'guiding to a specific target' by means of directly shaping individual behaviour and interaction both within the system and with the external environment in view of reaching a given state and obtaining specific outcomes.

To a different extent, both such classes of directed evolutionary processes imply the existence of an authority with superior intelligence capability, with the capacity to conceive, intentionally pursue and realize changes in the way the human system actually operates. Let us leave aside for the moment the problem of how such intelligence and authority can actually emerge, and focus on its rationale and the nature of its duties that is to consciously plan for change – of which the preservation of the status quo can be thought of as just a default, business-as-usual case – and to act consistently for its realization.

Defining a policy for change means to identify an end, the means to achieve it, and an implementation programme for applying the means to a specific reality. The means should be appropriate to the end or suitable to realize it. Noticeably, in real-world situations the relationship between end and means reflects a theory of cause–effect and cannot be simply assumed as a *datum* or fact. Determining the content of a policy in human societies is the result of a decision-making process in a context where the object of decision is inherently uncertain, as the future states of the environment and the system, as well as the processes aimed at generating novel states cannot be fully determined in advance.

As a matter of fact, the combination of cognitive boundaries and imperfect information about natural and social phenomena fundamentally limits our capacity to intervene deterministically in the evolution of human systems (Simon, 1957). This has an implication of primary importance: a rational policy for change must necessarily rely on the use of empirical evidence to support, update, and rethink its underlying theory of cause–effect. To the extent that planned change entails the achievement of a truly novel state, the only way to meaningfully apply means to such an end is to progressively incorporate in the course of policy making new information about the state of the system and to use this evidence to evaluate the consistency and effectiveness of the policy hypotheses and, if necessary, to revise its logic and processes. In the words of Sabel and Zeitlin (2012, p. 411), when uncertainty is at play:

> [...] the official decisionmaker does not know how to respond to current or emergent situations, but neither do the primary actors. The response,

correspondingly, is not to organize a system for polling informed insiders, but rather to organize joint exploration of the situation and possibilities for responding to it, on the assumption that joint and continuous learning – arriving at provisional results and then correcting them in the light of further inquiry – makes the risks associated with persistent uncertainty more manageable.

The actions undertaken to implement a policy produce results whose correspondence with the stated aims or objectives ought to be periodically evaluated against benchmarks using heuristic techniques defined – and periodically revised – as part of the monitoring activities. Policy making can be seen hence as a cyclical process whose iterations allow us to progressively uncover and learn the actual relationship between results and objectives, in turn informing us about the suitability of means to ends and the validity of the underlying theory of cause–effect. Such a cyclical view makes clear how 'articulation of a [programme] priority and its implementation cannot be separated; they are components of one dynamic' (Rip, 1997, p. 108).

Historically, analysts of public policy have been observing a persistent tension or gap between the rationales of those planning policy strategies and those putting them in practice (Bardach, 1977), a phenomenon often associated with the different interests and incentives of principal and agent (Jensen and Meckling, 1976). This would create a breakpoint in the policy cycle preventing information on results from feeding back into policy design.

We use the notion of *strategy* for change to denote the necessary experimental and cyclical approach to policy making. A strategy is a set of decision rules that allows users to progressively align results to objectives by means of incorporating and interpreting new information about policy implementation, including the possibility of re-defining or dismissing the policy process. A strategy is not a decision regarding a single postulated relationship between ends and means, but rather a set of rules leading to different decisions to be taken depending on the actual results and their interpretation.

The consequentiality of decisions in a strategy or the rationality of the process should be supported by a 'coding and wiring' system that organizes and conveys information and provides signals for policy action. Such a system is the monitoring system of a strategy in its analytical function. In this understanding, it is clear how monitoring is a *necessary*, *internal* function of the strategy. It is a pre-condition for the policy cycle and constitutes the primary lexicon and syntax of decision-making for strategy designers and managers; without it, the strategy would be mute and the policy would be silent.

In its very essence, an innovation strategy for smart specialisation (RIS3) is not different from the general model we have discussed. The insistent call for integrating monitoring systems in RIS3 by EU institutions and their strategic guidance is actually a consequence of the fact that, lacking such a system, a valid RIS3 can neither be devised nor put into practice (European Commission, 2012; European Parliament and Council, 2013).

The monitoring system of a policy strategy ought to express the selected socio-economic needs, the intervention logic behind the identified policy actions and the expected results in comprehensive but precise and synthetic terms; it should, in other words, provide an immediate representation of the strategic vision for socio-economic change and the means activated in order to achieve it. Interestingly, a monitoring system of this sort would exhibit the *emergent*, *external* function of advocacy.

In this acceptation, a monitoring system may be regarded as a device supporting the development and communication of narratives to gather and maintain consensus on the strategy choice of ends and means, on their need and socio-economic desirability and appropriateness. The importance of advocacy was clearly highlighted for instance in the context of the Lisbon Strategy of the EU (European Commission, 2004, p. 16):

> An ambitious and broad reform agenda needs a clear narrative, in order to be able to communicate effectively about the need for it. So that everybody knows why it is being done and can see the validity of the need to implement sometimes painful reforms. So that everybody knows who is responsible.

In the context of smart specialisation policy, the guiding principles of RIS3 design state that the monitoring system allows 'clarifying the purpose and functioning of the strategy and making it comprehensible to the broader public' and 'supporting the constructive involvement and participation of stakeholders through transparent communication' (Gianelle and Kleibrink, 2015, p. 3). Advocacy is the ultimate goal of such communication.

3 Closing information, implementation and legitimacy gaps

The collaboration between government bodies and non-governmental stakeholders and especially the private sector in co-creating and co-operating monitoring systems for territorial development strategies is grounded on a threefold rationale: (i) the need to inform strategic decisions with relevant knowledge from socio-economic actors that is often tacit and difficult to capture through statistical and analytical sources; (ii) the need to meaningfully link the design and implementation phases of the strategy and close the policy cycle; (iii) the need to provide input and output legitimacy to the strategy process. Stakeholder involvement plays a key role in determining how effectively the monitoring system can perform its analytical and advocacy functions.

In a context where uncertainty is an inherent characteristic of the object of strategic decisions, the future states of the socio-economic system, and the results of the processes set in motion in order to change the status quo, stakeholders broadly defined – being either organizations or individuals – represent a constituent component of the 'collective intelligence' required for the definition and implementation of the strategy and the associated monitoring system.

Because of their closeness to real-world phenomena and the policy's operational level, stakeholders can in principle gather evidence about the state of the system and the actual results of policy interventions faster than traditional government bodies or statistical offices.[5] Even more importantly, stakeholders and in particular entrepreneurs possess tacit knowledge regarding emerging, future-oriented activities and trends (Sabel, 1995). This knowledge is a valuable, often indispensable complement to objective analysis and official statistics in devising trajectories for change which can effectively respond to socio-economic challenges.[6]

The disclosure and aggregation of informal and uncodified stakeholder knowledge would emerge naturally in the context of smart specialisation though the entrepreneurial discovery process in which entrepreneurs and other socio-economic actors produce information about the target areas or domains for policy intervention. The importance of non-governmental stakeholders in this respect is apparent in Foray's words (Foray, 2015, p. 3): 'Administration and politics no longer play the role of omniscient planner but are prepared to listen to entrepreneurs, researchers and citizens in order to identify priorities and facilitate the emergence and growth of new activities.'

The same author, who has contributed substantially to the conceptual development of the smart specialisation approach, goes even further in emphasizing the centrality and the collective, bottom-up nature of the entrepreneurial discovery process (Foray, 2015, p. 24):

> Entrepreneurial discovery is the essential phase, the decisive link that allows the system to reorient and renew itself. Indeed, the entrepreneurial discovery that drives the process of smart specialisation is not simply the advent of an innovation but the deployment and variation of innovative ideas in a specialised area that generate knowledge about the future economic value of a possible direction of change.

The information on the choice of targets and types of interventions brought into the strategy design by stakeholders contributes to determine the overall causal structure of the strategy's monitoring system and the nature and boundaries of individual indicators. In turn, the involvement of stakeholders in the relevant strategic decisions, and especially on the *what* and *how* of monitoring, allows us to close the incentive and information gap between strategy design and implementation which usually characterizes situations in which stakeholders have no say on the strategic design and only are responsible for some aspects of implementation.

Stakeholder involvement in the development of strategies and the associated monitoring systems also helps confer legitimacy to the decisions taken in these contexts. In particular, research on collaborative governance suggests that the views and interests of non-governmental stakeholders should be more closely integrated in the policy design phase in order to enhance the legitimacy of policies and policy strategies (Scharpf, 1997, p. 14). In terms of legitimacy in modern democracies, Scharpf (2003) makes a very useful distinction between what he calls input and output:

> [...] legitimacy has come to rest almost exclusively on trust in institutional arrangements that are thought to ensure that governing processes are generally responsive to the manifest preferences of the governed (input legitimacy, 'government by the people') and/or that the policies adopted will generally represent effective solutions to common problems of the governed (output legitimacy, 'government for the people').

Policies in this understanding have to both deliver effective results to common challenges and to be responsive to societal needs and preferences. Consequently, any policy that is pushed through top-down by a public authority and produces impressive results cannot be deemed legitimate in the absence of full collaboration with concerned non-governmental organizations and individuals.

Admittedly, such cases of successfully implemented yet entirely imposed policies are likely to be rare. But what this distinction underlines, more importantly, is the intrinsic connection between collaborative process and policy outcomes (Romer, 1993, p. 389). After all, positive policy outcomes will very much depend on the motivation of those implementing them on the ground. Their motivation will be higher if they can at least partly set their own objectives (Mintzberg, 1994, p. 71).

Monitoring is commonly associated solely with output legitimacy, that is, it is meant to measure the progress towards reaching previously defined goals. In this acceptation, a transparent monitoring system that concisely communicates information about policy implementation achievements would contribute to building and maintaining dialogue with the stakeholders, empowering them to verify the actual progress made towards strategic goals.

In order to gain input legitimacy, however, the strategy monitoring system should be co-created and co-determined by stakeholders, and not only be an effective communication means to them. In other words, if we accept the dual nature of legitimacy in democratic policy contexts, the nature of the strategy development process and the associated monitoring system has to necessarily be collaborative.

Practitioners working on monitoring often focus on technical aspects and less so on broader governance questions. For instance, the latest edition of the *Frascati manual*, one of the central guides for collecting and reporting data on innovation policies, does not mention in any way how stakeholders can actively take part in monitoring exercises (OECD, 2015). Surveys of the 'end users' of policies are the only tool that can be considered a passive consultation of stakeholders who report on their activities and views.

Indeed, consultation has come to be used interchangeably with collaboration in the daily practice of policy making. Yet, '[c]ollaboration implies two-way communication and influence between agencies and stakeholders and also opportunities for stakeholders to talk with each other', which is not the case in consultations (Ansell and Gash, 2008, p. 546). Tapping the opportunities from innovation is limited largely by the need to organize 'collective action' which is difficult within existing political institutions and in the absence of new innovative institutions to facilitate this (Romer, 1993, pp. 346–7). Often, governments must delegate this task to more independent and knowledgeable institutions, but they are reluctant to concede power (Romer, 1993, p. 366).

A simple example of more collaborative arrangements can be found in the funding policy of Science Foundation Ireland, the prime research-funding agency in Ireland. The Foundation asks every grant applicant to define their desired impact in formal 'impact statements'.[7] Based on this self-set benchmark, selection committees can better assess the feasibility of the project and its results and longer term impact. In other words, a meaningful monitoring is established by entering a substantial and collaborative agreement between funding agency and beneficiary.

4 Current theory and practice of policy monitoring: From auditing to learning

The approach of contemporary scholarship to policy monitoring and the practical experiences in the context for instance of EU-funded programmes tend to concentrate around two different conceptualizations of monitoring activities, alternately seen as mostly a way to guarantee *accountability*, or a means to support *policy learning*. Considering the recent EU Cohesion policy developments, most analysts would agree that the smart specialisation approach requires a fully learning-oriented monitoring. However, this has yet to take strong and widespread roots, while audit-oriented thinking is still widespread.

Accountability has long been at the core of monitoring, usually as a legal obligation. In the framework of EU territorial policy, audit requirements have been a defining feature to ensure that programme and project managers are accountable for their activities. Criticism has been raised on several occasions that too excessive and rigid audit requirements focusing mainly on compliance may stifle innovation in EU regional development programmes. This kind of audit thinking in European regional development programmes also has had a major influence on the way programmes and projects have been chosen and implemented, and the way monitoring has been conceived.

Bachtler and Mendez (2011) argue that audit obligations have overburdened regional administrations, promoted too many risk-averse project applications and in the worst case even scared off promising applicants. It is curious to note that most of the academic literature on public administration using the term monitoring does originate from audit exercises. To give another example, Altman (1979) developed the idea of 'performance monitoring' as a response to the sharp increase in funding for social programmes in the U.S. American Great Society programme in the 1960s. Ensuring public money was spent well was a difficult task for local and state administrations that lacked the necessary resources and skills.

New public management scholarship has taken up and reinforced this approach by introducing detailed indicator systems for auditing and inspecting performance inside public administrations with the goal to make them more efficient and effective (Barzelay, 1997; Leeuw and Furubo, 2008, pp. 161–62). In policy studies, monitoring is usually associated with related sanctioning or enforcement mechanisms (Sabatier, 2007).

These strands of literature point to the question of how insights from monitoring translate into new decisions and adjustments. In other words, how governments learn from past failure and success is a crucial question. In order to truly move towards more reflective forms of governance, monitoring systems must ensure that 'complete knowledge and maximization of control are replaced by continued learning' (Mierlo *et al.*, 2010, p. 145).

The approach to policy monitoring we outlined in the previous sections clearly requires going beyond a mere auditing purpose and instead conceiving monitoring as an activity or a system of activities fully oriented to policy learning and stakeholder participation. This latter approach fits the smart specialisation principles and serves the purpose of creating sustainable policy cycles with the participation of stakeholders which in turn represent the necessary declination of a policy strategy for change.

As a matter of fact, policy learning through monitoring has received far less attention in the literature and in practice. Learning can be undermined if monitoring is mainly seen as having an audit or control function; quite to the contrary, this can even make the building up of trust and cooperation more difficult (see Hummelbrunner, 2006, p. 178). While using statistics to benchmark own performance with other territories that are structurally similar is a necessary pre-condition for policy learning, it is not sufficient (Navarro *et al.*, 2014). Indeed, participation and empowerment studies from the 1990s stress the need to actively engage concerned stakeholders and 'reflective practitioners' in 'communities of learners' (Fetterman, 2000, p. 9; Floc'hlay and Plottu, 1998; Plottu and Plottu, 2009).

Coupled with increasing attention paid to evidence-based policy making, scholarship on monitoring has been moving in the last decade towards broader and more systemic approaches that seek to capture the implementation of policies and their outcomes in a more holistic way (Mierlo *et al.*, 2010). This pays tribute to the complex nature of socio-economic systems and the difficulties in measuring their performance with single indicators (Borrás, 2012).

Following the definition of the Oxford Dictionary, an indicator is 'a sign that shows you what something is like or how a situation is changing'. Such signs can be derived from official statistics, but they may as well emerge from interactions with stakeholders with an intimate knowledge of how the situation is changing on the ground; while feedback from stakeholders can provide an external validation of collected statistical data (Plottu and Plottu, 2009, p. 346).

To promote learning, governments and stakeholders engage in an iterative process of what Sabel called learning-by-monitoring, in which the 'state instigates the firms to set goals with reference to some prevailing standard so that shortfalls in performance are apparent to those with the incentives and capacity to remedy them – the firms themselves – and new targets are set accordingly' (Sabel, 1993, p. 30). If those organisations implementing innovation measures have a certain degree of ownership in the setting up of monitoring, trust towards policy makers is more likely to build up. In the end, many different organizations will and should use monitoring data and related information for improving processes and projects and reaching out to a wider audience (Behn, 2003; Plottu and Plottu, 2009, p. 346).

5 Conclusions: Closing the policy cycle of smart specialisation

In this chapter we characterized the strategic process of designing and implementing policies for socio-economic change, especially smart specialisation policy, as a means of identifying and pursuing new possibilities for development and progress by way of adopting an experimental approach. In this context, monitoring should be understood as an evolving representation of the logic of intervention of the strategy. Monitoring provides the necessary information to analyze the constituents and causal relationships defining the strategy, and in this connotation it is essential for the achievement of the intended strategy outcomes. It can also have an emergent advocacy function towards stakeholders and the broader community of citizens and organizations which constitute the ultimate recipients of the policy strategy. Both these functions are important for the sustainability of the policy process.

A cyclical view of the policy process is the most meaningful way to conceive policy making in a world characterized by fundamental uncertainty about the future, and it is even more necessary when policies explicitly aim at pursuing innovation in the current state of affairs. In such a world, the actual relationship between ends and means is only progressively revealed as policy action unfolds, and the conceptual model on which the strategy is built should be continuously challenged against new information derived from policy implementation and adjusted accordingly. Strategy monitoring constitutes the wire harness that continuously collects and conveys information and provides signals for and feedback to policy action.

In the archetypical policy cycle, monitoring appears towards the end of different policy stages. Lasswell's seminal work on decision-making distinguished between seven different stages, out of which only the last two ones – appraisal of policy decisions, and their eventual termination or modification – refer explicitly to monitoring (Lasswell, 1956); albeit the first stage is primarily about gathering the necessary intelligence to form decisions which is de facto already part of monitoring. This stage model, although criticized by many for its overly functional and rationalist approach, has been a major influence on the way we understand contemporary policy making and contributed to the spread of a mostly audit-oriented conception of monitoring. In fact, if wrongly understood this model may seem to imply that policy makers have to think about monitoring only at the very end of both the policy design and implementation phases. However, these different stages in practice often overlap, occur in parallel or do not follow a linear logic.

Similar misperceptions have been observed by the authors of this chapter in their policy work on smart specialisation strategies in European regions and countries. Such a misapprehension can have unfortunate effects and actually make implementation and the follow up to success and failure an impossible task. The implementation gap of any policy strategy becomes wider if the strategy is not the result of commonly shared beliefs among all relevant stakeholders about the intervention logic that undergirds the entire exercise. Stakeholder involvement in strategy design and implementation and hence in strategy monitoring is necessary in order to close potential implementation and legitimacy gaps; it is instrumental for achieving an effective and sustainable policy cycle. In the context of smart specialisation, this implies that the entrepreneurial discovery process through which tacit knowledge about the states of the world is gathered, compared, integrated and distilled into decisions needs to be a permanent and recursive process that goes hand in hand with policy implementation and not just a phase of strategy design. A veritable apprehension of any policy for change, and the smart specialisation approach in particular, would need to pass from a conceptualization of monitoring as a phase of the policy cycle to a representation in which monitoring supports and enables the whole cycle. This can be explained by the uncertain nature of the relationship between ends and means that should be continuously considered and adjusted.

According to Sabel and Zeitlin (2012, p. 411), the cyclic nature of policy-making processes stems from the breakdown of the distinction between conception and execution; when the future states of the world are fundamentally uncertain, 'implementation becomes the conception' in the sense that the very implementation of policy measures may give new meaning to their original conception and rationale.

Innovation strategies for smart specialisation should incorporate the expectation that goals may shift during the implementation phase, otherwise there would not be genuine policy experimentation; indeed, 'it becomes impossible to speak of an 'original' goal' (Rip, 1997, p. 109). Monitoring has to be very much responsive to what is happening on the ground through information flows from stakeholders and the sharing of otherwise tacit knowledge. There is no value in monitoring progress towards what turns out to be an outdated and invalid goal or in investing resources in this direction.

Policy strategies are, thus, not set in stone and rigid, but rather emergent and adaptive and have to adjust to changing realities to facilitate learning (Mintzberg, 1994; Rip, 1997, p. 110). Similarly, the accompanying monitoring has to be an emergent strategic management tool co-created together with stakeholders. Without critical information from stakeholders, public agents alone are less likely to effectively identify and learn from experience and to identify failure and success.

In the context of smart specialisation, a direct implication of the cyclical, experimental nature of policy making and the loose distinction between policy implementation and conception is that, in order to 'close' the policy cycle, the entrepreneurial discovery process – understood as the central process presiding over the decisions on the intervention areas – should be carried out in a continuous time and be *reactive* to new information deriving from monitoring activities. The entrepreneurial discovery process would in other words be the default operation mode of the strategy governance, and not simply a phase of the strategy design or an activity performed in a definite time frame.

Collaborative governance and monitoring are better suited to deal with the 'diffuseness and the micro-politics of R&D policy making and implementation' (Rip, 1997, p. 115). Closing the policy cycle in this context also means creating a sustained 'web of institutions' that organize deliberation and collaboration (Sabel, 1995, p. 20); see Figure 7.1.

The main challenge for all parties involved in the policy making process is perhaps to favour in such a web of institutions the growth and spread of a

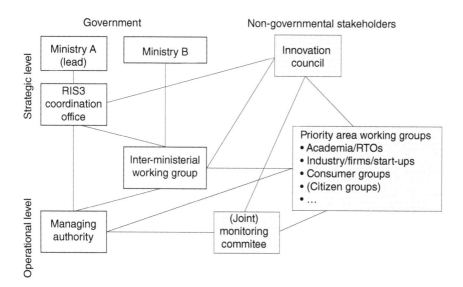

Figure 7.1 Web of institutions enabling deliberation and collaboration of innovation agents for smart specialisation

cultural attitude reflecting full awareness of the necessity of experimentation and which is therefore tolerant to failure (Lester and Piore 2006). The promotion and integration of such a stance at all levels of territorial governance should be a foremost goal of the authorities promoting smart specialisation in the European Union and beyond.

Notes

1 Policy advocacy is often supported by the use of composite indicators or indices representing an aggregate measure of a country or territory's performance. On composite indicators as advocacy devices, see also OECD (2005) and Saltelli (2007).
2 Interreg project KNOW-HUB, see www.know-hub.eu/blog/application-of-the-balanced-scorecard-methodology-in-lower-austria-s-economic-and-innovation-policy.html (accessed on 16/10/2015).
3 Innovation Index 2014, see www.statistik.baden-wuerttemberg.de/Service/Veroeff/Monatshefte/20150104.mha (accessed on 16/10/2015).
4 See www.jointventure.org/publications/silicon-valley-index/13-publications/silicon-valley-index (accessed on 16/10/2015).
5 One can argue of course that stakeholders are also at the same time interest groups that do not only pursue the public good. For the purpose of this chapter, we concentrate on the knowledge stakeholders possess and governments do not. In this sense, stakeholder involvement is positive. For a more detailed discussion on the multifaceted role stakeholders play in social change, see Friedman and Miles (2002).
6 Stakeholders are by definition interested parties in the strategy design and implementation process and their individual contribution is not unbiased nor is the information they provide. Involving a wide and diverse pool of stakeholders and engaging them in a collective, iterative process of entrepreneurial discovery and knowledge sharing is a way to increase the tacit knowledge base. At the same time, it reduces the likelihood that a single individual interest or perception prevails over the others. The information bias associated with the involvement of interested parties is also reduced by the need to compare and complement it with objective analysis and official statistics, see Friedman and Miles (2002).
7 www.sfi.ie/funding/sfi-research-impact/preparing-your-impact-statemen.html (accessed on 16/10/2015).

References

Altenberg, L. (1994). The Evolution of Evolvability in Genetic Programming. In Kinnear, K. (Ed.), *Advances in Genetic Programming* (pp. 47–74). Cambridge, Mass: MIT Press.
Altman, S. (1979). Performance Monitoring Systems for Public Managers, *Public Administration Review*, 39(1), 31–35.
Ansell, C. and Gash, A. (2008). Collaborative Governance in Theory and Practice. *Journal of Public Administration Research and Theory*, 18(4), 543–571.
Bachtler, J. and Mendez, C. (2011). Administrative Reform and Unintended Consequences: An Assessment of the EU Cohesion Policy 'Audit Explosion.' *Journal of European Public Policy*, 18(5), 746–65.
Bardach, E. (1977). *The Implementation Game: What Happens After a Bill Becomes a Law*. Cambridge, Mass: MIT Press.

Barzelay, M. (1997). Central Audit Institutions and Performance Auditing: A Comparative Analysis of Organizational Strategies in the OECD. *Governance*, 10(3), 235–60.

Behn, R. D. (2003). Why Measure Performance? Different Purposes Require Different Measures. *Public Administration Review*, 63(5), 586–606.

Borrás, S. (2012). Three Tensions in the Governance of Science and Technology. In D. Levi-Faur (Ed.), *The Oxford Handbook of Governance* (pp. 429–440). Oxford: Oxford University Press.

European Commission. (2004). *Facing the Challenge: The Lisbon Strategy for Growth and Employment* (Report from the High Level Group Chaired by Wim Kok). Luxembourg: Office for Official Publications of the European Communities.

European Commission. (2012). *Guide to Research and Innovation Strategies for Smart Specialisation (RIS3)*. Luxembourg: Publications Office of the European Union.

European Parliament and Council. (2013). *Regulation (EU) No 1303/2013 of the European Parliament and of the Council laying down common provisions on the European Regional Development Fund, the European Social Fund, the Cohesion Fund, the European Agricultural Fund for Rural Development and the European Maritime and Fisheries Fund and laying down general provisions on the European Regional Development Fund, the European Social Fund, the Cohesion Fund and the European Maritime and Fisheries Fund*. Brussels.

Fetterman, D. (2000). *Foundations of Empowerment Evaluation*. Thousand Oaks: SAGE.

Floc'hlay, B. and Plottu, E. (1998). Democratic Evaluation from Empowerment Evaluation to Public Decision-Making. *Evaluation*, 4(3), 261–277.

Foray, D. (2015). *Smart Specialisation: Opportunities and Challenges for Regional Innovation Policy*. Abingdon; New York: Routledge.

Friedman, A. L. and Miles, S. (2002). Developing Stakeholder Theory. *Journal of Management Studies*, 39(1), 1–21.

Gianelle, C. and Kleibrink, A. (2015). *Monitoring Mechanisms for Smart Specialisation Strategies* (S3 Policy Brief Series No. 13/2015). Spain: European Commission, Joint Research Centre.

Howlett, M. and Ramesh, M. (2003). *Studying Public Policy: Policy Cycles and Policy Subsystems*. Toronto: Oxford University Press.

Hummelbrunner, R. (2006). Systemic Evaluation in the Field of Regional Development. In B. Williams and I. Imam (eds), *Systems Concepts in Evaluation: An Expert Anthology* (pp. 161–180). Point Reyes, CA: EdgePress of Inverness.

Jensen, M. C. and Meckling, W. H. (1976). Theory of the Firm: Managerial Behavior, Agency Costs and Ownership Structure. *Journal of Financial Economics*, 3(4), 305–360.

Kauffman, S. A. (1993). *The Origins of Order: Self-Organization and Selection in Evolution*. New York: Oxford University Press.

Kleibrink, A., Gianelle, C. and Doussineau, M. (2016). Monitoring Innovation and Territorial Development in Europe: Emergent Strategic Management. *European Planning Studies*, 24(8), 1438–1458.

Lasswell, H. D. (1956). *The Decision Process: Seven Categories of Functional Analysis*. College Park, Maryland: Bureau of Governmental Research, College of Business and Public Administration, University of Maryland.

Leeuw, F. L. and Furubo, J.-E. (2008). Evaluation Systems: What Are They and Why Study Them? *Evaluation*, 14(2), 157–69.

Lester, R. and Piore, M. (2006). *Innovation. The Missing Dimension*. Cambridge: Harvard University Press.

Magro, E. and Wilson, J. R. (2015). Evaluating Territorial Strategies. In J. M. Valdaliso and J. R. Wilson (eds), *Strategies for Shaping Territorial Competitiveness* (pp. 94–110). Oxon; New York: Routledge.

Mierlo, B. van, Arkesteijn, M., and Leeuwis, C. (2010). Enhancing the Reflexivity of System Innovation Projects with System Analyses. *American Journal of Evaluation*, 31(2), 143–161.

Minelli, A. (2009). *Forms of Becoming: The Evolutionary Biology of Development*. Princeton; Oxford: Princeton University Press.

Mintzberg, H. (1994). *The Rise and Fall of Strategic Planning: Reconceiving Roles for Planning, Plans, Planners*. New York; Toronto: Free Press; Maxwell Macmillan Canada.

Nauwelaers, C. and Wintjes, R. (2008). *Innovation Policy in Europe: Measurement and Strategy*. Cheltenham: Edward Elgar.

Navarro, M., Gibaja, J. J., Franco, S., Murciego, A., Gianelle, C., Kleibrink, A. and Hegyi, F. B. (2014). *Regional Benchmarking in the Smart Specialisation Process: Identification of Reference Regions Based on Structural Similarity* (S3 Working Paper No. 03/2014). European Commission, Joint Research Centre.

OECD (2005). *Statistics, Knowledge and Policy: Key Indicators to Inform Decision Making*. Paris: Organisation for Economic Co-operation and Development.

OECD (2015). *Frascati Manual 2015*. Paris: Organisation for Economic Co-operation and Development.

Plottu, B. and Plottu, E. (2009). Approaches to Participation in Evaluation: Some Conditions for Implementation. *Evaluation*, 15(3), 343–359.

Rip, A. (1997). The Influence of the Initial Phases on Programme Dynamics. In M. Callon, P. Laredo, and P. Mustar (eds), *The Strategic Management of Research and Technology: Evaluation of Programmes* (pp. 105–16). Paris: Economica.

Romer, P. M. (1993). Implementing a National Technology Strategy with Self-Organizing Industry Investment Boards. *Brookings Paper: Microeconomics*, (2).

Sabatier, P. ed. (2007). *Theories of the Policy Process*. Boulder: Westview, http://site.ebrary.com/id/10510160.

Sabatier, P. A. and Jenkins-Smith, H. C. (1993). *Policy Change and Learning: An Advocacy Coalition Approach*. Boulder: Westview Press.

Sabel, C. F. (1993). *Learning by Monitoring: The Institutions of Economic Development* (Working Paper No. 102). New York: Center for Law and Economic Studies, Columbia University School of Law.

Sabel, C. F. (1995). Intelligible Differences: On Deliberate Strategy and the Exploration of Possibility in Economic Life. Presented at the 36th Annual Meeting of the Società Italiana degli Economisti, Florence.

Sabel, C. F. and Zeitlin, J. (2008). Learning from Difference: The New Architecture of Experimentalist Governance in the European Union. *European Law Journal*, 14(3), 271–327.

Sabel, C. F. and Zeitlin, J. (2012). Experimentalist Governance. In Levi-Faur, D. (ed.), *The Oxford Handbook of Governance* (pp. 169–183). Oxford: Oxford University Press.

Saltelli, A. (2007). Composite Indicators between Analysis and Advocacy. *Social Indicators Research*, 81(1), 65–77.

Saxenian, A. and Dabby, N. C. (2004). *Creating and Sustaining Regional Collaboration in Silicon Valley? The Case of Joint Venture: Silicon Valley* (No. Working Paper 2004–05). Institute of Urban and Regional Development, University of California at Berkeley.

Scharpf, F. W. (1997). *Games Real Actors Play: Actor-Centered Institutionalism in Policy Research*. Boulder: Westview.

Scharpf, F. W. (2003). Problem-Solving Effectiveness and Democratic Accountability in the EU. *MPIfG Working Paper*, *03*(1).

Simon, H. A. (1957). *Models of Man: Social and Rational*. New York: Wiley.

8 Bridging the gap between science, market and policy in Andalusia[1]

Inmaculada Periáñez-Forte and Clemente J. Navarro

Introduction

The process of elaborating the research and innovation strategy for smart specialisation (RIS3) in Andalusia has shown that it is possible to approach strategic regional planning in a different way. In particular, the setting-up of the entrepreneurial discovery process (EDP) during the elaboration of the RIS3 Andalusia has offered Andalusian companies the opportunity to reach consensus on a common vision for the future of the region and created commitment to the priorities for action. These priorities are projected to spark entrepreneurship and regional growth in Andalusia.

In order to avoid preconceived approaches such as sectors or clusters, a new governance structure was designed and an open questionnaire was distributed to the stakeholders involved in the S3 process. Following the logic of the EDP process, the questionnaire aimed at identifying the assets and existing resources, the business capacities and existing knowledge in the region. The objective was to extract from regional stakeholders' contributions unique proposals of specialisation opportunities for research and innovation (R&I) in the region.

This chapter presents the procedure followed by the Andalusian Regional Government in drawing up the Andalusian Innovation Strategy 2014–20 (RIS3 Andalusia), which today, the Andalusian Regional Government considers the basic element for building smart specialisation in the region. The aim of this chapter is twofold. The first objective is to illustrate the impact that the entrepreneurial discovery process has had – and is having – in Andalusia, including the changes that have been introduced during the process. The second objective is to stress that when it comes to the deployment of EDP, one size does not fit all regions.

To achieve this, section 1 provides an overview of Andalusia. It highlights the main characteristics, strengths and weaknesses of the region. Section 2 describes the procedure followed by the Andalusian Regional Government in drawing up the RIS3 Andalusia. Section 3 discusses some key factors for the success of the EDP in Andalusia.

The chapter concludes with two messages. First, it is possible to break with the past and approach strategic regional planning in a different way. Second, in order to ensure the success of the EDP in Andalusia – or any other region – and consequently, mobilise stakeholders' knowledge and integrate their perspectives into jointly developed shared goals and priorities, the differences, deficiencies and strengths of each region need to be acknowledged and individually addressed. At EU level, this means that the diversity across regions and countries in terms of size, clustering levels, legal and economic situations, and the state of RIS3 implementation, government and business culture makes it difficult to have a one-dimensionalisation approach to EDP across countries and regions.

1 An overview of the Andalusian context

Andalusia is the most populous region in Spain with over 8 million inhabitants followed by Catalonia, Madrid and Valencia. With an area of 87,597.7 km², Andalusia is larger than more than half the European Union countries and represents around 16.7 per cent of Spanish territory and 2.3 per cent of the EU. The Andalusian economic situation has been characterised by its lack of industrial diversification. Given its peripheral location, as the southern doorway to Europe between the Mediterranean and Atlantic, and its history, Andalusia has been a crossroads between three cultures – Christians, Jewish and Muslims.

Figure 8.1 Andalusian's characteristics

Indicator	Period	
Area (km²)		87,597.70
Total population	2013	8,421,274.00
Labour force (thousands)	1st Q–13	3,996.60
Working population (thousands)	1st Q–13	2,522.90
GDP (€ millions)	2012	140,757.00
Number of companies	2013	472,370.00
Working population with higher education and doctorates (%)	2013	34.2
R and D spending (% of GDP)	2013	1.1

Source: Andalusian Statistics and Cartography Institute (IECA), National Statistics Institute (INE).

*Elaborated by the Andalusian Innovation and Development Agency (IDEA).

Over the past two decades, Andalusia has developed at a good speed compared to other regions in Spain.[2] Andalusia has transformed itself from a region with a low-skilled population looking for opportunities outside the region into a host region for a large number of immigrants. Furthermore, in recent years, Andalusia has increased the skills of its human capital, a key factor that is allowing the region to evolve into an internationally competitive region.

Despite this, the economic crisis affected Andalusia harder than other regions due to its economic structure, heavily dependant on construction and tourism. In 2008, the deterioration of the labour market situation interrupted the increasing employment growth of the previous years, stressing the deficiencies of the regional system. Overall, despite of the improvement of its socio-economic context, the region still lags behind the European Union (EU) average in key economic and social indicators.

1.1 Andalusia and the EU funds

EU funding has been an important driver for the economic growth and modernisation of the region. The region has received the largest portion of the structural funds assigned to Spain over the last twenty years. An amount that has being increasing for each programming period, since Spain joined the EU in 1986. However, the economic crisis and the fact that beyond 2013 Andalusia was no longer a 'convergence region' but a 'region in transition' placed a strong challenge on the regional authorities and the entire regional system. At the time of writing, Andalusia has received € 14 billion for the programming period 2007–13, whereas the current programming period 2014–20 provides the region with € 13.4 billion – to be shared – together with Canarias, Castilla-La Mancha, Melilla and Murcia (Cohesion Policy and Spain, 2014–20).[3]

Together with the loss of the EU convergence region status and the impact of the economic crisis in the region, the increased competition from emerging economies has placed on the Regional Government of Andalusia the challenge to mobilise policies and strategies to contribute to the re-establishment of a sound economy and social cohesion (OECD, 2010).

Table 8.1 Evolution of European funds programme for Andalusia

Programming period	EUR million
1986–88	1,088
1989–93	2,781.1
1994–99	7,030.8
2000–06	12,297.4
2007–13	14,024.2
2014–20	7,722.6

Source: Andalusian Innovation and Development Agency (IDEA).

1.2 Andalusia and its governance system

The Spanish administration has three levels: central, regional and local (see Box 8.1).[4] The distribution of powers and responsibilities among the different public administrations is established under the Spanish Constitution, which is complemented with the Statutes of Autonomy of each autonomous region.

In the case of Andalusia, the region has eight provinces (Almería, Cádiz, Córdoba, Granada, Huelva, Jaén, Málaga and Sevilla) and a total of 770 municipalities. Concerning the distribution of responsibilities, the region may share powers with the central administration in areas such as education, universities, economic development, research, development and technological innovation.[5] For instance, the responsibility for research is shared by the central government and the regional (autonomous) governments.

Box 8.1 The governance structure of Andalusia

National Government

Government Office *(Delegación del Gobierno)*: represents the national government in the autonomous region. Its headquarters is in Seville with branch offices in each province.

Main functions: migration affairs; general coordination and promotion of scientific and technological research; public works of general interest or affecting two or more autonomous regions; regulation of academic and professional qualifications.

Judicial Power: Superior Court of Justice *(Tribunal Superior de Justicia)*: Highest judicial institution in Andalusia, Ceuta and Melilla. It has administrative, civil, criminal and social chambers. Its head office is in Granada with branch offices in Malaga and Seville.

Autonomous Region of Andalusia *(Junta de Andalucía)*

The **competences** of the region are exclusive or shared powers, depending on the policy area. The Regional Government of Andalusia has wide powers in agriculture and fishing; energy and mining; education and universities; health; urban planning; environment; social services; transport and communication; civil protection; culture and heritage and tourism. The competences of the region also apply to employment.

President of the Executive power leads and coordinates the Governing Council of the Regional Government, coordinates the administration and appoints the Regional Ministers.

Governing Council: holds executive and administrative powers. Council – president and regional ministers – holds weekly meetings.

13 Regional Ministries: presidency and local administration; economy and knowledge; financial and public administration; education; health; equity and welfare; employment, enterprise and trade; public works and housing; tourism and sports; culture; governance and justice; agriculture, fishing and rural development; and environment and territorial planning.

Legislative Power
Parliament of Andalusia: passes regional legislation, monitors and encourages the performance of the governing council and approves the region's budget. The Parliament is democratically elected every four years.
Other authorities independent from the regional government: the Andalusian Ombudsman, the, the Court of Auditors, the Regional Consultative Council, the Audiovisual Council of Andalusia and the Andalusian Social and Economic Council.
Provinces (8) Almería, Cádiz, Córdoba, Granada, Huelva, Jaén, Málaga and Sevilla.
Provincial Office (Diputación Provincial)
The selection of members at the provincial level is based on the results of municipal elections.
Main functions: Municipal coordination, legal assistance and advice. Assistance in fire and rescue service, waste management, water services, inter-urban transport etc. for the smallest municipalities.
Municipalities (778) City Council: Members are elected every four years in municipal elections. City Council is led by a mayor.
Main functions: urban planning; social housing, community social services; water supply and waste management; public lighting; fire prevention; public transport; maintenance of roads; customer service; tourism, culture and sport promotion; cooperation with other administrative offices linked to Andalusian heritage etc. Municipalities can collaborate in delivery of services (*mancomunidades*).

Source: Regional Government of Andalusia.

1.3 Andalusia and the S3

Andalusian economic development strategies based on promoting innovation and the emergence of the knowledge society contributed, before the economic crisis, towards bringing the region closer to national and EU averages in terms of overall economic performance. The impact of the economic crisis in the region, together with the loss of the EU convergence region status, helped the Regional Government of Andalusia to embrace smart specialisation as an opportunity to improve the competitiveness of the region.

The first steps towards the elaboration of the RIS3 Andalusia were taken around 2011, with different actions of the Regional Government of Andalusia, such as participation in the Smart Specialisation Platform (S3 Platform) of the Joint Research Centre, Institute of Prospective Technological Studies (JRC-IPTS) of the European Commission and the organisation of different activities and meetings related to smart specialisation. It would be widely acknowledged that Andalusia was on the frontlines of the development of the S3 approach and EDP concept.

According to the Regional Government of Andalusia, the elaboration of the Andalusian Innovation Strategy 2014–20 (RIS3 Andalusia) had a two-fold objective:

- to respond to the 'ex-ante' conditionality imposed by the European Commission for accessing Structural and Investment Funds (ESIF); and
- to comply with the Legislature Agreement upon which the Andalusian Regional Government builds, concerning the need for progress towards a new productive model based on innovation.

In line with these objectives, the RIS3 Andalusia was elaborated in coordination and coherence with the European Regional Development Fund (ERDF) Andalusia Operational Programme, with the Andalusian Economic Plan 2014–20 (Agenda for Employment and Strategy for Competitiveness), and with the rest of the regional planning instruments created under different sectoral policies.

The following section describes the procedure followed by the Andalusian Regional Government in drawing up the RIS3 Andalusia. The RIS3 Andalusia is considered today by the Regional Government of Andalusia, as the basic strategic planning instrument for building smart specialisation R&I priorities for the economy in the region. Furthermore, it extends the S3 methodology to other regional strategies such as the Andalusian Industrial Strategy. Section 2 places special attention on the governance structure designed and the deployment of the entrepreneurial discovery process to ensure the engagement of Andalusian stakeholders and obtain their commitment to the elaboration and coordinated implementation of the RIS3 Andalusia.

2 The S3 Andalusian experience and its EDP

The Regional Government of Andalusia has traditionally played a strong leadership role in steering the region towards a knowledge-based economy through significant investments in innovation, development of human capital and connectivity (OECD, 2010). Despite this, when the smart specialisation approach was introduced in Europe around 2009, its logic created a new challenge – an opportunity – on the Regional Government of Andalusia – and, regional policy makers in general. The S3 approach imposed on countries and regions the mobilisation and management of the knowledge existing in their territories and people and their feedback into public policy.

The logic of smart specialisation was clear, to bridge the gap between science, market opportunities and policy-making using the knowledge accumulated in the region. The definition of the EDP concept was straightforward, an interactive process that allows market forces and the private sector to discover and produce information about new activities, whilst government provided the right conditions to empower key actors to contribute to the strategic development of the region (Hausmann and Rodrick 2003). However, the conceptual stage of EDP did not address a number of challenges that have emerged over time through regional policy design and practices.

Hence, it seems fair to stress that it is not possible to evaluate the efforts made by Andalusia, and/or any other region across Europe, without a clear understanding of the challenges that the EDP represents in each region. In the case of Andalusia, contrary to other regions across Europe, the mobilisation of stakeholders of its regional innovation system could be considered particularly challenging given the size and density of the region. Andalusia is particularly dense in terms of governmental bodies, public research institutions, public universities (10), technological parks and centres, enterprises and the large group of different entities designed to bring research and innovation closer to companies.

2.1 Selecting stakeholders for an inclusive EDP in Andalusia

In the case of Andalusia, selecting stakeholders is a major challenge given the size of the region and the number of actors involved with its innovation system. Moreover, selecting and engaging the adequate actors in any EDP is an increasingly difficult task due to the cross-border, multi-disciplinary and cross-sectoral dimensions of emerging activities (OECD, 2013). The selection of stakeholders is a challenge that has not been clearly tackled when defining the EDP concept.

The challenge addressed by the Regional Government of Andalusia was to create a collaborative process to ensure the engagement of the regional stakeholders in the EDP to jointly design the RIS3 Andalusia. To achieve this, the Regional Government of Andalusia understood innovation actors in a broad sense, including large and small companies, independent innovators, technology and competence centres, universities and public agencies, science and business parks, etc.

For this difficult task, the region invited to the process those regional companies that had demonstrated a commitment to innovate, that is, companies that were investing in innovation projects or introducing new products/services to the market. Likewise, individual innovators were also taken into account and were selected among those actors assuming the risk of exploring new business opportunities in the region, such as starts-up/spin-off. Those stakeholders were considered to be the best placed in Andalusia to know or/and discover which are the region's most promising areas for specialisation and, above all, to be the real performers of the exploitation of these promising areas in the future.

Different ways of forming and managing panels were put in place. The objective was to ensure the engagement of a large number of stakeholders, as well as a fair number of initial ideas/areas pointing out the innovation opportunities existing in the region. According to the staff in charge of the organisation of the EDP, what was expected from the actors involved was commitment, cooperation, learning capacity and progress.

2.2 The governance and process of entrepreneurial discovery in Andalusia

The option favoured by policy makers in this case was clear: the more the merrier. To this end, Andalusian customised the RIS3 Andalusia phase sequence foreseen by the RIS3 Guide,[6] changing the order of the steps, starting with the definition of the governance of the EDP. The Regional Government of Andalusia believed that gathering the commitment – from the very beginning – of the stakeholders involved, especially from companies, was key to ensure the success of the process. In 2012, the Council of Government of the Andalusian Regional Government started with the elaboration of the RIS3 Andalusia under the following fundamental principles:

- To direct economic policy and mobilise public and private investment towards innovation-based development opportunities.
- To discover and exploit strengths and opportunities for specialisation and excellence in Andalusia.
- To involve the universities and regional actors in innovation, including the civil society, as the main driving force for structural change in the Andalusian economy.

Once the Council of Regional Ministers of Andalusia launched the RIS3 design process in December 2012, the Economic Policy Commission, (regional competent body which assumed the political leadership of the process), appointed the members of the Steering Committee. This Committee was chaired by the General Director of the Agency of Innovation and Development of Andalusia (IDEA) and the General Director of the European Funds, both at the Regional Ministry of Economy, Innovation, Science and Employment at that time. Today, after the last change of government, IDEA was moved to the current Regional Ministry of Employment, Enterprise and Commerce, whereas the European Funds remained at the Regional Ministry of Economy and Knowledge. Likewise, General Directors representing all the regional ministries concerned with innovation, research and development, entrepreneurial and industry, Andalusian universities' rectors, research institutes' presidents, the Andalusian network of technological spaces (RETA) and the public and private partnership for innovation (CTA) were also members of the Steering Committee.

The Technical Secretary role of the RIS3 was carried out by IDEA, which was charged with issuing all the working documents and the coordination of a task force featuring technical staff from all the regional ministries participating at the Steering Committee. This organisational design would guarantee interdepartmental coordination and coherence among all the regional strategies that were being developed in the region for the frame 2014–20, the Andalusian Industrial Strategy, the Andalusian Energy Strategy, the Andalusian Internationalisation Strategy and the Andalusian specific Plan for R&D&I. All of these regional strategies had to be aligned with the RIS3 Andalusia and the Operational Programmes in which Andalusia was involved within the European Cohesion Policy.

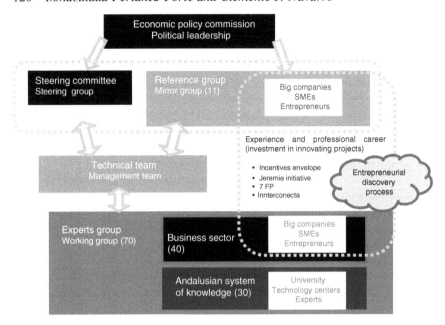

Figure 8.2 Andalusian RIS3 governance

2.3 Steering the EDP process

In order to create the RIS3 Andalusia, Group of Experts accompanied the Technical Secretary during the entrepreneurial discovery process – 70 people were invited: 30 representing technology and competence centres, universities, public agencies, science and business parks and 40 representing individual companies. In order to ensure transparency in the selection of the companies, three rankings were defined: one for start-ups, one for small and medium enterprises (SMEs) and one for big companies, all of them taking into consideration the following three criteria:

- The development of innovation projects in Andalusia.
- The technical assessment in the frame of European funded calls for innovation projects, over the previous five years: 7th Framework Programme for Research and Technological Development (7FP) and national and regional calls co-funded by the European Regional Development Fund (ERDF).
- The score of each company was calculated by adding the add-valued of the project in terms of the impact generated, measured by the incentive obtained and the total investment mobilised.

On the basis of these three rankings, the best 40 companies were invited to participate in the Group of Experts. From this selection, the first eleven were appointed as members of the Reference Group, which co-led the process, with the same decision powers as the Steering Committee.

Once this governance was set, all the working documents elaborated by the Technical Secretary were submitted to the different bodies using a web platform created for this purpose. All experts on the panel were actively involved in this mission, amending and documenting the drafts. All their contributions were duly registered, traced and commented on.

The first document was the Regional Innovation System Analysis and its Strengths, Weaknesses, Opportunities and Threats (SWOT) analysis. This document was approved separately by the Reference Group and the Steering Committee. Hereafter, the two bodies were merged into one called the Co-decision Committee.

2.4 Methodology and process of the EDP in Andalusia

Once the governance structure was established and stakeholders were engaged, a sound methodology was designed to make emerge from the discussion with experts, proposals of specialisation opportunities for research and innovation in Andalusia. In order to avoid preconceived approaches such as sectors or clusters, an open questionnaire was distributed to the experts together with an invitation to the kick-off meeting of RIS3. The purpose of the questionnaire was to map the existing assets, resources, business capacities and knowledge in the region. This exercise was associated with the ideas of Andalusia as: Crossroad territory; Healthy living space; Talented people; Sustainable territory; and Location of advanced industry.

All the answers provided by the experts to the questionnaire were the first inputs for the discovery process. Thereafter, the Technical Secretary analysed, interpreted and documented the results, interconnecting them and organising six entrepreneurial discovery workshops (ED workshops) in order to address the identified themes together with the experts. Based on the results of the questionnaire, the objective of these ED workshops was to discuss and vote on the initial ideas of the experts in terms of areas of opportunity for specialisation.

The ED workshops were developed according to a specific methodology, with the intervention of three main figures: a *Speaker* introducing the topics of the ED workshop and possible areas of opportunity, a *Driver* to stimulate discussions, and a *Rapporteur* collecting contributions as final conclusions for each one of them. At the end of the debates the opportunities and, for each of them, the existing barriers and capacities were collected. The experts voted on the possible impact of each opportunity for specialisation taking into consideration the following factors:

* opportunity in the Andalusian GDP;
* opportunity in the regional internationalisation;
* opportunity in job creation.

The consensus among stakeholders engaged in the EDP, of both the challenges to be addressed and the regional development model to be followed was agreed when setting the Common Vision. To do so, the Technical Secretary of the RIS3 submitted to the experts a 'cloud of tag' including terms that had been constantly used during the working sessions of the process. The Technical Secretary asked the experts to vote on the terms – according to their relevance as an opportunity for specialisation – and to add as many terms as they considered necessary. Experts carried out this exercise on the web platform and its result was considered very revealing. Furthermore, when the Co-decision Committee approved the Vision, the result of the exercise was used as a filter for the selection of the regional priorities, see section 2.5 Results of the EDP (8).

The results of the meetings and ED workshops were completed with in-house work involving an in-depth study of each of the proposals made. The proposals were documented, incorporating appropriate technical and statistical support, analysing their relationship with the priorities established in the Horizon 2020 European Framework Programme for Research and Innovation. This stage of the process was supported by specialists expressly brought in for each environment created, with the support of the Spanish R&D&I network, and the Technical Team of the Strategy. This work was contained in the Catalogue of Specialisation Opportunities in Andalusia, a document compiling 68 opportunities, reviewed by the RIS3 Andalusia group of experts, validated by the Joint Decision-Making Committee and subject to public examination.

In addition, a web platform was made available to all players in the process in order to facilitate online work, traceability and the management of contributions to the process (www.ris3andalucia.es).

2.5 *Results of the EDP: S3 priorities and tools*

The RIS3 Andalusia contemplates eight specialisation priorities which emerged from the opportunities identified as a result of the ED workshops, the in-house work and the joint decision-making process. These S3 priorities were considered the best options to transform the current economic model into a model based on knowledge and innovation. The priorities are now pursued through 36 lines of action.

The RIS3 Andalusia also includes a set of Axes in view of the implementation of the strategy, with their corresponding measures and instruments, which make up the core of the strategy programme. The measures were designed with direct links to one or more specific aspects of the specialisation priorities, with the objective of giving coverage to a number of present and future actions in order to achieve the final objectives of the strategy. Finally, policy tools designed are flexible, in order to allow governments to react, adjust or re-direct rapidly their public support to the new needs of the society.

Table 8.2 S3 priorities and lines of action

Specialisation priorities	Lines of action
P1. Mobility and logistics	L11. Research and Innovation into integrated logistics: Intermodality
	L12. Innovative business development in international value chains
	L13. New models of sustainable mobility and distribution
	L14. Incorporation of logistics not related to productive activity
P2. Advanced industry related to transport	L21. Advanced manufacture in the transport industry
	L22. Research and Innovation in new materials
	L23. Development of innovative products for transport industries
	L24. Transfer of technology and manufacturing processes
P3. Endogenous territorial resources	L31. Research and Innovation in the management of natural resources and the cultural heritage
	L32. New processes and products for the exploitation of agricultural resources
	L33. Mining integrated into the territory
	L34. Innovation to adapt the territory to climate change
	L35. Optimisation of ecosystemic services
P4. Tourism, culture and leisure	L41. Research and Innovation in innovative tourism products
	L42. Development of new tourism models
	L43. Research and Innovation in accessibility in tourism
	L44. Innovation in the cultural and creative industries
P5. Health and social welfare	L51. Development of the biosanitary business fabric
	L52. Creation of applications and technologies for new health and social welfare services
	L53. Advanced therapies and regenerative medicine
	L54. Population-based socio-sanitary research
	L55. Research and Innovation into healthy living and active ageing
P6. Agri-food and healthy eating	L61. Progress in food quality, traceability and safety
	L62. Functional and personalised foods
	L63. Exploitation of new opportunities in the blue economy and the green economy
	L64. Innovation in food industry processes and products
P7. Renewable energies, energy efficiency and sustainable construction	L71. Development of terrestrial and marine renewable energy sources
	L72. Smart energy networks
	L73. High-capacity energy storage systems
	L74. Energy efficiency in companies, housing and institutions
	L75. Energy sustainability in rural areas
	L76. New construction designs and materials and sustainable processes
P8. ICT and the digital economy	L81. New developments in ICT
	L82. ICT for business development
	L83. Development of new e-government instruments
	L84. Innovation in digital content

Source: Andalusian Innovation and Development Agency (IDEA).

Table 8.3 S3 axes, measures and priorities

Axes	Measures	Specialisation Priorities							
		1	2	3	4	5	6	7	8
Efficient competitive industry	Support for business R&D&I projects	•	••	•		•••	••	•••	•
	Incorporation of technologists and researchers	•	••	•		•	•••	•••	••
	Support for participation in international tenders	••	•••	••		•••	••	•••	•
	Integration of magnet companies	••	•••	•		•••	••	••	••
	Support for the incorporation of enabling technologies	•	•••	•		•••	••	••	••
	Implementation of Information and communications technology (ICTs) in industry	•••	••	•		••	•	••	
Key enabling technologies	Support for the generation of KET knowledge		••			•••	•	••	•••
	Encouragement of collaboration	•	••	•	•	•••	•	••	•••
	Internationalisation of the generation of Key enabling technologies (KET) knowledge		••			•••	•	••	•••
	New developments in ICTs	•	•	•	•	•	•	•	•••
Innovative SMEs	Innovative entrepreneurs	•	••	•	••	•••	•	•••	•••
	Protection of Industrial and Intellectual Property	•	••	•	•	••	••	•••	•
	Integration into global value systems	•••	••	•	•••	••	••	••	••
	Collaborative R&D&I	••	•	••	•••	•	••	•	••
	Implementation of ICTs in SMEs	•	••	••	•••	••	•••	••	
Overseas projection	Immersion in innovative environments	••	••	•	•••	••	•	••	•••
	Internationalisation of the generation of knowledge	•	••	••	•	•••	••	•••	••
	Internationalisation of companies	•	••	•	•	•	•••	•••	••
	International cooperation projects	••	•••			••	••	••	•
	Capture of innovative companies	•	••	••	•	•••	•	•	••
Education, talent and creative enviroments	Technology transfer	••	••	•••	•	•••	•••	••	••
	Support for excellence in research	•	•	••		•••	••	••	•
	Support for the generation of knowledge	••	••	••	•	••	•••	••	
	Enterprise culture	•	•	••	•••	••	••		•••
	Skill-building for innovation	•	•••	••	••	••	••	•	••
	Support for the formation of creative environments	•	•	••	•••	•	•	•	•••
	Culture of creativity	•	•	••	•••	•	•	•	•••
Social innovation	e-administration and e-government	•	•	•••	•	••		•	•••
	Support for knowledge management	•••	•••	•		••	•••	•	••
	Innovative public procurement	•	•	•			•••	••	••
	Promotion of new models of public–private cooperation	••	•••	•	••	••	••	••	••
	Support for new proposals for social organisation	••		••	••	•••	•	••	•••
	Pilot projects	••	•	••	••	••	•••	•••	•••
	Digital Strategy	•	•	•	•	•	•	•	•••

Axes	Measures	Specialisation Priorities							
		1	2	3	4	5	6	7	8
Networking	Support for the development of new collaborative approaches	••	••	••	•	••	•••	••	•••
	More intense participation in networks	•••	•	••	•	••	•••	••	•••
	Information Systems and awareness-raising for innovation	••	•	•••	••	•	•••	••	•
	Support for the maturing of business projects	•	••	•••	••	••	•	••	•••
Infrastructures for excelence	Research infrastructure	••	•••	•••		••	••	•••	•
	Spaces for innovation	•••	••	•••		••	••	••	•
	Communications infrastructure	•••	•	••	•••	•	••	•••	
	ICT infrastructure	••	••	••	•••	••	••	•••	•••

Source: Andalusian Innovation and Development Agency (IDEA).

Finally, the Regional Government of Andalusia designed a list of instruments to introduce the necessary changes and improvements to overcome the challenges identified[7] and reach the established objectives.[8] Their selection and design reflect their capacity to act on the target groups and players participating in the strategy: individuals, companies, knowledge agents and public administrations, aptitudes which derive from their effectiveness and efficiency in influencing the decision-making processes of these groups.

2.6 Monitoring and evaluation of the RIS3 Andalusia

Finally, the monitoring and evaluation system of the RIS3 was designed to engage stakeholders also in the monitoring and evaluation of the RIS3 Andalusia, taking into account the role played by the members of the system of governance. The aim is to allow the RIS3 loop to learn and change direction when needed. For this, the joint decision-making group (Co-decision Committee), composed of members of the Steering Committee and the Reference Group, is in charge of the monitoring and evaluation of the RIS3. This body has the support of a large number of economic and social actors in the region.

Overall, the process of elaborating the RIS3 Andalusia, including the creating of a monitoring and evaluation for the RIS3 Andalusia, has shown that it is possible to approach strategic regional planning in a different way. The opportunity now – and challenge – of the joint decision-making group (Co-decision Committee) in charge of the monitoring and evaluation system of the RIS3 Andalusia is to capitalise on the existing knowledge and long-standing experience in the monitoring and evaluation of regional strategies and policies embedded in other parts of the administration.

Section 2 aimed at illustrating the impact that the RIS3 Andalusia process is having in Andalusia and the changes introduced during the process. The next section focuses on some key factors for the success of the EDP in Andalusia.

Table 8.4 Policy instruments to support the RIS3 Andalusia

Type of instrument	Instrument	
Financial instruments	*Repayable*	*Non-repayable*
	Repayable aid Participation loans Ordinary loans Capital holdings • Business Angels • Risk capital (seed, launch and development) Pension funds (PPI) Thematic funds: technological entrepreneurs, business development, tourism and commercial SMEs, internationalisation, university enterprise culture, sustainable economy, productive spaces, cultural industries, renewable energies and energy efficiency Deposits and guarantees	R&D incentives • Companies • Business and non-business organisations Investment/spending incentives • Companies • Business and non-business organisations Innovation bonds Cost of deposits and guarantees Knowledge grants Provision to public bodies
Tax instruments	*Tax deductions*	
Advanced services	Monitoring of processes Support for entrepreneurship and innovation • Training • Coaching • Mentoring • Networking Advisory and impulse tools Tools to improve the capacity for innovation Market and technological prospectives Knowledge transfer partnerships Technology transfer Surveillance of markets and technologies Awareness-raising for innovation and entrepreneurship Support for inter-business cooperation Protection of industrial/intellectual property	
Innovation and entrepreneurial infrastructure	Knowledge generation infrastructure Knowledge transfer infrastructure Knowledge application infrastructure Entrepreneurial development infrastructure (accelerators, incubators) Public–private consortia for the development and maintenance of R&D&I infrastructure	
Innovative public procurement procedures	Conventional public procurement Pre-commercial public procurement Public procurement of Innovative Technologies	
Development of regulation	Regulations on procurement for innovation Regulations for the improvement of innovation processes Regulations for administrative simplification in innovation and procedures Regulations on public–private cooperation	

Source: Andalusian Innovation and Development Agency (IDEA).

3 Some key factors for the success of the EDP in Andalusia

The deployment of the EDP during the elaboration of the RIS3 Andalusia resulted in a new innovative and participatory governance model. The overall objective of this governance model was to help policy makers in the identification of the regional investment priorities for research and innovation. The process designed is aligned with Foray's explanation of the EDP provision as a crucial step for entrepreneurs to open and explore new domains of technological and market opportunities and to discover the innovation potential of a new activity. The ED process is equally important as a crucial process to provide information to the government and policy makers in order to prioritise across emerging activities and ultimately enable structural change.

In Andalusia, despite the fact there are still areas for improvement in the implementation of the EDP, a number of factors have emerged over the past few years explaining the success of the EDP in this region.

First, the Andalusian Innovation and Development Agency (IDEA), responsible body for driving, supporting, coordinating and encouraging the RIS3 process in Andalusia was strongly committed to the elaboration of the S3. It was also important that IDEA was well positioned in the region to mobilise stakeholders and resources to set a strategic framework for future actions (see Box 8.2).

Box 8.2 Strong leadership and commitment

The Andalusian Innovation and Development Agency (IDEA) is the regional development agency of the Andalusian Regional Government (www.agenci-aidea.es) and led the RIS3 Andalusia process. IDEA designed the methodology of the entire process and ensured the dynamisation of the stakeholders engaged. Likewise, IDEA drafted the RIS3 Andalusia and leads its monitoring and evaluation.

A key factor for success of the RIS3 Andalusia was the enthusiasm and strong commitment of the team involved in the organisation of the EDP. The open minded and energetic staff of the Agency were crucial not only to explore and understand the EDP concept, but also to engage and mobilise stakeholders for the success of the process. The importance of this leadership and commitment to the RIS3 Andalusia reveals the relevance of individuals and human capital willing to drive an organisation and ideas forward.

Source: Authors' elaboration.

Past studies had already announced that once the process of 'discovery' is initiated, the next challenge is to maintain the dynamics generated by the process itself (OECD, 2013). Some years later, further analysis is still needed to address this question in order to ensure the continuity of EDP created. For instance, incentives to keep stakeholders engaged – and/or to engage new ones – in the process and ways to maintain the EDP resistance to political changes. Unfortunately, the case of Andalusia does not answer this question.

The second key factor identified for the success of the EDP in Andalusia is the Collaborative Leadership generated by the mechanism followed for the elaboration of the RIS3 Andalusia. This Collaborative Leadership approach refers to a process in which entrepreneurs, companies, knowledge actors and the Regional Government of Andalusia work together. Based on this Collaborative Leadership process, the Regional Government of Andalusia achieved consensus with the stakeholders engaged in the process on a common Vision of the future of the region and created commitment to the S3 priorities and subsequent actions. Furthermore, the Regional Government of Andalusia considers this Collaborative Leadership approach essential to ensure a sound entrepreneurial discovery process in all steps of the RIS3 process, including the monitoring and evaluation of the RIS3 Andalusia (see Box 8.3).

In addition, the RIS3 Andalusia process itself has brought different benefits, equally important for the progress of the region. For instance, it has shown the need and benefits in the region of participating in international policy debates. Concerning the EDP in particular, the RIS3 Andalusia process has stressed, among others, the importance of:

- ensuring capability to learn and adapt to change during the process;
- strengthening trust among stakeholders and their commitment to the process;
- building on and connecting regional capacities.

Box 8.3   Collaborative Leadership

The concept of Collaborative Leadership requires the governance structure to be sufficiently flexible in the decision-making process so as to allow the stakeholders engaged to adequately undertake the role assigned during the process regardless of their own characteristics and capacities. The EDP itself generated 'Collaborative Leadership' dynamics in which entrepreneurs, companies, knowledge actors and the Andalusian Regional Government have worked together, complementing each other and the work carried out by opening up the strategy to all of the citizens of Andalusia. Two distinctive features characterise the EDP in Andalusia: the design of a *participatory* and *joint decision-making* process. This is part of the impact of the elaboration of the RIS3 and deployment of the EDP in Andalusia.

Source: Andalusian Innovation and Development Agency (IDEA).

Conclusions

This chapter concludes with two general messages which are supported by the case of Andalusia. The first message stresses that it is possible to break with the past and approach strategic regional planning in a different way. The second message is that when it comes to the deployment of EDP across regions, one size does not fit all.

In Andalusia, the process of elaborating the research and innovation strategy for smart specialisation (RIS3) proves that it is possible to approach strategic regional planning in a different way. In particular, the setting-up of the entrepreneurial discovery process (EDP) during the elaboration of the RIS3 Andalusia offered Andalusian companies the opportunity to reach consensus on a common vision of the future of the region and create commitment to the priorities for action. The process aimed at extracting from regional stakeholders' contributions unique proposals of specialisation opportunities for R&I in the region.

Given the particular regional context, in terms of size, density, clustering levels, legal and economic situation, loss of the EU convergence region status, impact of the economic crisis in the region, institutional commitment to the RIS3 – together with external drivers such as the increased competition from emerging economies – the demands placed and the opportunities offered to the Regional Government of Andalusia were high.

Hence, the strong commitment and leadership of the Regional Government of Andalusia and enthusiasm of the human capital involved resulted in an innovative and participatory governance model. The option favoured by policy makers in Andalusia was clear: the more the merrier to bridge the gap between science, market opportunities and policy making in the region. Some of the key factors for the success of the EDP in Andalusia are commitment and Collaborative Leadership during the process.

Summing up, despite the challenges that the Regional Government of Andalusia still has to tackle during the implementation and maintenance of the EDP, a number of achievements/lessons emerge from this case:

- Open, joint public–private participation and decision-making is possible.
- A solid basis to justify the priorities for specialisation is crucial.
- Flexibility in the process facilitates the progress.
- The RIS3 process and the dynamics created by the EDP strengthen the alignment with other regional economic planning activities such as the Andalusian Strategy for Competitiveness, Operational Programmes, Andalusian Industrial Strategy, Andalusian Research, Development and Innovation Plan, and the Andalusian Innovation and Development Agency's own plan (IDEA Strategic Plan).
- Innovation is possible in the process of defining economic planning.

These lessons, may be useful – or not – to other regions across Europe when deploying their EDP, depending on their own characteristics and context.

Notes

1 The authors would like to thank Carmen Sillero, Carlos Fernández-Palacios, Manuel Arroyo José Antonio Pascual, Mª Angeles Ruiz and Antonia Hermosilla for the material provided by the RIS3 Technical Secretariat (Andalusian Innovation and Development Agency, IDEA) for the elaboration of this chapter to the authors. This chapter also builds on extensive discussions and meetings with the Secretariat of the RIS3 and staff from different departments of the Regional Government of Andalusia.

2   Gross domestic product (GDP) and GDP per capita growth is above the national average, there is clear dynamism in enterprise creation and in capitalisation of talent by promoting higher education, and an economy that is becoming more and more knowledge oriented, with increasingly significant public investment in innovation.
3   The total amount invested in Spain by the EU Cohesion Policy is € 28.6 billion (current prices). The rest is allocated as follows: € 2 billion goes to less developed regions (Extremadura), € 11 billion to more developed regions (Aragón, Asturias, Baleares, Cantabria, Castilla y León, Cataluña, Ceuta, Comunidad Valenciana, Galicia, La Rioja, Madrid, Navarra and the País Vasco). The remainder goes to European Territorial Cooperation (€ 643 million), a special allocation for the outermost regions (€ 484.1 million) and the Youth Employment Initiative (€ 943.5 million),
4   The administrative organisation is described in more detail in the OECD *Reviews of Higher Education in Regional and City Development* Andalusia, Spain Self-evaluation report 2011.
5   An example of multi-governance collaboration in Andalusia is the Guadalinfo project. Started in 2003 and co-financed with the European Regional Developments Fund (ERDF), this project aimed at improving the digital skills of all Andalusia, especially in those municipalities with less than 20,000 inhabitants, fostering the integration of the region in the knowledge society. To that end, the regional government joined efforts with every Andalusian Provincial Office (Diputación Provincial) and the 692 municipalities with less than 20,000 inhabitants (out of 770 existing municipalities in Andalusia). It was an innovative collaboration of public administrations in the region. Guadalinfo extended the telecommunication infrastructures, including broadband Internet access, and the necessary technical means, resources and tools to achieve the complete integration of Andalusian citizens into the Information and Knowledge Society. A facilitator in every municipality has been assured as a key human factor to guarantee the use of the means and technical infrastructures furnished for the mobilisation of citizens. Currently, the Guadalinfo Network is composed of 692 centres of public Internet access in municipalities with fewer than 20,000 inhabitants, and other associated centres such as 65 centres located in disadvantaged neighbourhoods of larger Andalusian cities, and 22 access points in Andalusian Communities Abroad (CAEs) (OECD, 2010).
6   Guide on Research and Innovation Strategies for Smart Specialisation (RIS3 Guide) http://s3platform.jrc.ec.europa.eu/ris3-guide
7   Challenges: To significantly improve the propensity for innovation in Andalusian society; to make innovation a keystone of the identity of Andalusian society; to convert the Andalusian Knowledge System into the driver of economic growth in Andalusia; to position the private sector as the leader of innovative processes in Andalusia; to make Andalusia an international beacon in research, development and innovation within the priorities laid down in the Andalusian Innovation Strategy; to achieve full accessibility for all companies and citizens in Andalusia to new information technology and digital content; to ensure that optimum use is made of Andalusia's knowledge capital for the development of the region; to capture resources, skills and experience from outside Andalusia in order to reinforce regional knowledge capital and to encourage faster, stronger, smarter, sustainable, integrating growth; to make Andalusian public administrations highly innovative and use the best media, techniques and tools that technological development can provide for their services and relationships with citizens.
8   Objectives: To take R&D&I to 2.2 per cent of GDP; to take private sector R&D&I spending to 50 per cent of the total; to increase the intensity of innovation in innovative companies by 20 per cent; to increase the number of research personnel by 20 per cent; to double the number of innovative companies and the amount

they spend on innovation; to increase the number of patents by 50 per cent; to increase the Gross value added (GVA) of medium and high technology activities by 50 per cent; to increase exports of medium and high technology goods and services by 60 per cent; to reach 100 per cent high-speed broadband coverage and for 50 per cent of homes to have connections faster than 100 Mbps; to incorporate 40 per cent of Andalusian companies into the digital market; to achieve habitual Internet use for personal and professional purposes by 85 per cent of the population; to achieve 40 per cent Internet use by the public and 100 per cent by companies in their interactions with the Administration.

Bibliography

Barca, F. (2009), *An Agenda for a Reformed Cohesion Policy: A Place-based Approach to Meeting European Union Challenges and Expectations.* Independent report prepared at the request of Danuta Hübner, Commissioner for Regional Policy.

Cohesion Policy and Spain (2014–20). Available at: http://ec.europa.eu/regional_policy/index.cfm/en/information/publications/brochures-factsheets/2014/cohesion-policy-and-spain (accessed 27/02/2016).

Foray, D. (2014), *Smart Specialisation: Opportunities and Challenges for Regional Innovation Policy.* London: Routledge.

Foray, D. and Goenaga, X. (2013), *The Goals of Smart Specialisation*, S3 Policy Brief Series n° 01/2013, EUR 26005 EN, ISBN 978-92-79-30547-4, Luxembourg: Publications Office of the European Union, 2013. Available at: http://ftp.jrc.es/EURdoc/JRC82213.pdf.

Foray, D. and Rainoldi A. (2013), *Smart Specialisation Programmes and Implementation*, S3 Policy Brief Series No. 02/2013, EUR 26002 EN, ISBN 978-92-79-30541-2, Luxembourg: Publications Office of the European Union. Available at: http://ftp.jrc.es/EURdoc/JRC82224.pdf.

Foray, D., David, P. and Hall B. (2009), Smart Specialisation: The Concept, *Knowledge Economists Policy Brief*, No. 9.

Hausmann, R. and Rodrik, D. (2003), Economic Development as Self-Discovery, *Journal of Development Economics*, 72 (2): 603–633.

Mintzberg, H. (1994). *The Rise and Fall of Strategic Planning: Reconceiving Roles for Planning, Plans, Planners.* New York; Toronto: Free Press; Maxwell Macmillan Canada.

Nauwelaers, C. and Wintjes, R. (2008). *Innovation Policy in Europe: Measurement and Strategy.* Cheltenham: Edward Elgar.

OECD (2010), *Higher Education in Regional and City Development: Andalusia*, Spain 2010, OECD Publishing. Available at: http://dx.doi.org/10.1787/9789264088993-en.

OECD (2011), *Andalusia, Spain: Self-Evaluation Report,* OECD of Higher Education in Regional and City Development, IMHE. Available at: www.oecd.org/dataoecd/32/27/44666367.pdf.

OECD (2013), *Innovation-driven Growth in Regions: The Role of Smart Specialisation* 2014–20. Available at: www.oecd.org/sti/inno/smartspecialisation.htm.

Regional Government of Andalusia, *Economic Report of Andalusia* (2014). Available at: www.juntadeandalucia.es/export/drupaljda/INFORME_2014.pdf.

9 Implementing the entrepreneurial discovery process in Eastern Macedonia and Thrace

Elisabetta Marinelli, Mark Boden and Karel Haegeman

1 Introduction

Regional Smart Specialisation Strategies (S3) aim at developing regional competitive advantages following a vertical[1] prioritisation logic (Foray and Goenaga, 2013). Central to this prioritisation is the bottom-up identification of a limited set of priorities where regions believe they have potential to obtain a comparative advantage. Priorities are identified through the interaction of stakeholders across the quadruple helix of government, industry, academia and society at large. This is because entrepreneurial knowledge is most often distributed across a regional system. This cyclical and recursive process of identification and prioritisation is referred to as an entrepreneurial discovery process (EDP).

While several authors have examined the concept and rationales of EDP (Foray and Goenaga, 2013; Hausmann and Rodrik, 2003; Martínez-López and Palazuelos Martínez, 2014), few experiences of its actual implementation have so far been codified. This chapter starts filling this gap by describing the approach taken in the Greek region of Eastern Macedonia and Thrace (REMTh). The activities described are part of a European Parliament Preparatory Action (PA),[2] led by the European Commission's Joint Research Centre (JRC),[3] working in close collaboration with the Commission's Directorate General for Regional and Urban Policy. The PA ran between September 2014 and November 2015 and focused on the refinement and implementation of the region's Smart Specialisation Strategy for Research and Innovation (RIS3).

REMTh is one of the poorest regions in Europe and has been heavily hit by the crisis, making the implementation of a smart specialisation strategy all the more challenging. In this context, the Preparatory Action has also provided a test bed for advancing theories on smart specialisation and, in so doing, has devised lessons on S3 implementation for other convergence regions in Greece and Europe.

The case of REMTh allows for an empirical test of many of the observations raised in the more theoretical chapters of this book. In line with Foray (Chapter 1), this chapter shows how the Preparatory Action designed and implemented an EDP in which research and innovation activities were considered complementary to local assets, and in which the information generated fed directly into the policy process. The insights by Grillo (Chapter 5) also provide an interesting lens through which to interpret this experience. Indeed, the different expectations and working methods of stakeholders in the public, private and research sector can potentially be disruptive, and it is critical –to keep the EDP alive – to find ways to sustain their engagement. Finally, the chapters by Morgan (Chapter 4) and Rodríguez-Pose (Chapter 3) are critical in understanding the institutional dynamics behind the EDP in REMTh. In line with their observations, the approach pursued demanded considerable innovation and adaptation from the public sector, especially in its ability to act as a platform for dialogue and ensure trust.

Before proceeding further, it must be remarked that the Preparatory Action took place at a critical moment both for REMTh and Greece. Not only had the region little responsibility for R&D and Innovation policy in the recent past –and hence needed to enhance its own capacity – but political and financial instability affected the development of long-term perspectives. The Preparatory Action has hence provided many insights into the complexity of balancing the pressing short-term agenda in times of instability with the long-term outlook at the core of S3.

This chapter, which aims to facilitate the replication and adaptation of the approach to other areas, comprises five further sections: section 2 reviews the key socio-economic characteristics of REMTh and its S3. Section 3 summarises the activities of the PA. Section 4 describes the EDP implementation approach followed. Section 5 provides an initial evaluation of the approach based on the feedback of experts and consultants participating in the activities. Section 6 concludes by highlighting the main lessons arising from the experience.

2 Eastern Macedonia and Thrace: economic overview and S3 summary

The region of Eastern Macedonia and Thrace lies in the north-eastern part of Greece. It is bounded in the east by Turkey, in the north by Bulgaria, in the west by the Region of Central Macedonia, and in the south by the Aegean and Thracian Seas. Its population in 2014 was estimated at 606,225,[4] accounting for 5.6% of the national total.

As set out in the 2015 regional S3 strategy,[5] whilst REMTh is one of the most industrialised regions of Greece, it is also characterised by the highest share of primary sector (agriculture). Its service sector is based on non-traded and public services and tourism. The manufacturing sector is dominated by medium to low technology sectors (food industry, textiles and clothing, mining and quarrying, manufacture of pulp, paper and paperboard and tobacco products). Nevertheless there are some more technology-intensive industries, in the chemicals sector as well as in the manufacture of machinery and equipment.

With a GDP per capita of €13,100 in 2011 (at market prices), as compared to the national average of €18,500,[6] the region is one of the poorest of the country and is lagging well behind (70 per cent) the EU27 average. The economic crisis has had a significant effect and the unemployment rate increased dramatically between 2008 and 2011 from 8.8 per cent in 2008 to 24.2 per cent in 2014. The main sectors affected by the crisis (Regional Innovation Monitor, 2012)[7] are trade and services, but also manufacturing and construction.

In terms of R&D, with only €75.1 spent per inhabitant in 2011, the region is well below the national average of €125.1[8] with a very small private sector contribution. R&D expenditure is concentrated in two public tertiary education institutions: the Democritos University of Thrace and the Technical Education Institute of Kavala. The European Regional Innovation Scoreboard ranks East Macedonia and Thrace (grouped in the mega-region Kentriki Ellada) as a modest–medium innovator (the lowest of four performance categories) along with all other Greek regions except Attiki. The level of education of the workforce is relatively low with, in 2014, 20.5 per cent of the population aged 25–64 with tertiary education attainment (as compared to 28.1 per cent in Greece).[9]

2.1 S3 in REMTh – horizontal and thematic priorities

In REMTh, the definition of the S3, carried out between 2012 and 2014 by the local managing authority, identified the broad horizontal and thematic priorities summarised in Table 9.1. The former cover four critical elements of the local structure that need to be boosted. The latter are organised around two main pillars:

- the transformation of the agri-food cluster.
- the expansion and consolidation of the emerging sectors of the regional economy.

The identification of these areas of intervention represents the necessary and preliminary step to allow the EDP implementation described below. Furthermore, it represents a remarkable novelty for the region. Indeed, not only did the region not have any significant previous competence in the research, technological development and innovation (RTDI) fields, but to acquire them it needed to introduce novel ways of interacting with stakeholders at a time of decreasing trust towards the public sector.

3 The European Parliament Preparatory Action

The PA described in this chapter, conducted between September 2014 and November 2015, has built on the efforts and analysis made by the region between 2012 and 2014, with the aim of complementing and reinforcing them. It has revolved around three main aims:

Table 9.1 S3 priorities in REMTh – horizontal and thematic priorities

Horizontal priorities
• Upgrade of the institutional capacity of the Regional Innovation System and its constituent parts • Upgrade and retention of human capital • Targeted supply of knowledge, strengthening of the absorption of knowledge and induction of the entrepreneurial dynamics • Boosting the intensity and quality of intra-regional and inter-regional networking

Thematic pillar 1	*Thematic pillar 2*
Transformation of the agro-food sector	*Supporting the growth of emerging sectors*

1 Modernisation of the agro-food cluster and improvement of the regional added value with the use of technologically driven innovation
2 Improvement of regional added value through the adaptation and use of mature processes, organisational and promotional innovations, including the use of ICT, aid to sources of uniqueness (e.g. PDO products) and the upgrading of human resources
	1 Strengthening of technologically driven product or process innovation, preferably through KETs in the sectors:
	  • plastic–rubber products,
	  • pharmaceuticals,
	  • electronic/electrical equipment,
	  • innovative building materials,
	  • energy, environment and hybrid technologies.
	2 Provision of incentives for the installation of units of the above sectors in REMTh and encouragement of new innovative activity.
	3 Expansion of the tourist product through organisational and promotional innovations
	4 Development of promotional innovations for the strengthening of the branding of marbles and the expansion of markets.
	5 Attraction or support to investments in service enterprises which serve consolidated or emerging sectors of the regional economy such as:
	  • Certification of health claims in foodstuff, design of biofunctional foodstuff.
	  • Information and communication technologies with applications in the primary sector or industrial information technology;
	  • Industrial planning;

Source: Authors' elaboration based on the REMTh S3.

- to facilitate the refinement and implementation of the S3 strategy in a region heavily hit by the crisis;
- to serve as a model for other convergence regions in Greece and Europe;
- to test theories on smart specialisation.

These goals have been pursued through three streams of activity, aimed at:

- **ongoing mapping, stocktaking and assessment** of the development of the S3 strategy and identification of actions to ensure its smooth implementation;
- **testing and optimising an entrepreneurial discovery process (EDP)** by engaging stakeholders and policy makers in participatory exercises;
- **building capacity for a sustainable S3 development and implementation** by supporting a networking and collaboration culture among stakeholders and ensuring that access to relevant information and best-practice is duly shared.

This chapter focuses on the second of these streams, detailing the implementation of the EDP from the identification of innovative ideas (EDP focus groups) their refinement, the exploration of funding opportunities and appropriate policy instruments (Project Development Labs).

4 The entrepreneurial discovery process: from theory to practice

The concept of the entrepreneurial discovery process, as developed and used by the S3 platform of the Joint Research Centre,[10] is one of the pillars of S3. It is an inclusive and interactive mainly bottom-up process in which participants from policy, business, academia, as well as other sectors, engage with each other to identify potential new activities and opportunities. It is based on the recognition that the public sector does not have innate wisdom or the *ex-ante* knowledge of future priorities and that stakeholders' engagement is essential to establish realistic directions for local development.

Foray and Rainoldi (2013) place the generation of cross-sectoral information spill-overs at the core of the EDP. Partnerships and networks among stakeholders are critical to integrate fragmented knowledge, allow spill-overs to occur and ultimately open up new technological and market opportunities.

Clearly, there are several ways to support and encourage the generation of such spill-overs (see Kroll *et al.*, 2014 for a review), not least, because each EDP approach is context dependent. Within the REMTh Preparatory Action the EDP has been implemented through two sets of workshops:

- **The Entrepreneurial Discovery Process (EDP) focus groups** –a set of four events, with a sectoral focus, aimed at generating innovative ideas through the interaction between business, public and research sectors. These are described in section 4.1.
- **The Project Development Labs (PDL)** – a set of two further events aimed at processing the EDP ideas and moving them towards implementation, identifying funding opportunities and action plans for policy. These are described in section 4.2.

4.1 The EDP focus groups

The four EDP focus groups covered respectively the sectors of wine (November 2014), dairy and meat products (January 2015), tourism (February 2015) and marble and non-metallic minerals (May 2015). Each event lasted between one and one and a half days. Whilst the local authorities and a team of local experts engaged with regional stakeholders, the JRC identified key international experts and devised an appropriate methodology.

Each focus group followed the same basic methodological template, and used a combination of plenary and parallel sessions (See Table 9.3). However, the lessons derived from each event, as well as context specificities, were embedded in the design of the subsequent ones.

Plenary sessions were held at the beginning and at the end of the events. They included an introduction to the regional S3, an outline of the aims and approach of the Preparatory Action, as well as scene-setting presentations from international experts, with time also allowed for open discussion.

Table 9.2 Template of EDP focus groups

Plenary introduction
- *Presentation of the region and the regional S3*
- *Presentation of the project*
- *Presentation from international expert on the sector at stake*

1st parallel sessions covering four different parts of the sectoral value chain
- *Presentation by a national expert on the specific value chain building block*
- *Participatory exercise to stimulate interaction among stakeholders*

2nd parallel sessions covering four different parts of the sectoral value chain
- *Participatory exercise to stimulate interaction among stakeholders*

Plenary conclusion
- *Reporting back from the participatory exercise*
- *Presentation from international expert on the sector at stake*
- *Round-table and Q&A from the public*

Source: Authors' elaboration based on the REMTh S3.

Table 9.3 EDP focus groups parallel sessions

	Parallel EDP sessions			
Wine	Research and innovation focusing on technological improvements in wine	Research and innovation focusing on by-products of grapes and wines	Research and innovation related to green energy and the environment in the wine sector	Research and innovation in wine tourism
Meat and dairy	Research and innovation in animal husbandry	Food processing technologies	Research and innovation in dairy products	Organic meat and dairy products and sustainable production
Tourism	Four seasons tourism	Tourism and cultural heritage	ICT and tourism	Gastrotourism
Marble and non-metallic minerals	Research and innovation for energy and environmental optimisation of the marble production chain	Management of marble quarries and aggregates – Waste and environmental impacts		

Source: Authors' elaboration based on the REMTh S3.

The core of the EDP focus group approach, however, lies in the parallel sessions, which addressed different segments of the value chain of each sector (as defined in Table 9.3) and included presentations from experts and a participatory exercise.

4.1.1 EDP focus groups: methodology of the participatory exercise

In the parallel sessions, participants were grouped according to their expressed preferences and with the intention of achieving a mix of actors from:

- various different parts of the value chain;
- both the public and private research sectors;
- within and beyond the region as well from outside Greece;
- with policy or strategic perspectives as well as scientific and technological perspectives.

Each parallel group had a moderator and a rapporteur (tasked with reporting the outcomes of the parallel session to the plenary as well as with carrying out related follow-up activities). The exercise comprised a sequence of five core tasks and aimed at generating and selecting innovative ideas requiring expertise from different sectors (tasks 1 and 2), creating partnerships around them (task 3) and reflecting on their potential development, outlining the first steps necessary for implementation (tasks 4 and 5). Specifically:

Task 1 Individual generation of ideas: In task 1 each participant was asked to reflect and fill in a simple form with the following information:

• Personal profile (i.e. entrepreneur, private sector, researchers, etc.).
• Problem faced and potential innovative idea to solve it.
• External expertise/partners needed to implement the idea.

Task 2 Presentation of ideas: Participants were each asked to present their ideas to the rest of the group, highlighting the profile of the expertise needed for their further development.

Task 3 Formation of 'idea-partnerships': Each parallel group, building on the outcomes of Task 2, created a consolidated list of ideas, wherein similar or complementary proposals were clustered.

Following that, participants were asked to identify those ideas that they were interested in developing further by identifying their individual top three favourite ideas. Based on that, the group – guided by the moderator – proceeded to organise itself in different sub-groups or 'idea-partnerships'. These comprised (ideally) individuals from different sectors (i.e. research and industry) with similar interests.

Task 4 development of ideas (Phase 1): Each of the 'idea-partnerships' defined the ideas in greater depth, identifying the required contributions from different partners, developing initial considerations on framework conditions (legal problems, needs for human capital, capacities, etc.), on financial planning and on the 'next' steps.

Task 5 development of ideas (Phase 2): The 'idea-partnerships' then defined the concrete title for their idea, the subsector(s) of interest, a brief project description, a rough estimation of the resources needed, a timeline for the event, and the stakeholder groups involved. The work was conducted under a set of guiding questions and took into account the criteria for funding.

All in all, each of the four EDP workshops produced a set of entrepreneurial ideas, merging different sectors (research and business) and compatible with the local S3 strategies. The full list of ideas is reported in Table 9.4.

Furthermore, the discussion around each idea was recorded in a series of fiches, made available on the PA website and used for the stakeholders' consultation described in section 4.2.2 Box 9.1, contains an example of such fiches.

Table 9.4 Idea outputs of EDP workshops

Wine	Meat and dairy	Tourism	Marble and non-metallic minerals
1 Local grape varieties	1 Cluster for animal husbandry and agriculture	1 Regional/local tourism organisation	1 Geological and geophysical research in marble quarries; underground mining equipment
2 Vineyard network with GIS tools	2 Genetic mapping and genetic improvement	2 Off-season tourism	2 Integrated interventions for energy efficiency in quarries and marble processing facilities
3 Indigenous microbiota for local wines	3 Community supported farming and production;	3 Eco-tourism	3 Reusing quarry and marble processing residues and scrap
4 Prevention of Dekkera/ Brettanomyces bruxellensis	4 Vertical integration – slaughter houses in small farms	4 Innovative management of cultural heritage	4 Clustering across the marble value chain
5 Energy from wine	5 Religious certifications of meat and meat products	5 ICT based applications for thematic itineraries	5 Restoration of marble quarries
6 Food supplements and cosmetics	6 Production of certified traditional meat products and their promotion via marketing innovations	6 Personalised tourism	6 Planning/coordination of access to the raw material
7 Organic fertilisers from tsipouro	7 Innovative technologies in for local non-pig meat products with improved conservation	7 ICT tools for tourism	

Wine	Meat and dairy	Tourism	Marble and non-metallic minerals
8 Animal feeds from wine by-products	8 Sustained and integrated promotion of local, traditional fermented food systems from authentic microbial cultures	8 Digital business innovation in tourism	
9 Tsipouro-based liqueurs	9 Development of functional products based on local dairy products	9 Regional culinary centre	
10 Local varieties and local histories	10 Dairy/meat sectors clusters	10 History and cuisine	
11 Wine, gastronomy, culture and entertainment	11 Research and/or technologies for the production of new value added products		
12 Branding regional wines	12 Energy production from animal waste		
13 Wine-gastronomy/ cultural tourism	13 Network for collecting and managing data on the milk and dairy production chain		
14 Wine-value chain cluster			

Source: Authors' elaboration based on the REMTh S3.

Box 9.1 Example of output of EDP focus group idea

Local wine grape varieties

1 Brief description of the idea-partnership
The idea focuses on research on the potential of six to seven local wine grape varieties. Implementation comprises two steps: (a) the definition of the varietal character / potential of each variety and (b) the ways to enhance/maximise the initial potential during all stages of wine production, from vineyard site evaluation to the marketing of the final products.

2 Contribution of the different partners
The research will focus on varieties existing in established vineyards but can be extended to lesser known ones. Collection and description (both ampelographic and molecular) will be performed by specialised scientists and institutes (molecular biologists, plant pathologists and viticulture specialists). The participation of nursery facilities will ensure the propagation and delivery of the planting stock. For the definition of the varietal character (for both existing and promising varieties), laboratories specialised in grape and wine chemical analysis will be needed and tasting panels must be assembled and trained. To maximise varietal potential, viticulture and oenology experts will be necessary to plan and implement experimental protocols and evaluate the results. Grape growers and wine producers in the region will participate by providing vineyards and wineries for experimental implementation (experimental vineyard blocks, micro-vinifications).

3 First considerations on framework conditions
The main perceived obstacle to the implementation of the idea is the current legal framework, limiting the expansion of vineyards. Within the region, there are grape and wine producers that can support the idea with tangible assets (experimental cultivations and pilot wine-making processes) and human capital. Democritus University of Thrace (DUTH) could also support the action with specialised labs. Lack of infrastructure in the Department of Oenology at Drama might be supported by the participation of other labs at the Aristotle University of Thessaloniki (AUTH) and the Agricultural University of Athens.

4 First financial considerations
As the duration of the action at full scale deployment would be at least four years, only rough estimates of budget are feasible, and would be in the order of €2M.

5 Identification of first 'next' steps
These include: state of the art analysis regarding current knowledge on local varieties; evaluation of planting material and nursery facilities; and definition of areas and most important varieties for further research.

6 Initial interest of partners
Ten from industry and five from research / academic community

Whilst the above are the direct outputs of the EDP focus groups their outcomes are intended to be much broader. They involve facilitating access to international networks (not only in marketing and sales but also in research and innovation), promoting a culture of public and private partnership, increasing trust among stakeholders and the shared development of a vision for the territory.

4.2 Moving closer to implementation: project development labs and online stakeholder consultation

The project development labs (PDLs) were a set of two consecutive events, accompanied by a stakeholder consultation, aimed at moving the EDP ideas closer to implementation. The approach to this set of events was the subject of a complex discussion among the JRC and the Special Managing Authority and its eventual implementation evolved significantly from the original idea. Whilst the PDLs were first conceived to be centred on stakeholders' mobilisation, training and participation, this bottom-up dimension was ultimately downplayed in favour of a combination of a thorough technical reflection on funding opportunities and a smaller-scale stakeholder engagement, as described below. This evolution reflects the real challenges of aligning the concept of RIS3, the actual dynamics of stakeholder engagement and the administrative context.

4.2.1 The 1st Project Development Lab (PDL1)

PDL1, held in May 2015, assumed a technical focus and represented a first step to translate stakeholders' engagement into policy actions. Participation was limited to JRC and its subcontractors, the Special Managing Authority, representatives of regional and national government with expertise on S3, European Regional Development Fund (ESIF) and state-aid regulation, and representatives of regional higher education and research organisations.

The event explored exclusively the administrative dimensions of the EDP ideas, covering issues related to effectiveness, appropriateness, delivery mechanisms, project selection criteria, fitness to the national RIS3, state-aid rules and their implications for launching calls. A significant portion of the discussion was also devoted to clusters, since they were suggested in all four EDP focus groups.

The bridging of the EDP ideas to the formal policy process was organised through a *detailed mapping* of the delivery instruments that the Special Managing Authority intended to use. This was accompanied by an *evaluation* of whether and how the EDP ideas would fit under those instruments (as illustrated in Table 9.5). This sometimes required segmenting EDP ideas that fell under different investment priorities in the Regional and National Operational Programmes.

Table 9.5 Examples of allocation of ideas to available funding instruments planned under the Regional Operational Programme (Thematic Objectives (TO) 1, 2 and 3) and other instruments

| Idea ID | Description | Funding instruments fitting the idea components (and their total budgets in Euro) | | | |
		TO1	TO2	TO3	Other
WINE2	Vineyard network with Geographical Information Systems (GIS) tools		1.2c.3.2 eTourism / eCulture services for the Regional Authorities (€1.9m)		
WINE4	Methods to prevent the growth of Dekkera/ Brettanomyces bruxellensis against wine spoilage	1.1b.2.2 Technology transfer for the benefit of small and medium enterprises (SMEs) (€2m)			M04
MEAT AND DAIRY9	Development of functional products based on local dairy products	1.1b.1.1 New Product Development Grants for SMEs (€3m)	1.3a.4.1 Grants in support of the establishment and the initial operation of new, knowledge- or research-intensive enterprises (€15m)		
WINE10	Local varieties and local histories of wine			1.3d.6.2 Support of the establishment of collaboration networks in the fields of tourism and culture (€1.5m)	

Idea ID	Description	Funding instruments fitting the idea components (and their total budgets in Euro)			
		TO1	*TO2*	*TO3*	*Other*
MARBLE2 Integrated interventions for energy efficiency in quarries and marble processing facilities		1.3d.5.3 Support to SME business plans aiming to improve power efficiency in existing enterprises and introduce the use of renewable energy sources (€5m)			
MARBLE5 Restoration of Marble Quarries					CLLD

Source: Authors' elaboration based on the REMTh S3.

Note:

1 More than one instrument per idea means that this idea consists of multiple components which can be funded by one or more programmes.

The mapping revealed that two ideas were not sufficiently well defined to be further processed and one was incompatible with ESIF regulations. For the remaining ideas, 50 components were identified and linked to three main funding sources: 30 to REMTh's Regional Operational Programme (ROP), eight to the Operational Programme (OP) Competitiveness, Entrepreneurship and Innovation and 12 to the OP Rural Development (Agricultural Funds). In terms of ERDF investment priorities, 14 components were classified under 1b, three under 2b, two under 2c, three under 3a, 14 under 3d and two under 4b. Finally, some components were classified for potential implementation through Integrated Territorial Investments (ITI) or the Community-Led Local Development (CLLD) or Public–Private Partnerships (PPP). In conclusion, a majority of the idea components appeared to fit well in the ROP, hence validating the approach followed in the EDP focus groups.

Although PDL1 deviated from its original design, it proved to be beneficial in several ways. First, it revealed the complexities embedded in trying to translate stakeholders' engagement activities into technically sound policy actions. Further, it allowed the local Higher Education Institutions (HEIs) to become aware of the full range of ideas discussed during the EDP focus groups and to be exposed to implementation issues that might be relevant to them, particularly in planning technology transfer and mobility initiatives. Third, it highlighted some tensions between the 'theoretical' design of the S3 approach and the administrative framework of ERDF hence prompting a discussion on possible solutions. Notably it emerged that pursuing international dimensions of the S3 may prove difficult, as ERDF rules do not allow funds to go directly to beneficiaries outside the region. To overcome that, other tools should be considered, such as the outsourcing of part of the tasks to parties outside of the region (with the relevant external partners already identified in proposals); seeking self-funding consortium partners; or cooperation with other regions. Finally, PDL1 reinforced, among the participants, the need to include stakeholders across the policy process and led to the decision to use PDL2 as an opportunity to share draft calls with local actors and get their feedback.

4.2.2 Online stakeholder consultation

In between PDL1 and PDL2, the Managing Authority started developing draft calls and JRC launched an online stakeholder consultation, to allow stakeholders further input towards PDL2.

The consultation presented all the ideas included in Table 9.4, arranged by thematic area, together with a more detailed description as shown in Box 9.1. Prior to the event, PDL2 participants were required to browse the ideas and identify all those in which they had an interest. They were also invited to specify the type of engagement they were willing to have in each idea (ranging from simple interest to a potential investment) and to share additional comments. The results of the consultation were used to support the shaping of PDL2, and for the development of training material in the project.

A total of 134 stakeholders participated in the consultation, with a good spread across the quadruple helix: business (29), research centres (nine), universities (27), public administration (45), non-profit organisations (nine), and other (15). Their interests by thematic area were distributed as follows: wine (62), dairy and meat (56), tourism (86) and marble and non-metallic minerals (27). Each stakeholder could express interest in more than one idea.

The interest of business and other stakeholders in each idea is summarised in the four graphs below. The ideas that have most interest from all stakeholders also tend to have considerable interest from business. This is important as the private sector should have a pivotal role in the EDP.

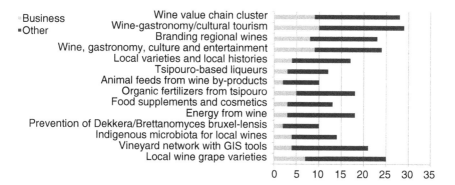

Figure 9.1 Stakeholders' interests on wine ideas

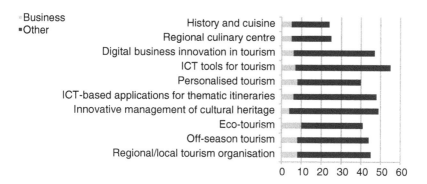

Figure 9.2 Stakeholders' interests on tourism ideas

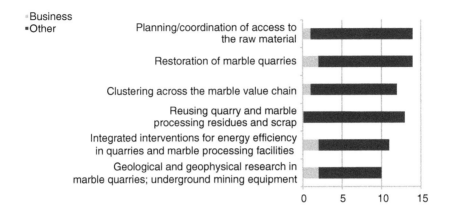

Figure 9.3 Stakeholders' interests on marble ideas

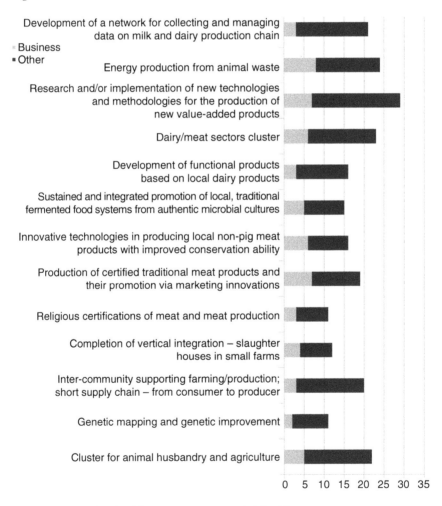

Figure 9.4 Stakeholders' interests on meat and dairy ideas

4.2.3 The 2nd Project Development Lab (PDL2)

PDL2 had two main groups of objectives:

- showing how the stakeholders' engagement in PDL1 fed back into the policy process by presenting and discussing the draft calls to be launched under Thematic Objectives 1 to 3 of the ROP (morning session);
- exploring the possibility of financing the EDP ideas (or some of their components) from other funding sources, particularly from Horizon 2020 (afternoon session).

As well as a detailed presentation and discussion of the draft calls, the morning session also included contributions on the linkages between regional and national RIS3 and the various forms of support (support for existing SMEs, targeted at increasing applied research, as well as actions for the promotion and dissemination of results, support for the creation of incubators for high-tech SMEs). Feedback and questions from stakeholders centred on a number of detailed technical issues. These included: the inclusion of managerial adequacy and efficiency among the selection criteria of the calls; compatibility of the calls with state-aid rules; how the specific needs of tourism as a sector and academia as a stakeholder are addressed; and whether there would be any mechanisms for proposals to Horizon 2020 which passed the thresholds but did not receive funding to subsequently receive ERDF funds.

The afternoon session aimed to explore the potential to fund (components of) EDP ideas under Horizon 2020. Prior to PDL2, the most voted on ideas in the online consultation were discussed with three National Contact Points for Horizon 2020,[11] who selected a sub-set of potentially eligible ideas. During the event, participants were split into four parallel working groups (one per EDP priority area) and conducted a participatory exercise focused on one of the ideas selected by the NCPs, who were presently available for support and clarification.

As the issue of funding criteria proved difficult to present and digest in the time allocated to the exercise, the sub-group discussion centred on the following three questions, rather than the six foreseen:[12]

- What specific part of the EDP idea could be funded through Horizon 2020?
- Which key international partners should be invited to join in a consortium?
- What are the main obstacles that will be faced in pushing the idea forward?

The outcomes were a series of fiches, an example of which is given in Box 9.2.

Box 9.2 Example of output of Project Development Lab 2

Cluster for animal husbandry and agriculture
Short description
The idea is about the production of milk and meat in clusters with the aim to produce high quality products at competitive prices and with specific comparative advantages linked to the regional advantages and unique characteristics.

PDL2 participants
This idea was elaborated by all six participants of the working group Dairy and Meat (there were no sub-groups in this session). Four participants were researchers and two were from the enterprise sector. The researchers had previous exposure to Framework Programme projects as participants, and one of them also had experience in proposal writing for FP projects.

Which specific parts of the idea could be funded under Horizon 2020?
The participants agreed that this idea is in principle a regional project. However, as the cluster evolves, there might be some research issues that could be considered for Horizon 2020 funding, such as the evaluation of the impact of the local biodiversity in milk quality, methods for measuring biodiversity and similar.

Non regional expertise needed
Although there is some research activity in the region in these two issues, the participants agreed that cutting-edge research would require the engagement of other Greek or European Universities. Possible Greek stakeholders include the University of Thessaly, the University of Thessaloniki, and the Agricultural University of Athens.

Key international stakeholders needed
Possible international stakeholders include the University of Wageningen, University of Ghent.

Key barriers for the development of the idea
The key barrier for the further development of the idea is the commitment of local stakeholders, mainly in the enterprise sector, to participate in and support the cluster.

PDL2 was the last stakeholder event of the Preparatory Action aimed at implementing the EDP. In aiming at closing the cycle between idea generation and policy implementation it also attempted to present the whole S3 process as an agenda for bottom-up change in regional development, one in which policy makers offer a platform for interaction as well as receptive ears to the needs of the stakeholders.

5 Preliminary evaluation

In order to gauge the extent to which the approach of the REMTh Preparatory Action has been successful in developing an EDP and, hence, bridging the gap between different sectors (public, private, research) a short evaluation questionnaire was sent to each of the 28 international presenters and Greek experts participating in the EDP focus groups and the three Horizon 2020 National Contact Points in the second Project Development Labs.[13]

The 15 eventual respondents were all positive about the capacity of the events to stimulate public/private interaction. The methodology followed was evaluated positively in terms of its ability to generate critical and entrepreneurial thinking, although a number of respondents mentioned that higher participation by the private sector may have further enhanced the outcomes by ensuring a stronger market-viability of each proposal.

Respondents were also positive about the networking opportunities offered by the EDP focus groups, although they highlighted that opportunities for international networking were limited. The evaluation in terms of logistical organisation was also very positive.

Finally, respondents were given the opportunity to provide extra comments. Among the suggestions was the production of an 'EDP Manifesto' highlighting the key lessons from the experience. Another suggestion was to narrow further the sectoral target of the working group, make available more preparatory material for stakeholders and devise better ways to identify the more engaged entrepreneurs.

> "The event delivered a real output for participants. The four working groups have tried to transform the ideas into a practical framework for the generation of several joint projects and ideas. One-to -one meetings, during the breaks also help for developing new ideas or business relationships."
>
> International expert

Whilst the feedback for the EDP focus groups is highly positive, the PDLs have been less successful at reaching the expected outcome. In so doing, however, they have provided crucial lessons for S3 implementation. The feedback from the National Contact Points on PDL2 indicates that there was a widespread feeling that the project-based discussion was too short and may have been better placed in the morning, when participants were fresh. Second, it appears that not all participants understood the need to focus on Horizon 2020.

This partly reflects the fact that stakeholders in the region seem to be more inward-focused. In the participatory exercises they had difficulties identifying opportunities outside their region and seeing the advantages of international networking. It also suggests some weaknesses in communication and the sharing of expectations in planning and promoting the event. Overall, experience reflects the difficulties – but also the necessity – of bringing together institutions and people that have not interacted before. The National Contact Points also reported that many participants were active and engaged. As a minimum, the exercise should have served to further diffuse understanding of the importance of innovation, international partnership and networking among regional stakeholders.

6 Lessons learned and conclusions for policy

In line with the stated aims of the REMTh preparatory action, the EDP focus groups and the PDLs have made clear contributions to the EDP in the region, generating momentum and changing perspectives. Particular success is evident in the ways the focus group approach has mobilised and engaged relevant stakeholders in priority sectors. It has allowed stakeholders to explore and catalyse the dynamics of the entrepreneurial process of discovery and to examine the key criteria to identify and pursue relevant projects for the region.

In terms of its impact on regional stakeholders, this process has led to an enhanced understanding in REMTh of what S3 can do, of the advantages of exploring selected priorities and of the benefits of international cooperation in research and innovation. The learning effect is also reflected by the region taking the lead on the organisation of the fourth EDP focus group on non-metallic minerals and on two further EDP focus groups[14] in September 2015. Good progress has also been made in the necessary building of awareness and trust in the region, as reflected in the momentum created and the sustained engagement in activities, as well as their concrete outcomes. The approach has subsequently been adapted for use in three other regions of Greece (Thessaly, Western Macedonia and Western Greece).

A number of more general lessons have also emerged. First of all, at the methodological level, the experience in the four EDP focus groups shows that it is critical to manage time sharply. The moderation of plenary and parallel sessions needs to ensure that all members of the audience provide feedback and ideas. Furthermore, in participatory settings, it is critical that the aims of the exercise are clearly laid out and that the events are perceived as a coherent purposeful package. Failures to take these issues into account may undermine substantially the whole process.

Second, it must be stressed that awareness, trust building and the mobilisation of stakeholders takes time: public authorities, business, university, research and technical institutes, users and citizens, and the European Commission itself needs to get used to exploring together opportunities, gaps and barriers. Within this context, there is also a key role for local 'champions' capable of catalysing stakeholders' engagement.

Third, each setting of application has specificities that cannot be ignored. The REMTh experience indicates that there is a need for alignment with both local policy and political needs and the necessary administrative procedures and associated calendar. Related to that, the complexities of implementation must not be underestimated and indicate a need for more clarity on funding availability and procedures (at the national, regional and European level), and in particular on the identification of appropriate selection, evaluation and eligibility criteria. This is especially important as some ideas, whilst effectively engrained in an EDP, may not be eligible under the ROPs. In this respect, the S3 Platform, hosted by the JRC, can be of help by facilitating the sharing of relevant experience among peers.

To conclude, the success of the project described in this chapter, is also due to the political support, reflected by the commitment to the process of the region's governor, as well as the close-knit collaboration with the regional administration. They have engaged stakeholders in a novel process, at a very difficult time for the country and the region. This highlights how for the S3 to deploy its long-term transformative potential, it is essential to understand how the EDP can become, on the one hand institutionally embedded in the local administrative practices, on the other sustainable across political cycles. Both points are essential to avoid that this long-term transformative process falls victim to short-term needs and agendas.

Acknowledgements

The work described in this chapter has been financed under an Administrative Agreement between DG JRC and DG REGIO of the European Commission (JRC № 33653-2014-09 REGIO № 2014CE160AT056), following a decision of the European Parliament.

The organisation of the events described in this chapter has been possible only through the close cooperation of the Regional Governor, the Special Managing Authority of the Region of Eastern Macedonia and Thrace, the Regional Innovation and Entrepreneurship Council, the Innovatia Systems team and the local consultants that supported us throughout the process. We would like to thank Governor George Pavlides, Yiannis Kesanlis, Panagiotis Koudoumakis, Vasileios Pitsinigkos, Petros Soukoulias, Michalis Metaxas, Yannis Tolias, Effie Amanatidou and Christos Emmanouilidis. The JRC-IPTS would also like to thank the board of critical friends, who provided feedback and suggestions: Nerea Anacabe Uriarte, Magdalene Häberle, Raquel Ortega Argilés, Leyla Radovanova, Javier Revilla Diez, Artur Rosa Pires and Antonio Viader. Finally, the JRC would like to thank all the national and international experts who participated in the EDP focus groups. The authors would also like to thank their colleagues in DG REGIO, particularly the geographical unit for Greece and the Competence Centre on Smart and Sustainable Growth, as well as Patrice Dos Santos, from the JRC, for their support.

Notes

1 Vertical prioritisation favours e.g. selected technologies, or fields, or a population of firms.
2 The project is implemented through an administrative agreement between DG Regional and Urban Policy (REGIO) and the Joint Research Centre (JRC) of the European Commission.
3 The work conducted has been documented at: http://s3platform.jrc.ec.europa.eu/remth.
4 Data source: EUROSTAT Population on 1 January by age, sex and NUTS 2 region.

5 The REMTh S3 is available in English at: http://s3platform.jrc.ec.europa.eu/ documents/20182/144300/REMTh+RIS3+EN/8ba9bd80-4877-4fa0-b634-e16fc10ec709, accessed 23 May 2016.
6 Data source: EUROSTAT Gross domestic product (GDP) at current market prices by NUTS 2 regions.
7 Data source: https://ec.europa.eu/growth/tools-databases/regional-innovation-monitor /base-profile/region-anatoliki-makedonia-thraki.
8 Data source: EUROSTAT Total intramural R&D expenditure (GERD) by sectors of performance and NUTS 2 regions.
9 Data source: EUROSTAT Population aged 25–64 with tertiary educational attainment level by sex and NUTS 2 regions.
10 The S3 platform is the Smart Specialisation Platform, a competence centre on RIS3 hosted by the Joint Research Centre: http://s3platform.jrc.ec.europa.eu/ home.
11 Specifically the NCPs covered the SME Instrument, Spreading Excellence, and Fast Track to Innovation, ICT and Tourism).
12 The other three questions were: 1. Which funding criteria can be met easily? 2. For which funding criteria is external expertise is needed? 3. Decide whether there is enough interest/critical mass to push the idea forward and if so appoint a coordinator for future steps.
13 The international experts participating in the EDP focus groups were asked the following five questions, and were also encouraged to give explanations for their replies, whether positive or negative:
   • Do you think the event was useful in stimulating the interaction between the research and private sector in broad terms?
   • Do you think the structure of the event was effective in generating creative thinking?
   • Do you think the event was useful in stimulating innovative entrepreneurial ideas for the region? (Please note, that the ideas should be innovative for the region, rather than on the EU or global levels).
   • Do you think the event was useful in opening up networking opportunities both at the national and international level?
   • Was the logistic organisation of the event satisfactory?
14 The two EDP focus groups targeted chemicals and electronics.

References

Foray, D. and Goenaga, X. (2013), *The Goals of Smart Specialisation*, S3 Policy Brief Series n° 01/2013, EUR 26005 EN, ISBN 978-92-79-30547-4, Luxembourg: Publications Office of the European Union. Available at: http://ftp.jrc.es/EURdoc/ JRC82213.pdf, accessed 23 May 2016.

Foray, D. and Rainoldi, A. (2013), *Smart Specialisation Programmes and Implementation*, S3 Policy Brief Series No. 02/2013, EUR 26002 EN, ISBN 978-92-79-30541-2, Luxembourg: Publications Office of the European Union. Available at: http://ftp.jrc.es/EURdoc/JRC82224.pdf, accessed 23 May 2016.

Hausmann, R. and Rodrik, D. (2003), Economic Development as Self-Discovery, *Journal of Development Economics*, 72(2): 603–633.

Kroll, H., Muller, E., Schnabl, E. and Zenker, A. (2014), *From Smart Concept to Challenging Practice – How European Regions Deal with the Commission's Request for Novel Innovation Strategies*, Working Papers Firms and Region No. R2/2014, Karlsruhe: Fraunhofer Institute for Systems and Innovation Research ISI.

Available at: www.isi.fraunhofer.de/isi-wAssets/docs/p/de/arbpap_unternehmen_region/2014/ap_r2_2014.pdf, accessed 23 May 2016.

Martínez-López, D., and Palazuelos Martínez, M. (2014), *Breaking with the Past in Smart Specialisation: A New Model of Selection of Business Stakeholders Within the Entrepreneurial Process of Discovery* (No. 1401). Universidade de Vigo: GEN-Governance and Economics research Network.

10 Continuous priority setting in the Norwegian VRI programme

Jens Sörvik and Inger Midtkandal

1 Introduction

Smart specialisation (S3) is the European Commission's approach to regional growth through research and innovation (European Commission, 2010a, 2010b; Midtkandal and Sörvik, 2012). A key feature of S3 is that regions should identify a limited number of priority areas for their activities. A more comprehensive approach in these areas should lead to structural change in the region. The priority areas should be niches in which the region has the potential to have a competitive advantage in the future. It can be in areas of strong regional capabilities or emerging fields in which the region through a collaborative effort of regional and external actors can develop lead markets through systemic innovation.

The priority areas are to be identified through entrepreneurial discovery processes (EDP). EDPs are processes in which stakeholders are engaged in identifying domains for future potentials (Foray *et al.*, 2009), but also opportunities and needs within a priority area and to design comprehensive and targeted sets of measures in roadmaps of aligned public and private activities. The relevant stakeholders are the ones that are key to developing the areas and implementing the joint strategies.

After a first review of EU smart specialisation strategies (RIS3) (Sörvik and Kleibrink, 2015), it is evident that few regions or countries have defined priorities as specific as outlined in RIS3 conceptual work (Foray, 2009, 2014; European Commission, 2012). However, given the nature of gradual development as understood by the EDP and the time needed to mature such processes, this might be expected. S3 is a continuous process of priority setting; both in refining the priority areas, and deciding the portfolio of areas. To manage these continuous processes, regions need to develop institutions to constantly adapt activities to a changing reality.

The S3 concept is still emerging and can be enriched by learning from past experiences with regional research and innovation. Since 2007, Norwegian regions have worked systematically with VRI (Programme for regional R&D and innovation); a programme which shares features with smart specialisation. Other regions can learn from their experiences, in particular when it comes to organising the governance of S3 priorities. The aim of VRI has been to empower regions with competences and responsibility for research and innovation (R&I) and to give regions more autonomy in designing targeted policy mixes. A key feature of VRI has been that based on a regional analysis, regions have identified a limited number of prioritised areas and targeted activities within these areas.

In this chapter we will from a S3 perspective in the first section outline the rationale for priority setting; how continuous priority setting can be designed and institutionalised in the context of smart specialisation. In the next section we will illustrate this with examples from the Norwegian experience, and discuss what practitioners of S3 can learn from these experiences, which we will then summarise in the final section.

One of the authors of this chapter has previously worked with VRI in the Research Council of Norway, has first-hand experience with the programme and has thus observed the many similarities between smart specialisation and VRI. The data for the chapter comes from interviews with representatives from six Norwegian regions, the Research Council of Norway (RCN) and project descriptions, annual reports and result reports from the six regions. The regional cases included are Agder, Møre og Romsdal, Nordland, Rogaland, Trøndelag, and Vestfold. These were chosen as interesting cases with some distinct features that could illustrate the diversity in organisational set-up and approaches to managing the priority areas.

2 Smart specialisation

2.1 What are smart specialisation and priority areas?

The concept of smart specialisation was first introduced in a policy brief prepared by an independent advisory group to the European Commissioner for Research and Innovation (Foray and Van Ark, 2007). Foray *et al.* (2009) further developed the concept, and argued that research investment in Europe suffered from fragmentation, poor coordination and insufficient critical mass. They also noted a clear 'me-too' syndrome: regions tended to make investments in the same fashionable areas, such as nano- and bio-technologies that often did not have any connection to actual regional capabilities. Their recommendation was to foster structural change through supporting the emergence of new activity areas by investing in areas of strategic importance depending on existing areas of strengths, connections and future potential. Later contributions like the 'Barca Report' (Barca, 2009) increased the focus on existing local capabilities, transforming S3 into a place-based concept, with a focus on fewer priorities and emphasising better coordination of regional policies and activities (McCann and Ortega-Argilés, 2011).

S3 draws on past policy experiences, most notably from Regional Innovation Strategies (RIS and RITTS) but incorporates a number of novelties. Smart specialisation should emerge from an EDP (Foray *et al.*, 2009), which is a bottom-up learning process aimed at identifying domains for future specialisation. Most often these priority areas mean developing niches in areas of related variety to existing capabilities (Boschma and Gianelle, 2014). The role of public authorities is to create the right conditions for and support the EDP. Entrepreneurial knowledge involves more than knowledge of science and technology, and includes knowledge of market growth potential and innovation needs. This is important in order to overcome problems with prior research and innovation policies, where investments in research did not lead to innovation (Foray, 2014).

S3 incorporates the thinking of innovation systems saying that innovation does not only take place within a company; also collaboration and the socio-economic context have an impact and traditionally non-R&D based companies can be innovative (Lundvall, 1992). Moreover, it is important to address the relationship between regional production structures (firms and innovation support) and knowledge generation subsystems (e.g. research laboratories, universities and vocational training) (Cooke, 2002).

Smart specialisation aims at promoting collaboration between public authorities in charge of innovation policies and relevant stakeholders involved in innovation. Additionally the users and beneficiaries of innovations should be involved hence bringing in a quadruple helix perspective (i.e., firms, universities, research centres, and civil society).

A RIS3 should target a number of vertically prioritised areas.[1] The idea is to support clustering, both in terms of growing the number of companies and employees in the area, as well as a means for joint action to manage common challenges and opportunities (Foray and Goenaga, 2013). When it comes to R&I and raising productivity there are significant scale returns to critical mass, with potentials for positive learning curves.[2] Due to technological lock-in effects, industry from a large enough region that are early movers can establish de facto standards that can lock out competitors from elsewhere (Scherden, 1998), or become a Lead market, i.e. a region where a market has emerged first and whose innovations are subsequently adopted by others (Beise, 2001, 2004). The gains from specialisation and potential spill-over effects are central. The policy mix chosen in S3 must therefore make sure it also allows for the entry of new actors to enhance agglomeration and support positive cluster externalities (Nauwelaers *et al.*, 2014).

Clusters can be conducive to innovation due to intense competition, knowledge spill-over, specialisation, user–producer learning and possibilities for joint action (Sörvik, 2010). With regard to joint action, in agglomerations there are enough actors with common interests and partners to engage in deliberative policies to have an impact. The systemic view to identify potentials, weaknesses and coordinated actions to overcome them is central to the S3 concept (McCann and Ortega-Argilés, 2014). To select priority areas is not about limiting public investment to a few and restricted number of areas per se or single projects, but it is about market creation or development. The idea is to foster strategic innovation agendas with multi-stakeholder engagement;

where the stakeholders jointly identify and design the agenda and hence secure commitment to implementation and together create the market. For this, a range of coordinated activities are required such as pilots, new technologies, skills development, test beds, standards, legislation (legal, fiscal, intellectual property rights and financial frameworks), and new services, in order to stimulate the emergence of system changes (Elzen *et al.*, 2004). This is particularly important in areas of systemic character, e.g. energy, where infrastructure, public regulations and even public services are instrumental. To be successful, policy experimentation and putting learning mechanisms in place are needed. Regions will not pick winning national champions or only one priority area, but a few. The process can be seen as betting on different races rather than picking winners (Hughes, 2012).

2.2 Priority setting

Priority setting is based on predictions combined with efforts in trying to shape the future. The development of new markets takes place in socio-economic contexts that are extremely complex to predict, as there exists no macro-theory which can guarantee correct predictions. There are also black swans of unexpected developments and/or myopia that prevent analysts from seeing bigger and long- term pictures, by overrating the present and near past for future developments (Scherden, 1998).

Theories and methods for prediction have moved away from pure forecasting towards emphasising processes (Martin, 1995). As it is impossible to know the future beforehand, but the decisions today have an outcome for the development of future scenarios, it is important to get the processes right (Rodrik, 2004). This is the core message from the experiences with Foresight, which is also a part of the S3 logic. Foresight systematically attempts to look into the longer-term future of science, technology, economy and society with the aim of identifying areas likely to yield economic and social benefits and connecting the visions and actions of the actors participating to also shape the future (Martin, 1995).

With an increased emphasis on open innovation and networked economies in which companies increasingly innovate in collaboration with external actors, this kind of systemic approach is very important. The process becomes an arena in which a common strategy can be formed, restoring some stability to firms' environments (Metcalfe and Georghiou, 1998). The main guidance document for how to operationalise smart specialisation into strategies, the RIS3 guide (European Commission, 2012) emphasises that the priority setting process should be carried out through collaboration between multiple set-ups of actors that have different pieces of information about the potential future, but also have the possibilities to shape the future.

The RIS3 guide points out the need for a quantitative approach (exploring the past and present using statistical indicators) in identifying areas of potential for economic growth, as well as a need to identify the relevant stakeholders and engage these in a more participatory and qualitative selection process and design of policy mixes. The quantitative analysis can identify trends and areas of potential, as well as establishing some transparency and common understanding of reality. However, the actors that will design and implement the strategies and potentially find new and fruitful cross-sectorial opportunities that can be hard to find in a traditional statistical analysis are fundamental.

In sum, it

> ... is not about telling people what to do, what are the right specialisations, but accompanying emerging trends and improving coordination by providing the necessary public goods (education, training) and creating additional incentives at certain critical bottlenecks to help the new activity to grow.
>
> (Foray *et al.*, 2011, p. 6)

2.3 Governing continuous priority setting

Priority setting takes place through rationalised and formal processes. However, the decision making process takes place in an institutional context that affects the outcome, such as informal negotiations between different vested interests (Olson, 1965/1971), path dependency in policy frameworks and organisational set-ups, cognitive capabilities and perceptions among involved actors (Nelson and Winter, 1982). Additionally, simply serendipitous decisions and external effects can have important influences (Pagels-Fick, 2010). This reflects the bounded rationality of political and economic actors, who in most cases do not possess complete information about all relevant factors when taking decisions (Simon, 1991). In public administrations, this has been associated with what Lindblom (1959) famously called 'muddling through', i.e. incremental change without any clear strategy or steering of the process.

The S3 approach can be seen as a mix of rational analysis and a negotiation of the interests of different stakeholders, while at the same time organising mechanisms for learning (European Commission, 2012). This can be seen as a form of organic planning that recognises the limitations of forecasting and target setting and provides a framework within which a region adapts its activities progressively. This requires a governance system and policy mix which can balance the interests of incumbents and emergent interests, as well as different stakeholder categories, such as academia and industry. The processes are not only about identifying priority areas, but also to modify these, therefore the governance mechanism needs to deal with constantly evolving combinations of teams.

Priority setting in S3 is a process with at least two layers; on an overarching level the portfolio of priorities is managed by identification, selection and de-selection; and in parallel runs the process of deciding upon how to develop each priority area specifically.

2.3.1 Overarching strategic level – continuous priority setting

The overall strategy development and overseeing of implementation is done at the overarching level. Here lays the responsibility to detect priority areas and potential partners, to choose new priorities and drop outdated ones. In order to take informed decisions, regions need to set up mechanisms for market intelligence, monitoring and evaluation. It is not likely that one single method will do, but rather a mix of indicators and qualitative follow up mechanisms is necessary (Gianelle and Kleibrink, 2015).

The overarching level should be guided or led by high-level groups of stakeholders (such as regional partnerships, governance boards or innovation councils). The role of such a group is to steer the RIS3 or to give relevant guidance. It should include key actors that have the ability to influence the regional economic development taking into account a triple or quadruple helix perspective in order to secure an on-going interaction between different sources of knowledge and practice. Normally actors with overarching strategic responsibilities would be involved, primarily regional development agencies or regional ministries, industry representatives, university and research institutes and NGOs or civil society representatives.

Transparent and open processes are crucial not to get caught by rent seeking vested interests aiming at preserving a status quo (Lindgren and Forsberg, 2010). Important measures to avoid this include motivating decisions with evidence based background studies, setting conditionalities and sharing decisions with a wider public and democratic elected bodies. The group should also be able to change its composition over time to incorporate new actors and interests, and not only be based on the network initiator's personal connections (Sotarauta and Bruun, 2002).

2.3.2 Priority area working groups – entrepreneurial discovery process

At the priority area level actors work with identifying opportunities and weaknesses within the domain; which activities to carry out and which policy mixes to deploy. The actors involved would include set-ups of quadruple helix actors linked to the domain. Particularly important are i) entrepreneurs with the understanding of combining knowledge about science and technology with knowledge of market potentials, ii) actors who can influence the outcome of the future, due to resources and influence in a community, and iii) stakeholders who have the capabilities to be forward looking (Sotarauta, 2009). In many regions there are leaders without a formal role, but with informal influence. They can set direction, mobilise resources from different sectors and levels towards common goals, and ensure that resources from other actors are committed, in a form of distributed leadership (Bennett *et al.*, 2003).

The working groups design the actual roadmaps and policy mixes for the priority area and implement them. To be successful in keeping the stakeholders committed it is important that there are specific benefits for all participants, both to incentivise actors to participate in the design phase but also to engage in the implementation phase.

Just like when selecting priority areas, the choice of which actors to involve can only partially be based on a quantitative approach. When moving on to work on the priority areas, it is not only important to have the right candidates; they must also be willing to participate. The willingness to engage can be seen as a litmus test of whether the process and activities are relevant to the stakeholders and that it is a correct priority area.

In developing the roadmap, there is a need to generate scenarios, a vision with clear ideas on how to reach the objectives and which activities should be carried out by the different actors engaged in the process. The S3 concept emphasises that regions should explore possibilities to include external actors in this process (European Commission, 2012). A good roadmap will support awareness, coordination, vision, and completeness (Kostoff and Schaller, 2001).

EDP is about the experimental approach in implementing the strategy, with step-wise trying out activities (e.g. piloting) and adapting to changing circumstances, muddling through. For this reason the monitoring and evaluation system becomes very important. The monitoring system should support an adaptive learning approach, where different activities can be tested and learned from and possibly lead to changed interventions (Gianelle and Kleibrink, 2015).

3 The case of Norway

3.1 The Virkemidler for regional innovasjon (VRI) programme

The VRI programme[3] was launched in 2007 as part of a process of building capabilities and transferring competencies for research and innovation to regional level in Norway. The idea was to restructure the available policy mix for R&I at regional level into a new, less standardised package with more regional autonomy and improved coordination with other regional strategies, tools and activities. In 2010 this process was further reinforced with the introduction of Regional Research Funds[4] and the restructuring of Innovation Norway's regional offices.[5] This chapter concentrates on the experiences of the VRI programme and what practitioners developing and implementing Smart Specialisation Strategies can learn from the VRI programme experiences.

The VRI programme has aimed at raising Norway's competitiveness and productivity by enhancing research and knowledge-based activities. This has been done at a regional level, with an ambition to strengthen industries by addressing their specific R&I needs, mainly through broad partnerships in selected priority areas with a focus on R&I for regional development and improved arenas for coordination of R&I activities. The midterm evaluation of the VRI programme was positive and concluded that VRI had been particularly beneficial in contributing to the development of the regional research and innovation system (Furre *et al.*, 2012).

The VRI programme offers a number of tools to mobilise and connect regional actors in R&I closer together and build capabilities for research and innovation in the triple helix system. The toolbox includes network tools for linking actors in emerging clusters, competence brokering to match companies and researchers in developing precompetitive innovation projects, mobility schemes for Higher Education Institutions (HEI) allowing staff and students to foster closer and more dynamic links with companies, and dialogue tools for trust building and tying stakeholders closer together through arenas for identification of common activities.

The VRI programme has operated in three-year cycles, making it mandatory for the regional partnerships to review their activities and potentially renew approaches and policy mixes for the upcoming programming periods. When applying, regions have been asked to indicate a selected number of priority areas based on an analysis of the region's strengths and challenges. The regions should outline which tools and actors would be involved to pursue the goals and meet the challenges in each priority area.

After eight years and two new renewals we can observe that regions have changed the mix of priority areas, as well as the activities within them. There is no clear pattern in the development, except that the priority mixes change over time and are adapted to changing realities. Some regions have increased the number of priorities while others have reduced them. Some have become more specific with tighter cluster collaboration and international ambitions, while others have chosen very broad priority areas, opening up to basically any kind of technological activity in order to catch new upcoming industries. Priority areas originally launched as modest pilots have grown to become successful cluster organisations whereas other priority areas have been closed down, due to lack of results.

The Norwegian experiences with the VRI programme are particularly illustrative for the RIS3 process related to the governance of continuous priority setting, design of policy mixes for priority areas, organisation of the process and learning mechanisms related to monitoring and evaluation.

3.2 Overarching strategic level – governance set up

The governance set-up for the VRI programme builds on Norway's regional partnerships (Johnstad *et al.*, 2003). These were, if needed, reinforced with representatives from research and education organisations. The Regional Partnerships are now normally triple helix consortia consisting of the county authorities, the regional innovation agency, business associations, labour unions, research institutions, HEI, and other relevant actors, e.g. regional level state representatives. The county has a particular role as the contractual partner with the RCN and the financial source for most of the co-funding of the regional VRI programmes.

The Partnership has been given the responsibility to set up a steering committee and to be jointly responsible for the design and direction of the VRI (VRI, 2007). The steering committee has had the responsibility to ensure that VRI is carried out in line with targets and allocated budget. It is the forum for strategic discussions and for agreeing on eventual adjustments, in agreement with the RCN. In general in VRI, the county has kept the chair of the steering committee in some regions while other regions have given this task to an industry representative.

An important bridge between the steering committee and the daily operational work in the priority areas are the regional VRI project leaders, priority area sub-project leaders and competence brokers. The overall project leaders are in some regions employed by the regional authority (Trøndelag, Nordland and Rogaland), in others in a regional research institute (Agder and Møre og Romsdal) or at the regional university (Vestfold).

3.2.1 Representation and operability

Over time some of the regions have modified the steering committee to reflect the change of the priority mix portfolio, e.g. Møre og Romsdal added new members when introducing the priority area on health and welfare innovation. VRI Nordland included additional stakeholders (two HEIs and an innovation company) after two periods in order to secure better involvement for the implementation (VRI Nordland, 2013).

The respondents reflect the trade-off between legitimacy and action when setting up the steering committees. More members complicate collaboration, but it is important to have members with a position through which they can influence the behaviour of regional actors and thereby secure the regional strategy.

Three main approaches handling the size and involvement of steering committees are visible; i) Agder has reduced the size of the steering committee over time; ii) Rogaland has kept the size while accepting that not all representatives are always present; and iii) de facto or informally working with two set-ups, a larger group which gives strategic guidance on fewer occasions and an active group with frequent interactions with the project leader (Trøndelag). While broadening of the steering committee could make it too large, most regions appreciate the representativeness and coordination effect that the large group of innovation related actors have.

3.2.2 Trust and coordination

Several respondents mention that one success factor has been a trustful working climate within the steering committee and between the steering committee and the priority areas. Also RCN underlines that the most successful regions have managed to establish governance mechanisms based on trust and a collective mind-set to work with the potentials and the greater good of the regions beyond the stakeholders' own interests. This can be illustrated by Vestfold taking out the priority area Water Cleansing from the VRI portfolio to give room for a new and upcoming industry while the CEO of the Water Cluster was chairing the steering committee.

The steering committees are perceived as good arenas for informal discussions on topics related to regional innovation and coordination of activities. Long and well established relations with good connections to other fields of public interventions for regional development both facilitates the implementation of VRI and the coordination with these interventions, e.g. regional development funds and national cluster and R&I programmes. The RCN respondents perceive that VRI has worked better when coordinated with other programmes and less so where it has worked in isolation as a separate regional project

At the same time some respondents (Møre og Romsdal and Agder) are concerned that the steering committees' long relations may hamper innovativeness, due to a lack of necessary new inputs to their processes. To counteract this Møre og Romsdal plan to alter their steering committee by bringing in new actors representing additional perspectives. Agder has abstained from adding new actors to maintain the current size of eight which they find optimal for operational purposes. However, to counteract lock-in, they keep as a part of their internal dialogue a constant reminder of the danger of being too introverted and highlight diversity when designing calls.

Stakeholder representativeness matters – it is of importance to bring the right institutions, but also the right people to the table. The organisational background of a project leader or steering committee leader seems less important as long as the stakeholders work in a trustful environment and manage to coordinate with other policy programmes. Vestfold has made a point of having the steering committee led by a representative of the private sector and by this creating legitimacy and securing engagement. Others claim that to have the county's business manager has been beneficial for legitimacy and coordination with other activities, as long as this person perceives his or her role and VRI as important.

3.3 Priority selection

When VRI was first launched in 2007, the regions were asked to build on existing related strategies and regional development plans. Hence the first set of priorities seems to have been based on pre-existing areas in regional development programmes and national cluster programmes.

Each new programming period in VRI has allowed and encouraged regions to rethink both priority areas and policy mix. The steering committees are central in the selection of priority areas, but have applied different reasoning for changes.

3.3.1 The rationale for intervention

The first selection of priorities reflected large and important areas of the regional economies. The regions aimed at areas of the regional economy which could benefit from increased research and innovation activities, to raise the regional enterprises' productivity and stimulate a more knowledge-based development. In addition, regions have emphasised that enterprises should have the capacity to engage in R&I processes and in the longer run continue on their own or with national or European programmes. Some regions have broadened their portfolio by adding non-technology based areas, like tourism/experience-based industry in Nordland and film industry in Vestfold.

VRI has had a mobilising element in starting R&I processes with new actors who could later continue to other programmes and activities. In several cases it has been about activities in already strong clusters with a need to raise R&I components, or to mobilise regionally important areas with a future potential not yet identified or prioritised by national programmes. The VRI programme has supported areas where an embryonic network of actors have grown into cluster organisations later included in national excellence and cluster programmes, like Vestfold Water Cluster.

Agder has aimed at both what they call path renewal (innovation and diversification within established industries, e.g. oil and gas and wood industry) and path creation (to support the creation of new areas) – like culture. In the initial phase traditional industries were not included, but later the region realised that these could benefit from renewal, e.g. by introducing Information and Communication Technologies (ICT) to the wood industry.

3.3.2 Modification of priority portfolio

The introduction of new priority areas has come from many sources, such as interaction of involved partners and embedded researchers, through top down political priorities, from requests by regional actors, and in some cases through statistical background analyses.

In Møre og Romsdal, e.g., a new priority area emerged from the interaction between VRI partners; the competence brokers were increasingly having interactions around the topic of health. To include health as a topic was suggested to the steering committee which agreed to add it for the following programming period. The priority area was later narrowed down to welfare technologies. There are also bottom-up cases where regional actors have approached VRI to become a priority area, as in the case of Nordland where actors around oil and gas approached the regional authorities.

In quite many cases the regional authorities have decided to add new areas showing unique potentials. In Vestfold there was a small number of small film-related companies, but the local research institute and universities did not have any capabilities in the area. RCN was initially not in favour of prioritising this area, but the regional authorities argued to include it and have seen the activities grow. Tunnel safety in Rogaland emerged as the region was about to build several new underwater tunnels and there was a need for new knowledge, new solutions and new companies to manage security.

Statistically oriented background documents have been used to different degrees in identifying priority areas. In Vestfold the regional authorities have prepared statistical background material for discussions of future priorities and to some extent the Water Cleansing cluster was identified this way. Through this identification and networking activities, the establishment of cluster organisations has been stimulated.

Nordland has prepared a RIS3 which is reflected in their latest VRI programme period. One of the key activities was to prepare profound background material in order to identify the more important regional priority areas. For this, they used a mix of qualitative and quantitative approaches, like exploring the export value of different sectors. It needs to be said that this more profound analysis did not lead to the identification of any new economic activity areas beyond the ones previously identified, but it contributed to a shift of focus of actors and activities within the area, e.g. to work more with the supply industry and competence building. This background study has been an inspiration for other regions which intend to do similar analysis. Møre og Romsdal has done an analysis of their innovation system and business structure and interviewed stakeholders from academia and industry to support their regional innovation strategy and VRI (VRI Møre og Romsdal, 2013). Also Trøndelag has searched for future potentials through analysing the innovation structure of the region and identifying specialisation among industry and strengths in the regions R&D capability. It served as a basis for partnership discussions before the third programming period (VRI Trøndelag, 2013).

Before the start of the second VRI period, Agder worked with OECD which had done a report about the region. One of the suggestions pointed to becoming more knowledge based and knowledge intensive. The result was that Agder kept their three original priority areas, but increased the focus on knowledge development within them.

In the renewal of priority areas, some regions have become more specific like Møre og Romsdal going from health and public sector innovation to welfare technologies. Quite a few regions have added a new open category, opening the programme to whatever could surge (Rogaland: new technology; Agder and Møre og Romsdal: emerging industries). The reason is a satisfaction with the VRI tools, in particular the competence brokers who have generated new R&I projects. There is also a desire to being open to support emerging ideas. For the same reason, Møre og Romsdal has located the project leader and competence brokers in a more neutral arena for innovation support than within a specific research institute connected to established industries.

A number of priorities have been closed down in VRI. Nordland has closed down two areas. In aquaculture they focused on the local cod industry, which was knocked out by the financial crisis. The salmon industry was still strong, but needed no support from VRI, so the priority area was ended. The second area was related to solar energy which was modified to focus on other sources of renewable energies when the solar industry moved to Asia. In Vestfold, Water Cleansing and Micro/Nano electronics were ended because they were perceived as strong enough that there was no need for VRI support.

The examples presented above do not necessarily illustrate an EDP where the industry is the driving force in identifying the priority areas, but rather broad stakeholder involvement in entrepreneurial regional processes. However, common for these new priority areas is that they have been taken on board due to close dialogue with industry and the openness to explore new opportunities. Furthermore, the involvement of industry is a requirement for the longevity of the priority area.

The governance set-up and an entrepreneurial spirit in the regional administration is crucial to allow new priority areas to rise and develop. The respondents also shared that in choosing priority areas, it will not work well if the stakeholders come together and try to divide the funds between themselves instead of identifying strong potential areas where they can contribute jointly. Likewise if selecting areas of strong regional political interest, it can not only be an additional way of funding areas of region responsibility sustaining clientelism, but needs to have an innovation perspective.

We can also note that in order to succeed with a priority area, it is not enough to identify the correct areas of activities with a future potential, but there also needs to be stakeholders interested in engaging in these processes. For instance when Nordland had to stop two areas of activities, local knowledge still existed, but there was nobody to take the processes forward.

3.4 Priority area management

How are priority areas managed and developed to reinforce their strengths and foster innovation? The different VRI regions have tried various approaches over the programming periods. Common is that activities are carried out in the different priority areas through a set of tools and with boundary spanning roles of the regional VRI team members. Regions are also to different degrees using reference or working groups representing triple helix constellations to support the priority area management.

3.4.1 Priority area working group or reference group?

Due to limited resources in VRI, it has been difficult to have working groups with triple helix representation develop strategic roadmaps for each priority area. However, quite a few regions have worked with reference groups to bring in the views of the larger stakeholders' community on needs and opportunities within each priority area.

Nordland is the region that has advanced the most established working groups for each priority area, working close to the region's clusters and discussing what activities to carry out. They had initial challenges in convincing industry to participate, but industry representatives have eventually come to see the value. Agder uses reference groups as a way of involving stakeholders and new actors to counteract lock-in. They aim at further developing the working groups to stimulate renewal. Vestfold desires more structured involvement of reference groups but indicate that at the moment there are not resources for this. Møre og Romsdal has had a reference group for public sector innovation, which met once per year.

In identifying and developing the areas, it is the perception among many of the respondents that industry could have been even more deeply engaged in developing roadmaps and work in a more systematic structured approach. It would also be beneficial to have deeper thematically focused dialogues than the steering committee manage in each thematic area. This is one of Nordland's success factors, as perceived by themselves.

3.4.2 Boundary spanners

Central in the VRI process are the project leader for the VRI programme. Some regions also have proactive priority area leaders. Key actors are also the competence brokers, who are boundary spanning intermediaries interacting with companies and research organisations in order to identify needs for R&I in companies and to generate new projects. The competence brokers are sometimes priority area leaders. They normally work part time with VRI and are employed by research institutes, HEI, incubators, and innovation support organisations.

The respondents emphasise that competence brokers need to be able to communicate and understand needs within both the research and industry community, and be able to continue and scale up projects with tools also outside of VRI. They also need the right incentive to interact with the partners to initiate new projects. Some regions felt they had made a mistake in paying their competence brokers upfront, taking away incentives to identify new projects.

Møre og Romsdal used to have specialists for each priority area, but has moved towards generalists working with innovation support as they are perceived as being better at seeing new opportunities, especially for new types of diversifying cross innovation. Experts are brought in as the projects advance.

Nordland underlines that skills, qualities and personalities are more important than the institutional background of the priority area leaders, but the role needs to be connected to central stakeholders of the different areas. It is however crucial to be able to communicate, have good networks and also spend much time visiting companies and research institutes.

3.5 Activity selection and policy mix

The national VRI programme has developed a common toolbox that regions can use. Regions may also develop their own tools, as long as they comply with European Commission state aid regulation.

In selecting activities and policy mix, there are two main processes. The first is the identification of what needs to be done and the next what kind of tools to use. There seems to be a slightly polarised approach between regions and use of tools; some regions seem to depart mainly from available tools and use the same for all priority areas. Other regions seem to depart from the needs of the priority areas, and tailor appropriate mixes to address the needs. The priority areas, and even the strategies, seem more important in Agder, Trøndelag, Vestfold and Nordland. Rogaland and Møre og Romsdal on the other hand seem more focused on the activities/tools, which is also indicated in that these latter two are opening up the VRI tools in new and open categories, thus reducing 'sectorial' limitations. Yet, in the area of tunnel safety, Rogaland has taken a strategic approach, using innovation procurement to develop new solutions, supporting networks and awareness raising among local industry about opportunities and engaged a professor in tunnel safety to develop the area together with the University of Stavanger.

While some of the regions have a more strategic approach, roadmaps for the priority areas seem to be lacking. Action plans for the upcoming years outline broadly which activities to carry out and which VRI tools to use. The tools vary between priority areas depending on their maturity. Dialogue tools are used to introduce opportunities of R&I to industry and to generate new ideas. More mature areas concentrate on initiating and carrying out projects.

A tool which has grown in popularity is the dialogue tool called think tank, where a region invites cluster representatives, companies and researchers to identify projects, within a particular area, but also to develop cross clustering topics. A good result coming out of the think tank is 7Sense in Vestfold, which is a company that sprang out of a meeting between farmers and Nano-tech researchers. The company now sells a sensor that detects when potatoes are rotting.

Vestfold has concentrated their tools on developing business clusters within prioritised areas. The policy mix is chosen in order to optimise synergies between opportunities, challenges, available tools and regional interests. Since the regional industry traditionally has had low R&D intensity, there has been a focus on building trust between industry and R&D environments (VRI Vestfold, 2013). Part of this is also to develop the university college as a partner, strengthening the connection to the regional partnership. To meet the challenge of the lack of a skilled labour force, the regional university college has adapted its curricula to offer relevant courses. Industrial professors (Professor II) are employed to strengthen interaction and student projects with industrial focus.

Different tools are used for strategy development before each new programming period, e.g. Agder has arranged dialogue meetings with clusters and stakeholders from the knowledge infrastructure. Even though the potential interventions are not so detailed, each priority area has got a specific policy mix, depending on previous experience, maturity and challenges of the industry (VRI Agder, 2013).

The region with the most specific plans, Nordland, responds that they could develop roadmaps for each priority area further in collaboration with stakeholders. At the same time they see a danger in planning too much ahead and becoming too formalistic, as they fear they would lose contact with reality. Nordland indicates that their imperative is to be responsive and listen to industry needs. They underline the importance of flexibility; to be experimental and to have the right tools available (VRI Nordland, 2014). Within their priority area renewable energy, flexibility was crucial when the entire solar energy industry collapsed. Due to their flexibility, the steering committee together with the priority area leader could immediately start activities to maintain competences and explore new potentials. Still, renewable energy was ended from 2014.

The need for further and more comprehensively developing the priority area strategies is also backed by the RCN. They would have liked to see the entire palette of available VRI tools used in a more targeted way, e.g. they believe the mobility programmes are being under-used.

3.6 Monitoring and evaluation

Monitoring and evaluations systems are key in a continuous priority setting process and in managing the regional VRI programme and the different priority areas.

The process of preparing a new programming period is maybe the most important learning phase of VRI. Learning and results from the last three years can be applied to a profound renewal of the regional VRI strategy. In a shorter time frame there are different types of on-going mechanisms that keep track of the process and offer learning. These include steering committee meetings, project reporting, annual reports to RCN as well as more profound and long term learning mechanisms such as embedded researchers and on-going and external evaluation.

The VRI projects send annual reports to the RCN with indicators following up the activities. These reporting activities seem to matter less for the development of the priority portfolio and for the priority areas as the indicators reflect long term effects not impacted by VRI in the present programme period. Nevertheless, companies that have received funding for innovation or in Vestfold have participated in think tank projects are asked to fill out an evaluation scheme to provide feedback to the project secretariat and the impact of VRI is according to RCN demonstrated convincingly through qualitative reflections on investments and activities in most of the reports. The midterm evaluation of VRI including also a survey of companies involved in VRI, has also been conducted; concluding that VRI has had positive impact and is on the way to meet its objectives (Furre *et al.*, 2012).

More important than the indicators seems to be the meetings of the steering committees. Here project and sub-project leaders report developments and stakeholders discuss future developments and yearly action plans. Before new application periods, past experiences are discussed together with the introduction of new political goals from other regional strategies.

Other approaches are e.g. Møre og Romsdal which has used a broad range of informative resources in their monitoring and evaluations. Based on a mapping of the innovation system carried out by external consultants, they have had informal and formal consultative meetings with all relevant stakeholders from the innovation system, academia, public innovation support, and industry.

Part of the learning process is also the national learning arenas and training for VRI project management organised by RCN and the dialogues between the regional steering committees and the RCN programme office.

Many of the respondents mention appreciatively on-going evaluation processes and researchers providing input to their processes. In Vestfold the embedded researchers have supported with analysis of the region's clusters while in Agder they have made sectorial analyses and given broader strategic advice. The relationship has supported the Agder research environment to become one of Norway's leading centres in innovation studies. In Møre og Romsdal, the embedded researchers stimulated the inclusion of furniture and public sector innovation as new priority areas. In Nordland the embedded researchers inspired Nordland to initiate the RIS3 processes.

It seems like the formal evaluation and reporting systems are less influential. The respondents emphasise the reporting to steering committees and the continuous dialogue between project leaders, competence brokers, cluster managers and other stakeholders as having the greatest effect on learning and further development and priority setting. Also dialogue tools can be influential in this sense and several regions point to the increasing focus on cross clustering stimulating also learning and experience sharing between the priority areas.

The RCN had wanted to see more early analyses, better prepared background documents with more and better information as a foundation for decisions; but acknowledges that VRI funding is limited. Regions cannot design too complex and costly monitoring and evaluation processes but must balance the costs.

4 Concluding discussions on VRI and RIS3

The VRI programme is not entirely comparable to S3. It existed before S3 was conceptualised, has had less funding[6] and has encompassed fewer policy intervention areas than envisaged within a RIS3. The idea in S3 to stimulate the growth of agglomerations to enhance spill-over effects and to develop new lead markets does not seem to be articulated equally strongly in VRI. In VRI the ambition is to enhance cooperation on innovation among regional actors, to promote research-based innovation and generate knowledge about innovation processes in the regions. Still there are quite a few similarities and VRI has generated experiences which give insight to the development and continuous priority setting processes of S3.

4.1 Overarching coordinating level

Like in RIS3 VRI work is carried out on an overarching strategy level and through activities within the priority areas. The dynamics, learning and trust within and between these levels are vital for the continuous priority setting process. The selection process at overall level is about selecting which races to bet on. The process is focusing on future potential areas finding a balance between different interests, taking into account those that are less strong in mobilising own interest. The more successful regional VRI programmes are those that have seen beyond the immediate needs of the participants of the steering committees and focused on the region's needs and potential and where they have managed good coordination with other regional development programmes and activities.

4.2 Institutionalisation of process

The process has been led by a strategic steering group of broad stakeholder representation overseeing the learning processes and key in the continuous priority setting. Managing size and manageable discussion have different solutions. The ambition has been to get legitimacy by including all the main stakeholders from the regional innovation system, including regionally influential actors that can invest in an area and ensure coordination, while at the same time maintaining a size which is operative.

Dynamic dialogues between the steering committee and other actors in VRI have the potential to bridge the gap between strategic management and activities in the priority areas. This institutionalisation of dialogue has stimulated trust, supported linkages beneficial to innovation and has created tighter regional processes with actors better empowered to work for regional innovation.

4.3 Priority selection and entrepreneurial process of discovery

Most regions began VRI with areas of strength that had been identified in other regional development strategies, or related their priorities to the regional clusters. Then every three years regions have modified their priority portfolio and the activities within the priority areas and the regional stakeholders together have been able to modify the priority portfolio, by dropping priorities, introducing new ones or refining existing ones in a more EDP manner. This adaptability and flexibility, based on various rationales, is a prerequisite also for RIS3 to work. In parallel, the regions have worked long term supporting the build-up of new areas and refining the activity within them. Success factors have been to manage vested interests to avoid getting locked into old structures and evaluate past efforts and realign the activities. A current tendency is to start looking at cross clustering in the regions and also opening up to newer and emerging activities, losing the vertical focus of priority areas. This is something RIS3 could learn from: to have a number of vertical areas, with longer term strategic roadmap efforts, supplemented with horizontal activities supporting individual projects with innovative potential, using well-functioning tools.

Some of the analytical background studies carried out tend to point to regional areas of strength and interest matching the ones that have already been identified more intuitively. However, new priority areas have been discovered through analytical reports and later developed into clusters, and background analyses bring transparency to the discussion around the potential for different investment areas. Nevertheless, Norwegian experience shows that in addition to an observable opportunity you need willing partners to work with it.

4.4 Priority area management and policy mix

Project leaders, priority area leaders and competence brokers have in VRI regions perceived as being successful all played important roles as boundary spanners in the regional innovation support system. The identified priority areas have been developed through strategic approaches or by using successful VRI tools, often linked to already established clusters. It is within the priority areas that the closest and broadest engagement with industry takes place.

Most regions have to some extent analysed the different priority areas, and then selected which tools to use for each area based on maturity and needs of the field. But there are ones who emphasise more the development of the particular priority areas and work more strategically in depth developing these. They coordinate the activities with other actors, in particular cluster organisations. These regions have been keener on having dedicated priority area leaders managing the activities within their respective priority areas. Other regions place successful VRI tools at the centre to initiate projects, also beyond more narrowly defined priority areas and as a complement to other tools in the system. They have priority areas of strength but are also open to use the tools horizontally in any kind of economic area. Some regions mix the approaches.

4.5 Monitoring and evaluation

There are different valuable sources for monitoring and evaluation apart from a good and adequate system of indicators reflecting roadmaps with coherent intervention logic. Standardised indicators are reported as having less impact for learning and as feedback for the continuous priority setting process in VRI. Lacking such a system, VRI has established learning mechanisms based on reporting mechanisms and embedded researchers. A positive learning experience is the renewal of the programme through the three years cycles, where the participants evaluate past efforts and realign the activities. This organic approach of interaction between steering committee, project leaders, priority area leaders and other boundary spanners provide, as long as the relations are based on trust, a continuous feedback to the development of the project that is cost effective, in proportion to available funds, and flexible.

4.6 Concluding remarks

Institutionalised governance with sound and deep stakeholder engagement, trust, open and dynamic dialogue, learning, coordination of funding, activities and implementation and flexibility to make necessary changes seem to have been crucial factors for continuous priority setting in VRI. These elements are to various degrees advocated also in the RIS3 Guide and in the communication from the European Commission. The governance aspect of regional innovation should not be underestimated and creates a great challenge and expectations for change on the management of regional processes in order to keep alive a continuous priority setting process and an overall entrepreneurial approach to regional research and innovation.

Notes

1 A RIS3 will also have horizontal policies where the region carries out policy interventions regardless of economic activity areas.
2 What is critical mass and what the size of an agglomeration might be in order to have an impact and to be beneficial differ from region to region and as well between sectors.
3 www.forskningsradet.no/vri.
4 www.regionaleforskningsfond.no.
5 www.innovasjonnorge.no.
6 Yearly national budget has been approximately 60m NOK/7m Euro. Of the total budget around 50 per cent is national funds, 25 per cent regional and the rest comes from company funds. The actual company contributions are higher and go beyond what is being administered through the overall VRI budget.

References

Barca, F. (2009), *An Agenda for a Reformed Cohesion Policy: A Place-based Approach to Meeting European Union Challenges and Expectations.* Independent report prepared at the request of Danuta Hübner, Commissioner for Regional Policy.

Beise, M. (2001), *Lead Markets: Country-Specific Success Factors of the Global Diffusion of Innovations.* Heidelberg: Physica-Verlag.

Beise, M. (2004), Lead Markets: Country-Specific Success Factors of the Global Diffusion of Innovations, *Research Policy*, 33(6–7), 997–1018.

Bennett, N., Wise, C., Woods, P. A. and Harvey, J. A. (2003), *Distributed Leadership.* Nottingham: National College of School Leadership.

Boschma, R. and Gianelle, C. (2014), Regional Branching and Smart Specialisation Policy, *S3 Policy Brief* 06/2014. Publications Office of the European Union.

Cooke, P. (2002), *Knowledge Economies: Clusters, Learning and Cooperative Advantage*. London: Routledge.

Elzen, B., Geels, F. W. and Green, K. (2004), *System Innovation and the Transition to Sustainability: Theory, Evidence and Policy*. London: Edward Elgar.

European Commission (2010a), *Europe 2020 Flagship Initiative Innovation Union*. SEC (2010) 1161, COM (2010) 546.

European Commission (2010b), *Regional Policy Contributing to Smart Growth in Europe*. SEC (2010) 1183 and Annex IV of the general SF draft regulation, COM (2011) 615.

European Commission (2012), *Guide to Research and Innovation Strategies for Smart Specialisation (RIS3)*. Brussels: CEC.

Foray, D. (2009), Understanding Smart Specialisation, in Pontikakis, D., Kyriakou, D. and van Bavel, R. (eds), *The Question of R&D Specialisation: Perspectives and Policy Implications*. JRC-IPTS, European Commission.

Foray, D. (2014), *Smart Specialisation: Opportunities and Challenges for Regional Innovation Policy*. London: Routledge.

Foray, D. and Goenaga, X. (2013), The Goals of Smart Specialisation, *S3 Policy Brief 01/2013*, Publications Office of the European Union.

Foray, D. and van Ark, B. (2007), Smart Specialisation in a Truly Integrated Research Area is the Key to Attracting More R&D to Europe. *Knowledge Economists Policy Brief No 1*. Brussels: European Commission.

Foray, D., David, P. and Hall, B. H. (2009), Smart Specialisation: The Concept. *Knowledge Economists Policy Brief No. 9*. Brussels: European Commission.

Foray, D., David, P. and Hall, B. H. (2011), Smart Specialisation: From Academic Idea to Political Instrument, the Surprising Career of a Concept and the Difficulties Involved in its Implementation, *MTEI Working Paper n. 2011.001*. Lausanne: École Polytechnique Fédérale de Lausanne.

Furre, H., Aase, M., Horrigmo, J., Flatnes, A., Borgar Hansen, T. Brastad, B. and Moodysson, J. (2012), *Alle skal med!? Midtveisevaluering av programmet Virkemidler for Regional FoU og Innovasjon (VRI)*. Oxford Research.

Gianelle, C. and Kleibrink, A. (2015), Monitoring Mechanisms for Smart Specialisation Strategies, *S3 Policy Brief 13/2015*. Publications Office of the European Union.

Hughes, A. (2012), Choosing Races and Placing Bets: UK National Innovation Policy and the Globalisation of Innovation Systems, in Greenaway, D. (ed.) *The UK in a Global World: How Can the UK Focus on Steps in Global Value Chains that Really Add Value?* BIS, CEPR and ESRC.

Johnstad, T., Klausen, J. E. and Mønnesland, J. (2003), *Globalisering, regionalisering og distriktspolitikk. Makt- og demokratiutredningens rapportserie*. Rapport 76.

Kostoff, R. N. and Schaller, R. R. (2001), Science and Technology Roadmaps. *IEEE Transactions on Engineering Management*, 48(2), 132–143. www.scienceofsciencepolicy.net/sites/default/files/attachments/22.pdf.

Lindblom, C. E. (1959), The Science of 'Muddling Through'. *Public Administration Review*, 19(2): 79–88.

Lindgren, G. and Forsberg, G. (2010), *Nätverk och skuggstrukturer i regionalpolitiken*. Karlstad University Press.

Lundvall, B-Å. (ed.) (1992), *National Systems of Innovation: Towards a Theory of Innovation and Interactive Learning*. London: Pinter Publishers.

Martin, B. (1995), Foresight in Science and Technology. *Technology Analysis & Strategic Management*, 7(2): 139–168.

McCann, P. and Ortega-Argilés, R. (2011), Smart Specialisation, Regional Growth and Applications to EU Cohesion Policy, Faculty of Spatial Sciences, *Economic Geography Working Paper*. Groningen: University of Groningen.

McCann, P. and Ortega-Argilés, R. (2014), The Role of the Smart Specialisation Agenda in a Reformed EU Cohesion Policy. *Italian Journal of Regional Science*, 13(1): 15–32.

Metcalfe, J. S. and Georghiou, L. (1998), Equilibrium and Evolutionary Foundations of Technology Policy, *STI Review*, No. 2.

Midtkandal, I. and Sörvik, J. (2012), What is Smart Specialisation? *Nordregio News*, No. 5.

Nauwelaers, C., Periáñez-Forte, I. and Midtkandal, I. (2014). RIS3 Implementation and Policy Mixes, *S3 Policy Brief 07/2014*, Publications Office of the European Union.

Nelson, R. R. and Winter, S. G. (1982), *An Evolutionary Theory of Economic Change*. Cambridge, MA; London: Belknap Press.

Olson, M. (1965/1971), *The Logic of Collective Action: Public Goods and the Theory of Groups*. Cambridge, MA: Harvard University Press.

Pagels-Fick, G. (2010), *Setting Priorities in Public Research Financing: Context and Synthesis of reports from China, the EU, Japan and the US*. VINNOVA Analysis VA 2010:08.

Rodrik, D. (2004), *Industrial Policy for the Twenty-First Century*, John F. Kennedy School of Government Working paper No. rwp04-047. Cambridge, MA: Harvard University.

Scherden, W. A. (1998), *The Fortune Sellers: The Big Business of Buying and Selling Predictions*. New York: John Wiley & Sons.

Simon, H. A. (1991), Bounded rationality and organizational learning. *Organization Science*, 2(1): 125–134.

Sotarauta, M. (2009), Power and Influence Tactics in the Promotion of Regional Development: An Empirical Analysis of the Work of Finnish Regional Development Officers. *Geoforum*, 40(5): 895–905.

Sotarauta, M. and Bruun, H. (eds) (2002), Nordic Perspectives on Process-Based Regional Development Policy. *Nordregio report* 2002(3). Stockholm.

Sörvik, J. (2010), *On the Effects of Institutional Arrangements for Innovation in Clusters: A Comparative Case Study of Sugar Clusters in São Paulo, the North East of Brazil and Cuba*, Lund Studies in Research Policy 2, Lund University, Sweden.

Sörvik, J. and Kleibrink, A. (2015), Mapping Innovation Priorities and Specialisation Patterns in Europe, *S3 Working Paper 08/2015*. Publications Office of the European Union.

VRI (2007), *VRI programme plan.* Research Council of Norway.

VRI Agder (2013), *Prosjektbeskrivelse* 2014–2017.

VRI Møre og Romsdal (2013), *Prosjektbeskrivelse* 2014–2017.

VRI Nordland (2013), *Prosjektbeskrivelse* 2014–2017.

VRI Nordland (2014), *Resultatrapport* 2011–2013.

VRI Trøndelag (2013), *Prosjektbeskrivelse* 2014–2017.

VRI Vestfold (2013), *Prosjektbeskrivelse* 2014–2017.

APPENDIX: Interviews

Botnmark, Anne Kari, VRI project leader Vestfold, University Colleges Buskerud og Vestfold, telephone interview 30th October, 2015.

Gjærum, Anja, Research Council of Norway, project coordinator VRI, informal talks March 2015 and interview 30th September, 2015.

Herse, Øyvind , VRI project leader Møre og Romsdal, telephone interview 6th October, 2015.

Kristensen, Karin VRI project leader Nordland, Nordland Fylkeskommun, telephone interview 16th October, 2015.

Lorentzen, Philip, Research Council of Norway. Special adviser VRI, informal talks in March 2015 and interview by videoconference 17th June, 2015.

Skogvold, Øyvind, VRI project leader, Trøndelag Forskning og Utvikling, interview, 1st November, 2015.

Strickert, Sissel, VRI project leader Agder, Agder Forskning, telephone interview 22nd October, 2015.

Uppstad, Hilde, VRI project leader Rogaland, Rogaland Fylkeskommun, interview, 1st October, 2015.

11 Smart specialisation entering the Finnish territory

Marja Nissinen

1 Introduction

In Finland, Smart Specialisation entered a saturated soil where regional planning was deeply rooted. Active regional development policies have been pursued since the 1950s; the present format dates back to the legislative reform of 1994 when programme-based regional development was started. The adoption of Smart Specialisation (S3) as an ex ante conditionality occurred at a point in time when the regular strategy processes were reaching their final stages or had been just finalised in regions. The perplexing newcomer raised the question whether one should treat S3 as integral part of the existing planning system, or whether one should launch a parallel procedure additionally. Regions opted for different solutions: a) some regions embedded S3 in the regional development plans prescribed by Finnish law; b) others prepared a separate Smart S3 document.

This initial collision of European and national strategy processes makes the actual realisation of S3 in Finland quite interesting. The existence of regional strategies and regional innovation policies is an indisputable fact, but do those regional approaches meet the requirement of S3? A critical factor in such assessment is the materialisation of the entrepreneurial discovery process (EDP). On one hand, EDP lies at the heart of the S3 approach, distinguishing it from traditional top-down industrial and innovation policies. On the other hand, the practical implementation of EDP is an intricate experiment everywhere. Therefore, this article is appraising the uptake of S3 by focusing on evidence on EDP in Finland.

At the end of the day, one must contrast a normative policy ideal with empirical reality while investigating the correspondence between field actors' practices and the academic–bureaucratic policy notion. The following questions emerge in the Finnish context:

- How did regions manage to comply with the new policy guidelines? Did the European Commission's message reach the regions? Were the tenets of S3 understood correctly and implemented properly?
- To what extent is the normative standpoint of EDP compatible with real-life experience? Does the blueprint correspond to the real world? Or does it occur that ambitions and actualities became disjointed?

- What are the enabling *versus* impeding factors of an EDP in practice? Where are its bottlenecks? What is the secret of success?
- What kind of context-specific factors can be intervening? What is their role and impact?

This case study continues from the point where Europe-wide surveys or statistical macro analyses stop since it aims to expose the particularities of policy design and implementation by opening the black box of a regional innovation environment. Case studies typically combine diverse analytical techniques and sources of evidence. In this case, too, evidence collection relied on a multi-methodological approach that incorporated various types of materials, ranging from open-ended expert interviews to participant observation and document review.

- The single most important source was a series of 27 interviews with 31 people that were carried out in three waves. Face-to-face interviews took place in August 2014 in Finland. Telephone or Skype interviews with Finnish interviewees were conducted in May 2015. Finally, three key persons of the European Commission's Smart Specialisation Platform were interviewed in July and November 2015. Each interview lasted for 50 to 120 minutes, on average about one and a half hours. The reliance on broad open-ended questions and conversation-like style followed from the wish to expose patterns and opinions that are neither derived from theoretical premises nor forced by the interviewer.
- Participant observation was facilitated by the diverse roles of the author who has worked both as a regional stakeholder and an EC employee. The time span covers the years 2009 to 2015.
- Oral evidence was complemented by respective documents, such as regional strategies, project reports, S3 guides and web information.

As Smart Specialisation rests on a bottom-up approach, this paper wants to live up to this principle. The leitmotif is to give a voice to rank-and-file field actors, which are all too often neglected in surveys and interviews. Instead of being limited to the official views of S3 process owners, these interviews encompassed all relevant stakeholder groups involved in EDP. Special attention was paid to ordinary grassroots agents who should be engaged in EDP either as targeted participants (e.g. companies, enterprise associations and universities) or as hands-on organisers. Many of the interviewees work in business support, project or innovation services related to regional development, having an immediate interface with local firms.[1]

Qualitative data was collected from eight NUTS-3 regions with different profiles and geographical locations all over the country. One of the regions was scrutinised more in-depth so that it served as a minor case of its own within the major case study. Moreover, anecdotal evidence and individual random examples were inserted from a few additional regions. Hence, the overall scope of the study covered about half of the Finnish regions. Finland comprises 19 NUTS-3 regions called *maakunta* in Finnish. As Finland numbers some 5.4 million inhabitants, the population size of Finnish regions is thus small.

Accordingly, the circles of 'the usual suspects' are very compact in many regions. The last mentioned fact is the reason why empirical findings are made anonymous by mixing together observations from several regions so that they cannot be connected with any specific place. Findings are grouped and classified by theme, not by region. The reader will not find a narrative that would be based on evidence from a single interviewee. As the ethical rationale is to protect confidential sources, neither the names of the interviewees nor their regions are published.

2 Setting the scene

2.1 Regional planning system by law

In Finland, regional development is intersectoral in nature. The responsibility for regional development rests with the state, municipalities and Regional Councils. Regional Councils are statutory joint municipal authorities maintained by the given region's group of municipalities. They operate as regional development and planning authorities according to the principles of local self-government. Regional planning comprises a Regional Development Plan, Regional Strategic Programme and Regional Land Use Plan.

- The Regional Development Plan is a forward-looking vision that outlines the desired long-term development for all sectors in the region (20 to 30 years) but also indicates the means to achieve the agreed goals. It is implemented through a Regional Strategic Programme and a Regional Land Use Plan.
- The Regional Strategic Programme is a medium-term programme prepared every four years by each Regional Council. It determines regional development targets, key projects and measures, and a financing plan for the given programming period. It acts as a coordinating umbrella that covers all the programmes implemented in the region.
- The Regional Land Use Plan creates the potential for regional land use and sets guidelines for achieving the desired development in the region in the long run (10 to 20 years). It steers systematic community development in municipalities.[2]

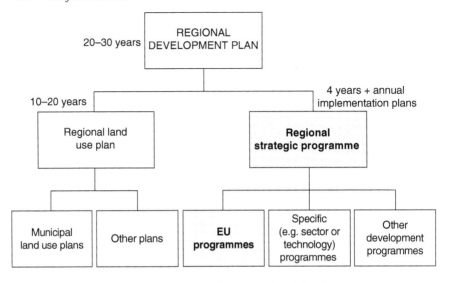

Figure 11.1 Decentralised regional planning system in Finland

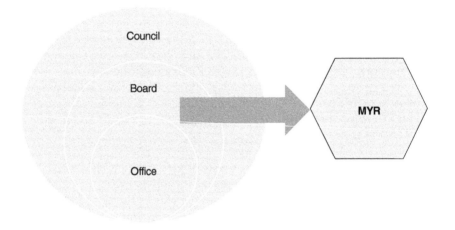

Figure 11.2 Organisation of regional administration in Finland

As for the organisation of Regional Councils, their decision-making and executive bodies – namely the Council and the Board – consist of elected politicians nominated by the member municipalities for a mandate of four years. The Council is the highest decision making body which represents the political will of the region. It elects the Board among its members to take care of executive tasks and interest advocacy. The Office, led by the Regional Mayor, assists the Board, for instance, in programme preparation and administration. The Office employs civil servants.

Regional Cooperation Working Group (Finnish abbreviation MYR) is a discussion forum which brings together various stakeholders on an equal basis. It is a statutory body nominated by the Board. MYR approves the annual Implementation Plan of the Regional Strategic Programme which determines the allocation of both the EU and national financing among the funding authorities. It discusses the main projects and initiatives of a region to ensure the coordination of different funds and regional measures. However, MYR is not the sole channel to engage stakeholders in regional planning. Regional Councils may likewise use other non-statutory networks, working groups or collaboration platforms as their task forces on a case by case basis.[3] On their web sites, Regional Councils stress the values of inclusiveness and a wide citizen perspective to facilitate an interactive, participatory strategy process. A quote from the portal of the Regional Council of Oulu summarises the message aptly:

> An essential part of all the regional planning is an open, transparent and intersectoral participation of different regional actors and decision makers. Regional Council's intension is to create a continuous, iterative strategic decision process that enables immediate functioning and step by step reassessment of strategies.[4]

2.2 Examples of implementation as described by Regional Councils

The preparation of regional strategies is an iterative process which consists of the alteration of collective drafting and circulation of the draft document for comments. The strategic focus is sharpening from round to round. Statistical background analysis and scenario work (foresight) lay its foundations while various steps are backed by surveys, consultations, hearings and workshops. The entire strategy process takes approximately a year (from ten to fourteen months). Two strategy processes are illustrated as *random* examples below, namely those of Lapland and Kanta-Häme. Both strategies include embedded S3 approaches.

Häme Programme is a combined document containing both the long-term Regional Development Plan and the medium-term Regional Strategic Programme. Its underpinning analyses were conducted in joint cooperation with two neighbouring regions, namely Päijät-Häme (east of Kanta-Häme) and Uusimaa (south of Kanta-Häme). In administrative terms, the three regions constitute the interregional collaboration area of South Finland; in popular terms, they constitute the extended metropolitan area of Greater Helsinki.

A major output of the strategic cooperation between Kanta-Häme, Päijät-Häme and Uusimaa was a common future vision for the greater metropolitan area. This interregional foresight exercise preceded the strategy preparation by individual regions, taking place in August to November 2012. The process and its respective report were titled *Wings and Roots*. The three regions recognised

Table 11.1 Process of preparing a regional strategy in Lapland, 2013–14[5]

Timeline	Activity	Content
26 March 2013	Foresight seminar • Webropol survey	• Analysis of the business environment • Assessment of the old strategies • Scenarios based on global phenomena and weak signals
21 May 2013	Council seminar • Webropol survey	As above
Evaluation and preparatory steps		
23 September 2013–1 October 2013	Survey	Initial guidelines
3 October 2013	Workshop	• An early draft • Scenario themes (10 phenomena)
11–13 November	Strategy camp	Narrowing down the scenarios 11 November from ten to six 12 November from six to four 13 November concretisation of four phenomena
December 2013	• Outline for a strategic framework • Strengths, weaknesses, opportunities, and threats (SWOT) • Analysis of the business environment	
16 December 2013	Workshop	• Specification of the content • Formulation of the intent
December 2013–February 2014	• Hearings of municipalities (meetings), and collection of feedback from citizens (www.lappi.fi, Webropol, fb) • Public announcement ⇒ draft available both on the web site and on the notice board 17 December 2013–17 January 2014, possibility to get a hardcopy • Feedback from January to May 2014 • A concise visual presentation of the strategy in February	
February 2014	• Preparation of impact and environmental assessment – Available both on the web site and on the notice board	
March–April 2014	• Consultations of stakeholders	
April–May 2014	• Writing of the strategy	
20 May 2014	Council	• Discussion • Approval • Communication

Table 11.2 How *Häme Programme* was prepared: important dates in 2013[6]

Timeline	Step
4 February	Board decision to launch plan/programme preparation
13 February	Foresight forum
March–April	Interim evaluation of the present programme
4 March	MYR, referral debate
15 April	Board, referral debate
14 May	Youth Council workshop, spearheads of the region
27 May	Council meeting
28 May	HämePro workshop, spearheads of the region
3 June	MYR, hearing
June	Negotiations with sub-regions 1
10–11 August	Fair *Elomessut*, Häme Arena (major public/civic events)
19 August	Board, spearheads and priorities
August	Negotiations with sub-regions 2
9 September	Board's working seminar, spearheads and priorities of the programme
9 September	MYR, hearing
16 September	Board, proceedings on the draft programme
23 September–25 October	Draft programme available and accessible to the public
24 October	HämePro workshop, Häme way of working
28 October	MYR, finalisation
11 November	Board, a programme proposal to be submitted to the Council
25 November	Council, handling of Häme Programme

common development themes, worked on views of common possibilities and paved the path for a deeper cooperation. To cite an example, they produced jointly a scenario analysis of future training needs in the entire collaboration area. The results of *Wings and Roots* were processed into a strategic training package for civil servants and local elected officials in Uusimaa region.

The three regions hired a consulting company to carry out the *Wings and Roots* project. The consultants were responsible for the scenario work, the blog of the project, and finally the report writing. They designed and implemented a series of six large workshops.[7]

One of the methods used by the consultants was replicated in a workshop with the Youth Council of Häme. It was based on a card deck. There was a pack of picture cards which displayed different kinds of images, photos and symbols that were unrelated to the given region. The workshop participants, who were divided into small groups, browsed the card decks to search out pictures demonstrating the future of their region. After selecting a picture, they had to explain what it means, what kind of future it symbolises and why they picked it up. Then the selected pictures were grouped thematically under broader headings by the groups. The second task for the groups was to point out a few priorities among them. The third round was to discuss what kinds of activities might lay behind the selected pictures or what kind of future they represent.

Last but not least, let us highlight a peculiar participatory exercise. Two infant schools arranged a future day on the initiative of the Regional Council. Six-year-old children were requested to draw what their region Häme will look like when they are adults. The drawings revealed that children think about housing, work and leisure time just like adults. The children's drawings were used as illustration on *Häme Programme*.

As far as *Häme Programme* is concerned, the Regional Council of Häme accentuated the engagement of citizens and stakeholders. From this point of view, the Council's active presence in big public events, like the fair *Elomessut* and the so-called *Mafia Cruise* (an annual happening of an enterprise network with some 900 participants, hosted by the regional development company), can be cited as channels to access the public. On both occasions, the Regional Council of Häme had a stand where it lured people to participate in its survey which contributed to priority selection. Respondents were given a list of 30 priorities. Respectively, they received ten points to be shared between these priorities according to their own preference. They could either concentrate their points on a few priorities or distribute them evenly between a number of priorities. Both the fair *Elomessut* and the *Mafia Cruise* generated about 300 replies each. All the municipal councils filled in the same questionnaire, which resulted in 70 to 80 responses. The raw data generated by the surveys were visualised by bar charts.

The Regional Council used HämePro network as a task force in preparing *Häme Programme*. The role of HämePro network was more significant than MYR's. It gathered together various development organisations and interest groups of the region:

- Regional Council of Häme;
- Centre for Economic Development, Transport and the Environment (ELY Centres)[8] of Häme and Uusimaa;
- Linnan Kehitys Ltd (regional development company), Forssa (Sub-) Region Development Centre Ltd, YritysVoimala (development company owned by four municipalities), TechVilla (technology centre), RTOY (incubator);

- HAMK University of Applied Sciences, Tavastia Education Consortium, Forssa Vocational Institute, Hyria Vocational College;
- Units of the University of Helsinki in Häme: Lammi Biological Station, the University of Helsinki Centre for Continuing Education;
- Natural Resources Institute Finland;
- Häme Chamber of Commerce, Riihimäki-Hyvinkää Chamber of Commerce, Association of Häme Entreprises;
- Union of Agricultural Producers and Forest Owners, ProAgria – Rural Advisory Services.[9]

The *Häme Programme* and all related documents can be found on the portal of the Regional Council of Häme. In addition to reading them, one can watch a video which displays the core elements of *Häme Programme*. The Chair of the Council, the Chair of the Board, the Regional Mayor and the Development Director (Vice-Mayor) present it audio-visually.

3 An alternative angle to regional strategy processes[10]

3.1 Stakeholder reflections

The opinions and subjective perceptions of individual actors diversify our picture of the strategy process. A Regional Council may be pleased with its accomplishment because regional actors frequently refer to its strategy when they justify their activities, which the Council considers a sign of success. At the same time, critical tones are voiced in the field.

Regional Councils tend to have weak links to the business sector and are sometimes even shunned by companies. Every now and then, one hears comments from external observers that the strategy process did not really involve companies, no matter what the documents or the representatives of the Regional Council claim. The direct engagement of individual firms forms a common bottleneck even when other stakeholders are joining the process. Public bodies still cooperate primarily with other public bodies. Company involvement mainly takes place through intermediaries, like business associations and development companies. As it is indeed hard to attract companies, Regional Councils easily turn to the few responsive firms every time. A commentator describes the way things are in her region:

> Whenever the Regional Council tries to mobilise firms, it always proves very difficult even though the topics like land use, planning of transports and logistics should be relevant for companies. These issues should interest them but they don't. Why not? The use of time is a factor but also the legacy of tradition. Companies remember the past when the Regional Council did not want to work with companies but neglected them. Therefore, the Regional Council cannot rally them with the exception of few. The Regional Council is considered to be an extremely bureaucratic public sector bastion.

A widespread belief is that in reality, the strategy is created by a small insider group of the 'usual suspects'. In smaller regions, the same 'talking heads' sit in each committee and task force. The roles are highly personalised: an informed citizen can list the names of the regions' key figures without difficulty while the VIPs hold their positions for decades. As an interviewee puts it succinctly: 'They are the ones whom everyone greets in the street.'

Many firms and citizens mistrust their own abilities to influence the decision-making. Some have previously gained negative experiences which convince them that it makes no difference what they say. Even when public hearings are organised and all people can articulate their grievances openly, the average citizen may conclude in the end that strongly critical or deviant, non-conformist interventions are 'sanitised' away from the final versions. Hence, involvement appears a non-serious theatrical exercise to them.

Another shortage is the exclusion of civil society organisations that address non-economic matters. Respectively, sectors and topics that are unrelated to the regions' established strongholds receive relatively little attention. The opinion leaders focus on traditional sectors that are considered to be central for job creation, money flows and power – at least in terms of conventional wisdom. Healthcare, wellbeing, culture and creative industries are less interesting to the 'usual suspect' than, say, metal industry. A similar bias concerns start-ups and micro firms especially if they come from maverick fields.

The share of active networkers among the stakeholders is limited. When a university of applied sciences investigated stakeholder networks, the results showed that contacts were concentrated in the hands of a few activists who were the only actors with extensive networks. The silent majority remains more or less passive. Furthermore, even advanced, export-oriented companies sometimes keep a low profile in their regions so that developing organisations hardly know about their existence.

A further aspect concerns the guiding influence of a regional strategy: its immediate impact on enterprises is limited, which reduces company interest in it. It only facilitates an overall framework for business development. Moreover, Regional Development Plans are regarded as vague declarations of intent without any concrete substance. Views of the private sector are filtered through the interpretation of civil servants. When the strategies are submitted to the political decision-makers, edges are ironed out at the end. One returns to a safe, familiar mode that irritates no one. It means watching a rear-window: strengths of the region will be notified to continue their further development. Radical turnouts appear impossible. An interviewee summarises the typical character of a Regional Plan as follows:

> Quite a lot of tradition, a little bit new, plenty of wishful thinking. Statistical background analyses are rigorous but when one moves to the foresight part, future visions get highflying, utopian and unrealistic. They seem to stem from [someone's] eloquent pen rather than from a foresight method.

MYR is regarded as a mere rubber stamp which gives its blessing to ready proposals put forth by civil servants. The members of a MYR have neither time, motivation nor expertise to contribute to programming and strategy work. Discussions within MYR have hardly any influence: processes follow their own track while civil servants are in control. Funding authorities are not willing to open their decision-making process.

From the perspective of the man in the street, Regional Councils are invisible and void. Most ordinary people have never heard of them. Their usefulness is also questioned in political debates from time to time. The upcoming social welfare and healthcare reform, of which the government of Finland reached an accord in early November 2015, should address some of these concerns.

3.2 Bottlenecks of Entrepreneurial Discovery Process

Stakeholders are being involved undeniably, but do Finnish strategy processes meet the criteria of an EDP? The question of inclusiveness can be approached from four angles at least: 1) Do Regional Councils reach a sufficient number of individual enterprises? 2) Is the contribution of enterprises (and other stakeholders) to setting the priorities adequate? 3) Is the process open, established, inventive and transformative enough? 4) Does the process avoid or eliminate the traditional fallacies? EDP is neither 'coffee for all' nor 'picking winners from above'. It also means breaking away from established lobbies and rent-seekers. Or do we again witness the 'usual suspects' around the table?

3.2.1 Enough enterprises?

Discussions with Regional Councils revealed that at least some of them acknowledge and admit shortages in their processes vis-à-vis entrepreneurial discovery. An interviewee referred to the distance between companies and his institution. A similar challenge was faced in Kanta-Häme. Although Kanta-Häme applied fresh, imaginative methods in its interaction with stakeholders and energetically tried to reach them through various fora, the accumulation of company feedback lagged behind the success rate with other types of agents. An outside observer confirmed that the efforts of the Regional Council of Häme were enterprising to catch the attention of enterprises.

At some stage, the Regional Council of Häme picked a sample of 12 to 15 small and medium sized enterprises (SMEs) from different branches and sent out an email enquiry to them. The sender counted on the power of personal relations since he chose firms in which he knew the CEO. He expected them to answer due to acquaintance. To his disappointment, the response rate remained low. He received only 2 to 3 decent, useful replies. Then he ran out of time which explains why he could not retrieve the replies in person. In hindsight, he concluded that he should have agreed on appointments and visited the companies to meet the entrepreneurs face-to-face.

3.2.2 Enough influence?

A good practice comes from the west coast where the Region of Satakunta composed a technology strategy five to six years ago. This region is a stronghold of export industry and thus outbound oriented. The preparation of the technology strategy was a separate process which was carried out independently of the Regional Development Plan/Programme. Although the Regional Council was in charge of leading the exercise, the chamber of commerce and enterprise associations played a key role. Consultation of the industry succeeded excellently according to the assessment of an interviewed stakeholder. In addition to the business community, the regions' higher education institutions took part to provide a scientific angle. Finpro's foresight know-how was also utilised during the work.

A working group was established for each major industry branch or technology area, such as automation, metal or forestry. Access to working groups was open to everyone; active persons found their way there without hindrance. While there were about ten working groups and each of them comprised five to ten participants, dozens of volunteers were engaged in the preparation of Satakunta's technology strategy. The broad base gave strength to the strategy process. The working groups drew up all the relevant issues. An iterative process lasted about half a year, consisting of a number of rounds that sharpened the focus step-by-step. The contributions of the working groups were compiled into a report which was jointly approved. Finally, it was admitted by the Board of the Regional Council.

In general, too, the permanent working groups or committees of enterprise associations and chambers of commerce are regular discussion fora where the business community takes a stand and expresses its opinion on current issues. The mentioned business organisations intervene actively and belong to significant influencers in regions. One should nevertheless keep in mind that they are lobbying organisations by nature and their staff are salaried employees.

3.2.3 Enough inclusion?

Especially in weaker regions, some persons working for development organisations may think that their industry base does enable a bottom-up process. In cases where most companies are small or micro-sized, their markets are local, they are not growth-oriented, they represent low tech or service sectors, and the educational level of entrepreneurs is low, it is hard to mobilise them. Such firms tend to be stuck in their daily routines instead of following trends in the outside world. Developers can become frustrated and discouraged by the lack of motivation shown by their reluctant customers. Developers may also doubt the entrepreneurial knowledge of the local companies. At the same time, if developers get too enthusiastic about the latest policy fashions or highflying technologies, such as key enabling technologies (KETs), a top-down approach is a risk.

A different rationale came up in the context of an Innovative Cities programme (INKA) application in one region. Although business representatives were kept informed and they were consulted to ensure their commitment, they were not invited to participate in the preparatory group that was responsible for hands-on strategy writing and negotiations with the Ministry. Because the strategy process 'dove' into the depths of sophisticated development activity, it was reasoned that the interest and patience of enterprises would not last out. Thorough consideration preceded this decision of exclusion which was not made light-heartedly. Moreover, it was argued that one knows in advance what companies think since each firm looks after its own vested interest or the profit of its sector.

A commentator expressed her concern about start-ups in emerging fields: are they taken seriously or are they being ridiculed if their business ideas deviate from the conventional mode? According to this observer, new business models evolve on the wasteland in the margin, at the outskirts of society. Only when those newcomers grow and reach enough volume, do they start becoming accepted by the establishment. The commentator continued that it might be better if these new start-ups are not embraced by the system too early because it could suffocate their fresh elements by forcing them into the old mould.

3.2.4 Enough consensus for the sake of the common good?

Even in regions where the formal process appears perfectly sound on the surface, some stakeholders may view it with scepticism. Different parties may describe the same occurrence in opposite ways. Truth is subjective. An illustrative example is the selection of an INKA priority when the Innovative Cities programme INKA replaced the Centre of Expertise Programme (Finnish abbreviation OSKE). The case under consideration shows how the re-prioritising for INKA led to a fierce power struggle between the interest groups supporting various OSKE clusters. In the face of the inevitable deselection, each interest group was naturally lobbying for its own field.

- *Winners' interpretation*: A person representing the winning side described the selection process as fair, inclusive and comprehensive in terms of its scope. According to him, all pertinent dimensions were taken into consideration in a balanced way. The process was felicitous, although the debates were intense, even heated, since the viewpoints were far away from one another.
- *Losers' interpretation*: The view of a losing party differs drastically from that of the winner's. According to the bitter accusations of the unsuccessful lobby, personal relations, jiggery-pokery behind the scenes, a battle over powers and dissemination of misinformation characterised the process. No open, free discussion was allowed despite the promises. By contrast, any counter-arguments were silenced by an influential clique

that favoured the competing cluster. In reality, a small closed group took the decisions. The disappointed critic concludes: 'A Triple Helix may drift into an impossible situation when personal reasons are killing the debate.'

Another kind of flop follows when a region fails to select among numerous priorities. Instead, it ends up having overly broad, all-encompassing priorities that enclose everything. Such a hybrid strategy simultaneously represents continuation of the old rather than industrial renewal. An observer comments upon the end result in his region: 'All that existed before was simply bunched together.' Nor is the interviewed observer aware of open consultation rounds or events to unfold RIS3 philosophy. According to him, the leadership of the region became defensive in relation to Smart Specialisation. The regional bosses regarded RIS3 as a typical futility of Brussels that is nothing but a nuisance. Things are good the way they are. In this case, the combination of indisposition and self-complacence may be perhaps explained by the region's economic history which offers an indisputable success story of the past regional development policies.

4 Lessons from 'proxy' exercises[11]

According to a few interviewees, part of the problem is that Regional Councils lack the tools and skills to approach enterprises. In this section, seasoned developers share their tips to attract business actors. Their experience stems from regional development projects that target enterprises and have parallels with EDP. Those projects can be treated as proxies.

4.1 Building contacts

Winning the trust of local companies is a long-run challenge. It is not enough if one shows your face once or twice a year in a meeting or a seminar. Long-term presence is a must which requires regular participation in apparently meaningless, unimportant events. Successful 'salesmen' of their cause are not only sociable and outgoing but also eager to take part in all kinds of activities. Local origin is an advantage because an indigenous native possesses inherent networks and understands people's mentality. Personal relations are important for contact-making and trust building.

An advisable option is to do the marketing of a project through a channel – i.e. a partner organisation – that companies trust and appreciate, such as a local business association. Moreover, cooperation with business actors helps formulate the invitation in appropriate language so that the target group understands all its words and finds the message appealing. It goes without saying that complex bureaucratic jargon and obscure, amorphous statements should be avoided; they do not only leave recipients cold but also annoy. The good old KISS formula works best: keep it short and simple. A project manager told me how an advisor re-wrote an invitation as follows: 'Do you want to make money? Juha (*a well-known person of high standing in local business circles*) will also be there. You should join us, too!'

The core issue is to find a persuasive argument why it makes sense to invest time and to pinpoint the benefits from participation. The primacy of convincing reasoning can never be stressed enough since all interviewees underscored it as a prime key to success. One must show in advance a tangible gain in utilitarian terms. Firms define the gain from their perspective, meaning that their business should profit from the offering in the short-run. Only a few growth enterprises are interested in future prospects. 'Nice to know' knowledge does not sell. The essentiality of a concrete focus implies that a possibility to contribute to regional development is not an appealing argument.

Sending invitations by email does not usually suffice to stimulate responses or registrations. One should hire staff to call or visit targeted companies. Through discussion, one can reach a common understanding of a mutual interest. Personal contact also enables the organiser to answer questions, which, in turn, provides useful information about misconceptions. Occasionally, developers organise special actions to encourage nudging and stimulate ideas or collaboration. Innovation competitions, followed by an innovation camp, can be cited as examples of such actions.

Some interviewees emphasise the importance of knowing one's target group to be able to select the right participants and ensure an optimal mixture of people. It is better to think ahead that a certain person should attend the envisaged workshop rather than send 1,000 invitations of which ten random attendants will be filtered. The deliberate selection of participants divides opinions. Its helpfulness probably depends on the objective of a workshop. According to a popular theory, the right participants are always those who happen to arrive. Some people believe that the most active players get selected automatically.

One should attract motivated, genuinely interested participants. If a person is forced to attend the workshop because the boss sent him/her there, the initial attitude is hardly propitious. An optimal composition may include students or other young people who often provide fresh and unprejudiced but viable solutions. According to one interviewee, young students used to bring up the best ideas in foresight workshops.

4.2 Event planning and implementation

Every successful event begins with careful planning and preparation:

1 The event should not last too long. A whole day workshop is critical; half a day is recommended. On the other hand, there should be enough time for team work. Hence, one should not set a task that is too heavy and time-consuming for the available time frame.

2   The scope of the event must be restricted in such a way that it is narrow, focused and practical enough. Too general, indefinite a topic or a broad perspective will frustrate both the participants and the instructor/moderator. Of course, the topic should appeal to the audience.

3   The choice of a moderator is of crucial importance. The moderator should appear sympathetic to the audience, instead of irritating the participants. He/she should be skilled, customer- or user-oriented and sensitive to case-specific needs. Instead of recycling the same standard package from workshop to workshop, he/she should tailor it according to the audience. Customisation becomes visible in the examples and the terminology he/she uses in concretising his/her methods.

Two illustrations exemplify the points made under bullets 2 and 3 above:

* Instead of developing visions of the countryside of future, one focuses on a certain production line, such as 'beef cattle in Häme in 2025', 'milk production in Häme in 2025' or 'a cowshed of tomorrow'.
* The moderator or the instructor should move on the same wavelength with the audience. For instance, an entrepreneur who is running a machine-building company and bears responsibility for the livelihood of his employees' families will not get excited about ecological argumentation how one can take a bike and buy eggs directly from a farmer. Naively simplistic examples are considered derogatory.

The array of various participatory methods is widely known and used in regional projects. Developers themselves usually possess many of those skills but outsourcing is equally common. Different foresight methods, encompassing both workshops and surveys, are frequently applied but also Delphi, peer review, network analysis and process management methods are used. Strengths, weaknesses, opportunities, and threats (SWOT) analysis and benchmarking are self-evidences to the extent that they are hardly counted as specific methods. Formal committee meetings usually rely on a free-form debate based on an agenda.

As far as the popularity of foresight is concerned, some regions have cooperated with the Finland Futures Research Centre (FFRC). This renowned institute enjoys a good international reputation as well. FFRC has either contributed to the development of a project methodology (e.g. Kanta-Häme) or to the revision of a strategic approach (e.g. Uusimaa). The challenge of inserting a foresight angle into an idea workshop is that the future is indeterminate by definition because one is talking about something that does not exist yet. Therefore, the framing of the task is particularly important because otherwise there is a risk that the discussion remains at a general level.

Acceptance of playful participatory methods polarises the audience. Some people like them, regarding them as relaxing fun that nurtures creativity and helps take a break from daily routines. Others, by contrast, condemn them as childish nonsense and a waste of time. Normally, just a few persons take an extreme position on the opposite poles whereas most people can be located in-between.

In any event, the moderator should get to the point straight and fast so that companies recognise the utility of being there. If they do not find participation useful, they will leave the workshop during the day or will not come again the next time. Even when they are motivated to attend to begin with, they will easily withdraw if the workshop does not correspond to their expectations. Business people are more impatient, demanding and critical than public sector employees because time is money for them. The value added must be substantial and instant. Public sector employees, by contrast, can use more time for these kinds of activities because public relations constitute part of their job description.

In terms of substance, public sector employees treat matters from a wider perspective than firms. The former think of the development of an entire industry whilst companies consider their own business. The level of knowledge varies from individual to individual, which makes it impossible to generalise categorically. Personal qualities are decisive both in the public and the private sector. In any branch, one can find CEOs of small companies that are keenly following global markets. However, the share of such growth-oriented companies is low. Micro-sized service companies in the social sector (e.g. private nursing homes) or subcontractors that operate in three municipalities maximum are not interested in the outside world. If the owner of an SME is not keeping up to date, nobody else in the firm is doing it either. Low education tends to restrict possibilities to monitor (international) trends but exceptional entrepreneurs manage to overcome this handicap. To repeat the point, much depends on the personality of an entrepreneur. Access to information is no obstacle nowadays; all depends on one's attitude. In general, trendy hype technologies, such as 3D printing, are known quite widely but deeper science-based knowledge is already more scarce.

Knowledge-sharing becomes a challenge as soon as one gets closer to business secrets. Firms have no problem talking about general matters but when real business opportunities, like promising product development ideas, come into the picture, company representatives get silent and cautious. The new generation of micro entrepreneurs from certain branches, like design and consulting, are an exception to this rule.

Experiences from product development workshops suggest that brainstorming exercises generate plenty of ideas but more than 90 per cent of them bring about nothing new. Less than 10 per cent count to valuable discoveries. When a group selects an idea for further refining at the next stage, it never picks up a radical innovation but a proposal that can be realised with existing machines or technologies. The most inventive discovery is rejected because it would require new production methods. The problem is where to take resources for a full turnaround. In other words, group decisions play it safe.

Last but not the least, the final challenge is to ensure continuation of the process under consideration. During the last session of a workshop, participants should agree who will take the responsibility for the next steps to bring forth their project. If nobody is explicitly in charge, the good intentions will dissolve and nothing will happen. This hazard is particularly high if the project or workshop management is outsourced to a consultant.

The responsible person should be committed, resilient, enthusiastic and optimistic. He/she should have strength to move on when things get tough; he/she should not be risk-averse but ready to stand up for what he/she believes; he/she should encourage others when they lose their faith. Although the person needs to be persistent, he/she should be simultaneously flexible and diplomatic. He/she should understand and accept the rules of the game in his/her region.

4.3 Analysis of impediments

The challenges described above lead us to question *why* it is so difficult to attract enterprises, especially SMEs. Many regional developers regard close involvement of enterprises in a long-lasting strategy process as unrealistic: the interests do not meet. The interviewees offer consensually very similar explanations irrespective of their background.

In small and micro enterprises, the lack of time is the obvious major hindrance. When the owner-CEO is engaged in the production process and business management his/her room for manoeuvre is limited. When the human resources are scarce, the labour input of a single person is crucial.

It is no longer easy to involve large companies either, although they often employ business development managers, corporate relations managers or the like who can participate in these types of exercises. However, when companies have rationalised their operations already for years by cutting down their staff in constant reorganisations, the remaining personnel is under a heavy work load. They must consider carefully how to use their time. Pressing obligations that are directly related to their job targets take precedence. What is the carrot for them to participate? People also change jobs more frequently than in the past. Finally, the quarterly financial narrows the line of thinking in companies. Generally taken, the time span of regional strategy work differs from that a firm.

Furthermore, globalisation has changed the ownership structure of large corporations. In the 'good-old days', the ownership of capital was personalised and patriotic so that the local factory was owned by a family and led by the patriarch of that family. These patriarchs were usually passionately dedicated to the development of their region, exploiting their political influence on its behalf. After selling the large companies to faceless international equity investors, decision-making power escaped from regions to far away headquarters in Europe. A director who comes from an international organisation has no interest in contributing to regional development. Local factory

managers lack the authority to decide anything. An interviewee put it succinctly: 'A snotty brat leads our industry from an office in Stockholm.'

The industrial structure of a region affects the prerequisites for an EDP
while its profile influences the quality of entrepreneurial knowledge and
growth orientation. In a region characterised by export industries, large companies and a high tech concentration, an average company is different from
a typical business player coming from a region dominated by low tech SMEs
and service providers focusing on the local market. According to Statistics
Finland, roughly half of the Finnish enterprises pursue innovation activities.
Viewed from a life cycle perspective, the development stage of the region's
company stock is another decisive factor. If companies have reached the
phase that they compete with established technologies in settled markets,
they are less open to the adoption of radically new technologies.

As firms are mainly interested in developing their own business, they see
less benefit in talking to the guys of a Regional Council than to a regional
technology advisor of Tekes (the Finnish Funding Agency for Innovation).
A dynamic, industrial growth region which also hosts a vivid start-up community has solved the dilemma of enterprise involvement by working on the
terms of companies. The Regional Council relies – side by side – on multiple
channels and forums of which some are formal, others informal. The clue is
to be present as a listener wherever firms are interacting. In the case of young
start-ups, virtual social media platforms play a central role, such as Mobile
Monday for example. In any case, building trust is the key issue. The logic of
this region's approach can be best highlighted by an anecdote:

> When OSKE was terminated, it turned out that most enterprises had
> never heard of it, although the cluster programme ran for 20 years and
> was considered to be a success story. Should the regional developers feel
> that they had failed miserably? No, on the contrary! They had accom-
> plished its job perfectly because it is the express task of public bodies
> to filter the policies in such a way that companies need not bother their
> heads with a bureaucratic programme jungle.

A similar argument was likewise suggested by a regional development man-
ager from another region: 'Firms do not care about regional strategies. We
who develop projects chew them over and try to offer them to firms.'

5 Conclusions and hypothetical explanation

The reported empirical findings from Finland expose the challenges in engaging enterprises. The exact judgement of the Finnish achievement depends on
the level of ambition as regards EDP. However, there is no unambiguous
yardstick against which to measure the Finnish performance since neither
the academic concept nor the policy guides define rigorous criteria for an
optimal EDP. Keeping this reservation in mind, one is nevertheless inclined

to conclude that all the results of this interview round are hardly compatible with a priori ideal models. There still seems to be room for operational improvement despite the propitious prerequisites like advanced institutional mechanisms, administrative tradition in stakeholder consultation and pronounced emphasis on a user-driven innovation policy that favours Quadruple Helix cooperation. Finland – as a relatively egalitarian, consensus-oriented society with corporatist traditions – is usually believed to do well in integrated collaboration.

Some interviewees say that formal organisational arrangements or inter-institutional agreements do not suffice alone to stimulate genuine interaction if endogenous enthusiasm is missing. Nor is an institutionalised process an automatic guarantee of inclusive engagement of various parties on an equal basis if cabinet politics and personalised power relations are concentrating the real decision-making in the hands of the few.

There are examples where a smallish region re-invents the wheel again and again by establishing new collaborative platforms one after another. Those attempts create nothing new because the same usual suspects gather together and continue working in an old-established way. The only effect is that the regional innovation system becomes a complex, incomprehensible jungle with overlapping activities. Rather than work with actual policy issues, the efforts will be wasted on continuous organisational reforms. An interviewee refers to 'the emperor's new clothes'. He equates it to the regular introduction of new titles for what one is doing although the real functions are not actually changing.

Even in a small, homogenous country like Finland, no fully uniform pattern exists countrywide. The selection of strategic priorities has resulted in a heterogeneous set of regional spearheads: sectors/sub-sectors, technology fields, all-sweeping frameworks, vision-based concepts, horizontal functions... The wide range of practices partly reflects terminological bewilderment and semantic misunderstanding that follows from imperfect adoption of the S3 approach in some regions. In a few cases, the deviant definition of a priority type may be a deliberate choice which complies with another underpinning policy paradigm. The majority of regions nevertheless seem to have internalised the meaning of a S3 'domain' in an exemplary fashion.

Instead of final answers or universal solutions, the empirical evidence from Finland pinpoints potential bottlenecks in the implementation of EDP. They are the blind spots that require more attention from the developers of the S3. Practical guidance, accompanied by social innovations, would be beneficial for the following aspects, among other things:

- *How* to mobilise a great array of ordinary enterprises to contribute to a long-standing strategy process?
- *How* to rally an industrial transformation? Even in a case of a flawless procedure, it appears unlikely that enterprises will opt for any profoundly radical renewal.

- *How* to abolish the influence of lobbies and rent-seekers? *How* to break the hegemony of the local 'kings' and their courts?

The right way of communicating with enterprises holds the key to successful stakeholder involvement. The reviewed approaches and tricks look familiar to anyone who has done any kind of promotion either in the private or the public sector. In other words, those ground rules are widely known among people; their reporting epitomises no originality. They belong to the category 'everyone knows' among the field actors under consideration. Should an architect of a policy concept like EDP also know how to approach enterprises for the sake of a realistic grand design?

Practical men are constantly complaining about the bureaucratic jargon of the public sector which they encounter, for instance, when companies apply for project funding or when farmers apply for agricultural subsidies. Universities and development organisations recruit project advisors whose foremost task is to 'translate' the EU or ELY language into Finnish. Rhetoric plays an astonishingly significant role in distracting companies from publically funded projects. According to an interviewee, the style of the administrative language – e.g. its adherence to special terminology and artificially abstracted upper level notions – is considered to be a means of exercising power.

As far as regional innovation policies are concerned, EDP brings the friction between development organisations and their unwilling clients into the lime-light. One way to portray this discrepancy is to treat it as a cleavage between 'innovators' (= the real actors, such as industrial researchers and technology developers) and 'innovation cheerleaders' (= consultants and public bodies promoting innovation). On many occasions, the two are driven by different motives and they do not even speak the same language with the result that those to be assisted may not appreciate the help to be offered. Such incompatibility is often treated as an absorption capacity problem, but it implies an assumption that the target group is the guilty party. The cleavage between 'innovators' and 'innovation cheerleaders' could be alternatively viewed as a collusion of practice-based bottom-up knowledge (partly tacit) and academic-bureaucratic top-down knowledge (related to the official policy line).

Notes

1 The Nomenclature of Territorial Units for Statistics or Nomenclature of Units for Territorial Statistics (NUTS for French Nomenclature des unités territoriales statistiques) is a geocode standard for referencing the subdivisions of countries for statistical purposes. The standard is developed and regulated by the European Union, and thus only covers the member states of the EU in detail. The Nomenclature of Territorial Units for Statistics is instrumental in the European Union's Structural Fund delivery mechanisms. The NUTS classification is a hierarchical system for dividing up the economic territory: NUTS 1, 2 and 3 respectively, moving from larger to smaller territorial units. NUTS 3 small regions for specific diagnoses.
2 Finland. Ministry of Employment and the Economy (2009).

3 Association of Finnish Local and Regional Authorities (2014).
4 Council of Oulu Region (2015).
5 Regional Council of Lapland (2013).
6 Regional Council of Häme (2013), p. 33.
7 MDI Consultancy for Regional Development (2013).
8 The *Centres for Economic Development, Transport and the Environment* are responsible for the regional development tasks of the central government.
9 Interview with the Regional Council of Häme.
10 Based on the interviews.
11 Based on the interviews.

Bibliography

Association of Finnish Local and Regional Authorities. (2014) *Regional Councils – Financing and Organisation*. [Online] Available from: www.kunnat.net/fi/kunnat/maakunnat/rahoitus-organisaatio/Sivut/default.aspx [Accessed: 11 January 2016].

Council of Oulu Region. (2015) *Regional Development and Planning*. [Online] Available from: www.pohjois-pohjanmaa.fi/regional_development_and_planning [Accessed: 11 January 2016].

Finland Ministry of Employment and the Economy. (2009) *Regional Planning*. [Online] Available from: https://www.tem.fi/en/regional_development/national_regional_development/regional_planning [Accessed: 11 January 2016].

MDI Consultancy for Regional Development. (2013) *Future Vision for the Greater Metropolitan Area – Workshop Series 'Wings and Roots'*. [Online] Available from: www.mdi.fi/showroom/laajan-metropolialueen-tulevaisuustarkastelu-siivet-ja-juuret-pajasarja [Accessed: 11 January 2016].

Regional Council of Häme. (2013) *Häme-ohjelma. Strateginen maakuntaohjelma 2014+*. Hämeenlinna: Hämeen liitto. [Online] Available from: http://hameenliitto.fi/sites/default/files/hame-ohjelma_lopullinen_28.11.2013_1.pdf [Accessed: 11 January 2016].

Regional Council of Lapland. (2013) *Lapin liiton Maakuntastrategia 2040 ja Lappisopimus (MAO) 2014–2017. Osallistumis- ja arviointisuunnitelma*. Rovaniemi: Maakuntahallitus 16.12.2013. Unpublished meeting document which used to be available online but has been removed. [Accessed: 18 November 2015].

12 Impact of the entrepreneurial discovery process on the decentralisation of innovation policies in Central and Eastern European Member States

Krzysztof Mieszkowski

1 Introduction

After World War II Poland, the Czech Republic, Slovakia, Hungary, Romania and Bulgaria belonged to the Soviet Bloc. These countries experienced centralised political and economic systems and specialisations imposed within the Council for Mutual Economic Assistance. During that time, the Research, Technology Development and Innovation (RTDI) system was highly centralised with the leading role of a special minister or a committee for science and technology. The democratic centralism allows for feedback from bottom to top, but RTDI actors had very limited impact on decision-making process (Meske, 1998). At the beginning of 1990s the democratic political and economic transformation began in these countries,[1] but the regional territorial dimension and stakeholders' participation became more important in light of their EU adhesion prospects around 2000 as they began to digest the European Union (EU) Cohesion Policy approach.

Regarding innovation policy, the EU started in 2000 supporting the development of regional innovation strategies in the countries in question (Klepka, 2005). For the financial perspective 2007–13 the concept of Regional Innovation Strategy was continuously promoted (EC, 2006) and implemented in the Czech Republic, Hungary, Slovakia and Poland (OECD, 2011). For the years 2014–2020 if a Member State wants to use European Structural and Investment Funds for RTDI investment, it has to submit to the European Commission (EC) with its *smart specialisation strategy (S3)*. The EU regulation requires that S3 should be developed within an *entrepreneurial discovery process* (EDP) which can be established at national or regional level (EU, 2013).

The choice between national or regional levels was a subject in the negotiation process reflecting the consideration of the regional dimension in operational programmes. On the one hand, this approach helps to fit S3 strategies better within national and regional governmental, economic, social and cultural specifics. On the other hand, it brings regions many challenges on how to do it right due to different responsibilities, administrative and citizen involvement capacities to prepare and then implement such strategies.

In this context, the World Bank policy brief *Smart Decentralisation of Innovation Policies* calls for *smart decentralisation*, which means a search for the right division of labour between national and regional levels to improve efficiency of innovation policy at both levels, especially through implementation of coordination tools which enable to build critical mass (Guimón, 2013).

The main goal of this chapter is to codify the phenomenon of (de)centralisation in innovation policies relying on S3 development and EDP in the countries in question. It investigates the division of responsibility between national and regional levels, national and regional governance structures and interactions within them and coordination mechanisms as well. Stress was placed on ways of involving stakeholders as they shape the EDP.

The preparation of the S3 strategies brought new opportunities for a regional dimension in RTDI in all post-communist countries. But in order to observe the clear regional dimension of these processes the number of such countries was limited to those which have significant territory and a chance for development of clear regional governance structures and policies. These pre-conditions determine possible decentralisation of state power and responsibility towards regional level regarding the economic development policy.

2 The matter of decentralisation[2]

Decentralisation is a process which can appear within Multilevel-Governance (MLG). According to G. Marks (1993) (as quoted in Żurek, 2013, p. 90), MLG is the system with constant negotiations among governments on different territorial levels. The structure is a result of creating institutions and reallocation of decision-making processes *up* towards supranational levels or *down* to lower levels. It can be assumed that MLG is a multi-level governance system where there exists a combination of supranational, intergovernmental and sub-national institutions and a certain level of centralisation and decentralisation of responsibilities (Żurek, 2013).

Following Pollitt *et al.* 1998 (as quoted in Brandy, 2002 p. 3) decentralisation, broadly speaking, means the shifting of decision-making rights or responsibilities away from the centre. Usually, decentralisation includes the dissemination of decision-making authority from a smaller to a larger number of actors. This also applies to the decentralisation of operations, resources and the allocation of rights more generally. This might include the rights to: initiate or propose, ratify, veto, set conditions, determine in the event of a dispute, deal with exceptions, allocate resources, etc. (Brady, 2002, p. 3).

Following White and his literature review on decentralisation in a more narrow sense the *government* decentralisation means a transfer of authority from the central government to regional governments. Depending on its scope we can deal with *de-concentration, delegation* and *devolution*. The decentralisation can be classified as well as *political, administrative,* or *fiscal* (White, 2011). While digging in the literature, decentralisation can be *competitive* or *non-competitive, external* or *internal,* and *horizontal* or *vertical* (Pollitt *et al.,* 1998) etc. It might refer to changing a shape of a state structure and *a reform* decentralising public administration. If there is no explicit decentralisation reform *silent decentralisation* might occur (Dubois and Fattore, 2009).

The decentralisation is very visible in the EU and the USA and this phenomenon has been also recommended for other countries in Latin America, Africa and Asia by international institutions like the World Bank (Bardhan, 2002) and the United Nations. For instance the United Nations Development Programme supported several programmes which considered the Decentralised Governance for Development. In its origin the programme focused on the empowering of sub-national levels of society to ensure that local people take part in and benefit from their own governance institutions and public services (UNDP, 2004).

For the purpose of this study, the focus is on *political* decentralisation in terms of *delegation* or *devolution* which can be *competitive* and *non-competitive, external* or *internal* and probably *silent.*

3 Participation in decentralisation

Political decentralisation, as a sign of democratisation, tackles particularly the issues of citizens' involvement and ways on how to identify and address their interests and needs. Furthermore, this approach should give citizens more importance in public decision-making processes which means more influence on the design and implementation of policies (Manor, 1999, p. 9). The decisions, which are made with greater participation of citizens, will be better informed and more appropriate to address different interests in the local society than those made at national level (The World Bank, 2015). This belief is used to convince governments, in less-developed countries, to devolve central control and authority towards boosting civic involvement in local governance processes (Panth, 2011).

Even if this approach seems to refer to democratic elections of local representatives, the participation cannot be only understood like that or as a public hearing itself. It seeks continuous involvement of citizens in decision-making processes on a policy design which will respect their interests. The manners to enable this participation can be: *information, consultation* and *co-operation, active participation* (Grävingholt *et al.,* 2006), and even *co-management* (Chase *et al.,* 2000).

The good implementation of the participation approach depends on: (a) the vitality of the public sphere or political environment, (b) the culture and political history of the country, and (c) the capacity and incentives of both civil society organisation and local governments to interact and interface meaningfully with one another (Panth, 2011). Furthermore, the participation system should consist of: (a) institutionalised mechanisms of participation, where channels of interactions are somehow formalised; (b) inclusiveness, which means involvement of a wide range of stakeholders representing the public and private sectors and the civil society; (c) stakeholder legitimacy, which means that all representatives of groups of interests should have their legitimation. Finally, mechanisms for participation should ensure openness and transparency of this process (Grävingholt *et al.*, 2006).

The participation issue is one of principles of the smart specialisation concept. The smart specialisation process should avoid the government failures which are often caused by the top-down and centralised bureaucratic processes of choices and selection (Foray & Goenaga, 2013). This exercise postulates involvement of representatives of innovation users, consumers, citizens, relevant non-profit organisations and workers (within the quadruple-helix model (Carayannis & Rakhmatullin, 2014)). The main idea is that entrepreneurial actors could suggest the potential areas for future regional or national economic development which are based on R&D activities and innovation (Foray *et al.*, 2012). The process should help identify the main innovation players who should facilitate the discovery of the most promising activities for regional innovation and ensure their involvement at a later stage of the smart specialisation process (Rodríguez-Pose *et al.*, 2014). S3 governance structures should ensure inclusive participation of all regional stakeholders when it comes to the decision on the future development priorities by collaborative leadership. This means that each of them can participate not only in discussions but also in the decision-making process. In order to deal with potential conflicts of different interests and opinions, the process should be moderated and managed by people and organisations with knowledge and skills to deal with interdisciplinary issues and different actors. The governance structure should be managed by steering/managing groups and relies on thematic and specific working groups (Foray *et al.*, 2012).

4 (De)centralisation phenomena in the countries in question

The measurement of decentralisation is an issue itself due to the lack of comparable data. Existing indicators rather show the spending at regional level which does not clarify how much the decision-making process is advanced (Guimón, 2013). According to some past studies there is a difference in confirming the existence of decentralisation, in terms of institutions, self-ruling, shared-ruling and finally decentralisation of powers, for science, technology and innovation (See Table 12.1).

In all countries, the intensity of decentralisation depends on the political regime. Historically, these regimes have been evolving and differentiating depending on the countries' circumstances and political factors. There are some studies which try to assess the level of decentralisation. In this chapter four of them are discussed.

According to the method developed by BAK Basel Economics, which was used by the S3 Platform and Orkestra – Basque Institute of Competitiveness – for the purpose of its Regional Benchmarking Tool, the most institutionally centralised countries were Bulgaria and Slovakia, then Romania and

Table 12.1 Decentralisation assessments in selected countries

Country	Institutional decentralisation (1)	Regional Authority Index (RAI) (2)				Decentralisation of powers for science, technology and innovation (STI) (3)	RIM-Plus assessment of regional innovation policy governance (4)
		Years	Self-rule	Shared-rule	RAI		
Bulgaria	25	1991–2006	0	0	0	n/a	(a) – no (b) – no; (c) – centralised and fragmented; (d) – top-down
Czech Republic	50	1993–1999	0	0	0	elected regional authorities, no decentralised STI policy, but with RIS	(a) – medium (b) – high; (c) – centralised (d) – bottom-up
		2000–2006	7	0	7		
Hungary	44	1990–1993	8	0	8	non-elected regional level/decentralised state agencies, no decentralised STI policy, but with RIS	(a) – low or none (b) – low; (c) – centralised; (d) – bottom-up, participatory
		1994–1998	9	0	9		
		1999–2006	10	0	10		
Poland	48	1990–1998	2	0	2	elected regional authorities, with some decentralisation of STI power and resource to regions, with RIS	(a) – medium–low; (b) – high, but not independent; (c) – centralised (d) – top-down
		1999–2006	8	0	8		
Romania	43	1991–1993	6	0	6	n/a	(a) – low or none; (b) – low or none; (c) – centralised and fragmented; (d) – participatory
		1994–1997	7	0	7		
		1998–2002	11	0	11		
		2003–2006	10	0	10		
Slovakia	36	1993–1995	0	0	0	elected regional authorities, no decentralised STI policy, but with RIS	(a) – low (b) – low or none; (c) – centralised and fragmented; (d) – participatory
		1996–2001	1	0	1		
		2002–2006	6	0	6		

Source: Author's elaboration based on (1) Benchmarking tool data: Müller, U. and Haisch. T. (2009) *From Subsidiarity to Success: The Impact of Decentralisation on Economic Growth, Summary and Conclusions,* BAK Basel Economics.; (2) Hooghe *et al.,* (2009) *The rise of Regional Authority. A comparative study of 42 democracies (1590–2006)*, Amsterdam, August 2009; (3) OECD, *OECD Reviews of Regional Innovation, Regions and Innovation Policy,* 2011; (4) https://ec.europa.eu/growth/tools-databases/regional-innovation-monitor/report/innovation.

Note: (1) BAK Basel Economics, the Decentralisation Index, min. score 25 and max. score 66, (Müller and Haisch 2009); (2) self-rule means the authority exercised by a regional government over those who live in the region; shared-rule means the authority exercised by a regional government or its representatives in the country as a whole; Regional Authority Index sum of self-rule and shared-rule scores (2009); (4) The criteria is as follows: (a) the degree of regional autonomy, (b) the autonomy in RDTI policy, (c) the set-up of the regional governance system, (d) the nature of the process of strategy development.

Hungary, and finally Poland and the Czech Republic (S3 Platform, 2015). The Regional Authority Index (RAI) whose aim is to measure self-ruling and shared-ruling confirms the mentioned order for Bulgaria and Slovakia but changed the order for Poland, the Czech Republic, Hungary and Romania (Hooghe *et al.*, 2009). The results of these studies show how varied ranks of countries can be according to the decentralisation idea as such and its degree can be changed through the years.

The OECD study on RTDI policy (2011) categorised its devolution of competences and resources into four categories:

a significant control of science, technology and innovation (STI) powers and resources by regions;
b some decentralisation of STI powers;
c no decentralisation power but Regional Innovation Strategy (RIS); and
d no decentralisation power or innovation projects.

This categorisation can be distorted by the following factors: (a) allowance to spend money does not mean freedom in decision-making, (b) the degree of decentralisation of RTDI policy can be different than for others, (c) different aspects of this policy might be decentralised differently as well, and (d) finally even small decentralised competences of regions might have an important impact on this regional policy (OECD, 2011). According to this study the most decentralised RTDI policy is observed in Poland, then the Czech Republic and Slovakia, and Hungary. For Bulgaria and Romania this kind of assessment was unavailable.

The Regional Innovation Monitor (RIM) and current Regional Innovation Monitor Plus (RIM-Plus) studies include the aspect of regional innovation governance, decentralisation of RDTI policy and stakeholders' involvement following the assessment logic:

a the degree of general regional autonomy;
b the regional autonomy in RDTI policy;
c the set-up of the regional governance system; and
d the nature of the process of strategy development.

The RIM initiative is to monitor the regional RDTI policy in a more continuous way for the policy purposes of the EU in order to provide a more updated picture of the regional dynamics in this theme.

5 The case studies settings

Following the findings of OECD and RIM initiative studies the two following questions examining decentralisation matters during previous and S3 processes can be raised:

1   Has S3 EDP had an impact on further decentralisation of RTDI policy in these countries?
2   Is the partnership principle of Cohesion Policy deepened by EDP processes?

The scope of these studies includes the division of labour between decision-making powers at national and regional levels to conduct S3 processes, governance structures and stakeholders' participation. For the purpose of this analysis decentralisation processes are considered from the perspective of:

* *Governance system* – transferring authority from central government to the regional level:
    - How is the governance system organised and what are its institutional capacities? (Foray *et al.*, 2012; Karo and Kattel, 2015).
    - Process managers/leaders (Edelenbos and Klijn, 2005; Ackermann and Eden, 2011; Foray *et al.*, 2012).
    - Creation of authorising environment (Bryson, 2007), building mutual trust between public administration and stakeholders (Yang, 2005).
* *Stakeholders' participation* – increasing the participation of stakeholders in the decision-making processes. Are the processes inclusive, dynamic and interactive?
    - Who is taken into account? (Foray *et al.*, 2012):
        * Stakeholders in a *narrow view* or a *broad view*; *claimers* and *influencers*; *actual* stakeholders versus *potential* ones; stakeholders *with power*, *of dependence* or *of reciprocity* (Mitchell *et al.*, 1997).
        * Identification and selection of stakeholders: key stakeholders, attention to stakeholders, stakeholders' analysis (Bryson, 2007); selection of stakeholders by sorting criteria for narrowing the number of them (Mitchell *et al.*, 1997).[3]
        * Stakeholders' attributes: *power, legitimacy, urgency* (Mitchell *et al.*, 1997).
        * Stakeholder legitimacy: stakeholder *fairness* and *moral foundation*; stakeholder *obligation* and *status*; *normative* and *derivative* stakeholders, *non-stakeholders* (Phillips, 2003).
        * High importance of *civil society participation* (Lépineux, 2005; Burby, 2003).
    - Decision-making process (Edelenbos and Klijn, 2005):
        * The level of formalisation of the process design: detailed organisational arrangement.
        * Action and style of process management: the level of dominance and activities of process managers over stakeholders, the level of flexibility.
        * Recognisable influence: impact of stakeholders on variety of ideas and problems, solutions, development of plans.

- Deepen participation through the level of open access of stake-holders to the process and actual participation.
- Widening participation by letting stakeholders' contribute to: a set-up of the agenda, a development of ideas, a decision-making process.
- A relation between interactive process and regional or national authorities: initiation, confirmation, feedback, regional/national authorities' participation.

These two perspectives help to illustrate the impact of the entrepreneurial discovery process on the (de)centralisation of RTDI policy in the countries in question. The EDP can be characterised as *an inclusive and interactive process,* in which stakeholders decide on new activities (priorities) and there is an arrangement of new ideas and an *ex-ante* assessment of their economic impact. During the entrepreneurial discovery process, entrepreneurial knowledge is highlighted and integrated through connections and partnerships among different stakeholders and governments assess their outcomes and empower actors to explore and open up new domains (Kyriakou and Periáñez-Forte).

For the purpose of providing assessment of the (de)centralisation processes from centre to regions in selected countries the studies follow the categorisation provided by Perry and May, and OECD. The first one distinguished four regional dimensions in RTDI policies depending on the passive or active role of regional actors. According to the typology, regions can be:

a   *stages*, regions are seen, but regional units are not participants;
b   *implementers*, where regional actors implement nationally defined policy;
c   *partners*, where regional actors co-decide on RTDI agendas; and
d   *independent policy-makers*, where regional authorities set RTDI agendas (Izsak, 2012).

6 Governance system

The region can be defined as a unit of territorial organisation of the state, which should cover significant territorial surface and include a significant number of inhabitants. According to strict definitions, a region should be homogenous in terms of economy, society and culture. Within its territory, policies should be carried out by regional authorities (Elżanowski *et al.*, 1990). Often regions, which are defined by political decisions, do not meet the requirements which are included in this definition. They are heterogeneous, multicultural and their internal economy is diverse in terms of development and diversification. Furthermore, the expected self-governance is limited by national law or does not even exist. The chapter as well as EU cohesion policy refers to the regions which are defined by NUTS methodology at second level (EU, 2013). As presented in the table, besides Poland, the NUTS2 level regions of selected countries do not correspond to the territorial administrative units which can be considered as regions in these countries (Table 12.2).

Besides Poland this lack of equality between the cohesion policy regions and administrative regions can have a negative impact on the development of regional smart specialisation strategies in terms of sharing responsibility, collaboration, coordination, common governance, capacities, interests and needs. Guimón's policy brief calls for smart decentralisation which means optimal national–regional division of competences in innovation policies and the use of efficient, flexible, and transparent multi-level governance systems. The problem is to find the right extent of decentralisation policy instruments for different regions within different countries. According to this assumption, decentralisation should be considered as a flexible and asymmetric process in each country (Guimón, 2013).

Successful policies depend on the capacities of actors. Many regions do not possess human and material resources to deal with strategic processes in the right way, considering even those which are quite experienced with the allocation of European funding. In many self-governed regions, regional policy is a matter of negotiation within the regional governance system (Kroll, 2015).

The EC previous RIS programmes took into account development or improvement of political–administrative competence at the regional level. It is assumed that the success of regionalisation of RTDI policy depends on implementation of political competence (Koschatzky, 2005). In some countries the national states supports the development of regional innovation strategies by calls, guidelines or other incentives. The evidence also shows that the mandate and resources are not enough, and the external support might be destructive to building regional awareness and commitment of regional stakeholders (OECD, 2011). Europeanisation of RTDI policies and governance systems has created the capacity for policy-making and implementation in Central Eastern Europe (CEE) since 2000. RTDI policy routines have been traditionally relatively centralised in CEE and there has been little regional and sectoral focus (Karo and Kattel, 2015).

Table 12.2 Arrangement of regions in considered countries

Country	Poland	Slovakia	Czech Republic	Hungary	Bulgaria	Romania
Number of regions (NUTS2)	16	4	8	7	6	8
Number of regions according to national law	16	8	14	20	28	42

Source: Author's elaboration based on http://ec.europa.cu/eurostat/web/nuts/overview.

7 Stakeholders' participation in RTDI policy

According to the OECD studies and recommendations any input from firms and other civil actors into regional development strategies is crucial. The involvement of companies in the innovation policy processes helps to address problems to increase benefits from public instruments to support innovations. The mentioned networking nature of innovation is another argument for wider stakeholder involvement for strategy development. In the application of innovation the civil society can play a lead role. There are different institutional forms to ensure private sector and civil society participation. Their representatives participate in Boards of Directors, Innovation Councils, and Growth Forums. Of course there are several obstacles to implement this approach like a limited number of regional champions, a lack of time from SMEs representatives, a lack of access to the right information, a lack of public sector capacities, or even a lack of involvement of universities in business-oriented R&D networks. Besides the positive aspects there is a risk that too high an impact of private influence might miss the public needs, so there is a need to balance it (OECD, 2011). To overcome these obstacles the creation of trust and a fair environment for learning is important. The involvement of the business sector might be facilitated by public–private partnerships. Particularly SMEs should be the target group of innovation promotion (Koschatzky, 2005).

The critical issue for decentralisation is wide public participation, but it often depends on the educational level of the population as well as on how well they can satisfy their basic needs. Consequently, based on its level of development, the nature of a country's RTDI policy will vary (Mercado, 2012).

So far participation in the EU system of multi-level governance has been materialised within partnership principles which empowered sub-national actors and social partners in network-creation and institution building within the framework of national rules and current practices. For this purpose the process should consider the regional and local authorities, the economic and social partners, and any other relevant competent bodies within this framework (Getimis, 2003). But often the flow of EU Structural Funds centralised the system contrary to the EU's intentions. The SF priorities were determined at the top and only implementation of them will be delegated top-down (Dubois and Fattore, 2009).

8 The case studies

8.1 The case of Poland

The chapter now examines the Polish smart specialisation process in more depth. In Poland smart specialisation processes have been exercised at national and regional level. There is a clear distinction between these two levels in carrying it out. Some attempts to coordinate them occurred from national level but without any intentional synergies so far. The national and two regional cases of Wielkopolskie and Pomorskie[4] were examined in terms of governance structure and stakeholders' participation in comparison to the previous strategic processes regarding the RTDI domain. The starting point and key elements of the national smart specialisation exercise are pointed out in Table 12.3.

Table 12.3 Key elements of smart specialisation process at national level – Poland

Aspect	Matter	Insights
Past RTDI strategies	Starting point	• The RTDI relevant strategies were drafted by Minister of Science (follower of Scientific Research Committee) or by Minister of Economy from perspective of science or economy and adopted or not by Government.
S3 Framework	Documents	• Strategy for Efficiency and Innovativeness of Economy (objectives, directions of activities, responsibilities at ministers' level) • Enterprises Development Programme (executive document, policy mix) • National Smart Specialisation (appendix to executive document)
Governance system	Leader	• Minister of Economy, (since Nov. 2015 - Minister of Economic Development, Vice-Prime Minister)
	Stakeholders	• Minister of Science and Higher Education, • other ministers • local authorities, • social and business partners, • NGOs • trade unions • Joint Committee of the Government and the Local Self-government authorities

(continued)

Table 12.3 (continued) Key elements of smart specialisation process at national level – Poland.

Aspect	Matter	Insights
Stakeholders participation in EDP	Selection of smart specialisations	• Consultation on the Strategy for Efficiency and Innovativeness of Economy: 30 entities involved • Business consultation on the result of Foresight technologiczny przemysłu – InSight2030: 14 meetings with 87 participants. • SWOT analysis workshops with social and economic partners: 106 participants of business chambers, research institutions, business supporting institutions and public administration. • Individual consultation with workshop participants. • Workshops on the results of cross-analysis between the quantitative and qualitative with consultation results.
Stakeholders' participation in continuous EDP: the concept of working groups around smart specialisation areas	The initiation of working groups	The launch of working groups dedicated to each smart specialisation area as forums for exchanging information, opinions and experience.
	The membership and selection of members to the groups	Each group contains 30 members from business, business supporting institutions, research institutions and Ministry of Economic Development. The recruitment process is based on two steps. Step I – the call for expression of interest to participate in working groups, meetings with interested entities, open calls for membership of working groups. Step II – application submissions, application assessment by Ministry of Economic Development, Steering Committee approval of Ministry of Economic Development proposal. The membership of each group can be changed if modification of the smart specialisation areas on Steering Committee approval. The observers can contribute to the work of the working groups. They can be invited by the chair or a member of the working group.

Aspect	Matter	Insights
	The management of the groups	The groups are managed by a chair who is elected from their members (internal election with ordinary majority of votes). The role of chair is to manage the working groups.
	The tasks of groups	The working group delivers recommendations and conclusions regarding national smart specialisation and innovation policy. Furthermore, these groups provide information wrapping-up work of the group and effects in implementation of each smart specialisation quarterly. The meetings of the groups are supposed to be called quarterly as well.
	The new groups formulation	There is an option to select additional, ad hoc working groups for emerging smart specialisations and organising common meetings of different working groups on the motion of the chair or a group member.
	The confirmation of eligibility	Participation in the working group does not exclude a member from applying for funding from the calls.
Stakeholders' participation in continuous EDP: the concept of Smart Lab carried out by World Bank	Pilot project	• 500 interviews with enterprises in 4 regions. • 120 interviews carried out by regional consultants. • 14 Smart Labs involving 60 enterprises. • Involvement of representatives from ministers, public funding agencies, VC funds, business supporting institutions, regional authorities.

Source: Author's elaboration based on Ustawa z dnia 6 grudnia 2006 r. o zasadach prowadzenia polityki rozwoju, Dz. U. 2006 Nr 227 poz. 1658; *Założenia systemu zarządzania rozwojem Polski*, Rady Ministrów, 2009.; Krajowa inteligentna specjalizacja (KIS), Rada ministrów, 2014; Regulamin naboru i prac Grup Roboczych ds. krajowych inteligentnych specjalizacji (GR ds. kis), Ministry of Economy, 2015; www.smart.gov.pl, accessed on 08/01/2016.

In the past the authors' perspective and consultations with their own communities meant that the strategic documents reflected the interests of communities and referred to the issues of others but not in the coherent way of common objectives. Mainly consultation and information sharing were employed as a way for stakeholders' involvement. The transparency of the process was not as important as an effect as such.

The implementation of the smart specialisation concept in the RTDI strategic process at national level occurred during the new design of RTDI documents. So the requirements of the concept including EDP had to be implemented. Even if there was a clear legal obligation to make an effort to consult publicly projects of strategies beyond government with groups of stakeholders (Sejm, 2006), which was mainly imposed before S3 exercise, the first work on the new RTDI strategic documents attracted only 30 entities (MG, 2013, p. 164). The result of this legal requirement could not be considered as good enough in terms of EDP implementation, increasing participation and decentralisation. In the further work on national smart specialisation areas more sophisticated forms of stakeholder participations were employed.

Analytical selection of first areas of specialisation was supported by the stakeholders' participation in the form of consultation and workshops. Further work on them was structured by forming 19 working groups.[5] For better manageability of the process the number of people was limited which means some necessary decentralisation limitation. Currently about 500 representatives are members of these groups[6] with balanced participation of business and research institutions. Dominance of public-dependent institutions in this kind of RTDI policy-related exercise was always the case for Poland (Mieszkowski and Kardas, 2015).

The procedure of identification and selection of stakeholders is ensured by the open recruitment process. The final selection is done by the Steering Committee for National Smart Specialisation. This committee coordinates the national work on smart specialisation. The membership of groups can be changed which means there is a *mechanism for verification of stakeholders*. The group can be extended by inviting observers which creates the possibility of *widening participation*. As management of these groups is in the charge of business and research representatives,[7] the operational management is separate from the public authorities. The degree of participation reaches the level of *active participation* leaving the right for final decision to the committee.

There is a path for new smart specialisation area initiation, but each new initiative should be supported by a number of stakeholders interested in establishment of that specialisation.[8] Participation in the policy process does not exclude members from the calls for projects. Additionally in the national process instead of working groups a more project-oriented model of Smart Labs was commissioned to an external institution which can be considered as another EDP method.

The details of the S3 process in Wielkopolskie and Pomorskie is presented in Table 12.4a and Table 12.4b.

Table 12.4a Key elements of smart specialisation process at regional level – Wielkopolskie

Regional innovation strategy	Smart specialisation strategy
Governance	
• Leader: Self-government of the region.	• Leader: Self-government of the region.
• Steering Committee: 5 representatives of public administration, 3 of research institutions, 3 of social-business chambers, 4 of business supporting institutions, 1 of banking institution, responsible for strategic decisions.	• The operationalisation of the strategic process commissioned to the Poznań University of Economics.
	• Working Group for RIS Implementation, Smart Specialisation and S3 Action Plan: 71 participants (45 enterprises).
	• Regional authorities: 23 participants
	• Expert panel: 13 people.
• Coordinator of the strategic project: Poznań Science and Technology Park Adam Mickiewicz University Foundation – business supporting institution.	• 3,500 interviewed companies
	• 100 in-depth interviews, 80 per cent of them with companies with aim to precise the smart specialisation areas
	• Working groups for pre-defined 6 smart areas: 214 enterprises.
	• Information meeting on S3: 115 participants (45 enterprises).
• Project partners: Marshal Office, ZAB Branderburg, Region Marche (1 polish public authority and 2 foreign ones).	• Participants during public consultations: 189 of enterprises, research institutions, business supporting institutions and local authorities
	• Forum for Smart Specialisation: 61 participants.
• Regional experts gathered in 3 groups coordinated by Wielkopolską Izbę Przemysłowo-Handlową: first group included 4 representatives of economic university, the second one 3 representatives of government, the third one 1 representative of chamber, additionally 2 foreign experts.	• The Internet Forum for S3
• 5 working groups including up to 20 members.	

(continued)

Table 12.4a (continued) Key elements of smart specialisation process at regional level – Wielkopolskie.

Regional innovation strategy	Smart specialisation strategy
Process	
• The main responsibility of experts was to prepare the diagnosis of problems and suggestions as solutions • Working groups' tasks was preparation of analyses for particular sectors based on research and experts' proposals and recommendations for elements of the strategy. • During the work on the strategy the 13 best examples of innovative enterprise were identified among tens of enterprises audited and interviewed. They were considered as core for future innovation centres.	• Research on innovative needs of enterprises. • Working Group meetings on an update of previous RIS and the method for selecting regional smart specialisation areas, the pre-defined smart specialisation areas to clarify their definition, identification of their value chains, elaboration of SWOT analysis, identification of key development factors, decision on activities supporting their development. • Meetings with local authorities to unify the work on strategy among differentiated sub-regions. • Expert panels to discuss the identified areas and further proceeding with them. • The value chain approach implementation and selection of the best participants for further S3 development. • Feedback meetings on S3 to discuss the progress on S3. • Pilot activities like: Voucher pilot programme (119 enterprises) with focus on cooperation between research institutions and enterprises in pre-defined areas of regional smart specialisation; trainings for researchers in 12 enterprises to test the model of transferring knowledge from research institutions to enterprises. • The workshop for enterprises in order to check the possibility for inter-sectoral cooperation within the areas of smart specialisation. • The consultation with stakeholders to receive feedback on the updated S3 and policy instrument design. • Forum for Smart Specialisation to discuss final draft of Wielkopolskie S3 and Wielkopolskie Forum for Smart Specialisation.

Source: Author's elaboration based on http://innowacje.wlkp.pl/index.php, accessed on 08/01/2016 and http://iw.org.pl/regionalna-strategia-innowacji-dla-wielkopolski-na-lata-2015- 2020-ris3, accessed on 05/06/2016.

Table 12.4b Key elements of smart specialisation process at regional level – Pomorskie.

Regional innovation strategy	Smart specialisation strategy
Governance	
• Leader: The Executive Board of Pomorskie region • The process was commissioned to a Consortium of 2 public bodies, 4 universities – one of them coordinator – and 1 research institution • Steering Committee of 4 representatives of public authorities, 2 research institutions, 4 representatives of socio-economic chambers, 3 representatives of business supporting institutions, 1 enterprise. • Other stakeholders	• Leader: The Executive board of Pomorskie region via the Department of Economic Development of the Marshal Office • Judgment panel for partnership competition of 1 regional authorities representative and 6 members combining business, academic and business supporting institutions experience. • Partnerships as consortia of regional entities including any kind of entities but with preference for business and scientific entities including 369 partners in total of which 65.58% are enterprises, 13.01% universities, 8.13% NGOs, 4.34% research institutions.
Process	
• 13 powiat and 2 municipal conferences in order to inform enterprises and local authorities about the targets of drafted strategy and facilitation of common cooperation among them. • Identification of innovation needs of enterprise – research which involved 266 enterprises. • Identification of 96 teams at universities and 36 teams in research institutes important for regional economy. • 10 audits in research institutions in order to identify restructuring and development needs. • 5 sector meetings involving selected enterprises to initiate cooperation among them and let them specify their expectation towards RIS • 2 conferences which presented the goals of the strategy and project proposals.	• Debates and consultations on partnerships creation • Definition of the economic profile of the region – research study • The first call for regional smart specialisation areas. • Assessment of proposals and recommendations • The final call for regional smart specialisation areas • Decision on the final partnerships representing smart specialisation areas. • Negotiation around the scope and instrument supporting development in smart specialisation areas. • Signing the partnership agreements for smart specialisation areas for 3-year period with possibility of extension.

Source: Author's elaboration based on: www.ris-pomorskie.pg.gda.pl, accessed on 11/01/2016.

In both strategic processes of Wielkopolskie the governance and process was initiated and led by the self-government of the regions. It was a result of the legal obligation imposed by the law (Sejm, 1998; 2006). But the operation was commissioned to an external contractor. The comparison of stakeholders' scope and their numbers involved between the RIS process and the S3 process seems to confirm a great attempt made to widen participation in strategic process imposed by smart specialisation requirements.

Similarly to the case of Wielkopolskie in Pomorskie S3 governance included a wider number and scope of stakeholders from a very fair bottom-up perspective compared to the previous RIS process. Even if the S3 process was managed from a self-government perspective the involvement of people with a mix of business, research and innovation backgrounds to assess the process reduced the role of public authorities or research insititutions. It confirms decentralisation on decision-making level. The process was competitive and comprehensive with the inspiration of top-down analysis which met the condition of decentralisation based on competition. The open tender for consortia of the smart specialisation areas and parnerships allows stakeholders to contribute to the policy-making process in a direct way.

8.2 The case of Bulgaria, the Czech Republic, Hungary, Romania, and Slovakia

In Bulgaria, the S3 process has been carried out at national level, but some efforts were made on increasing participation and communicating the strategic process by going down to the public at large. The role of local bodies is visible, but probably more than feedback from their side should be expected. When the role of the Wold Bank is finished, it is unsure if there is enough capacity to carry on the process by authorities on their own.

In the Czech Republic, it looks like the national smart specialisation exercise was rather facilitated by two regional activities in this field (Prague and South Moravia). This helped open a door for regional bottom-up approaches that are to be integrated at the national level into the common national S3. This caused difficulties for regions with lower administrative capacities in the field of RTDI. The scale of the problem is related to the existence of regional innovation agencies. Several forms of participation were employed in this processes. According to official declarations, the participation of stakeholders was significant.

In current Hungarian circumstances, the lack of strong regional authorities could be compensated by the existence of regional innovation agencies. As they are quite dependent on external funding, they were interested in being involved in the S3 exercise finally carried out at the national level. According to participation statistics, there was a wide scope of activities and stakeholder participation. Here, only the increase of stakeholders' participation can be considered as decentralisation in the centralised RTDI system.

Romania seems to have made a great effort to increase participation of stakeholders into the process at the national level. With the one obvious exception, the final development of regional smart specialisation strategies is pending. This cannot confirm the existence of clear decentralisation from the national to regional level in the RTDI field.

Slovakia also looks to have made a great effort to attract enterprises in the group of stakeholders. The strong position of Bratislava Region over the others due to their lack of RTDI capacities undermines nationwide decentralisation efforts. There has been no serious consideration of regional efforts to address the RTDI regional dimension.

8.3 General findings from all cases

Comparing the observations from case studies with the mentioned typology which considered the role of regional levels, the Polish regions can be considered as fair *independent policy-makers* regarding S3, some Czech regions and Bratislava region as *partners*. In Hungary and Romania the position of the regional level can be located between the role of *partners* and *implementers* and for Bulgaria as *stages*. In all cases there was an effort made to widen stakeholders' participation and to go beyond consultation towards more interactive forms of discussion and decision-making.

Most likely the S3 ex-ante conditionality as the official obligation caused re-centralisation of previous rather regionalised RIS processes. This led to the set-up of the national level commitment to the S3 exercise by national authorities. Probably the lack of local capabilities regarding RDTI policy also might have disenabled to keep the previous decentralisation approach in case of such important strategic exercise for most of countries in question. The process leaders and managers tried to attract varied and balanced pool of stakeholders to the process in order to implement entrepreneur discovery process.

In all these countries it is difficult to say if the efforts of addressing the right stakeholders were sufficient enough and finally the best representations around the S3 processes were really attracted. In the Polish case there is a lack of evidence for active and visible promotion of the attractiveness and importance of the S3 exercise via old and new media in order to attract the attention of society. The process promotion was mainly channelled through chambers and through contacts gathered in the databases of the main partners. Furthermore, there is no easy public access to the minutes and reports which could illustrate the discussion of working groups. The released information does not present the insights from the process so it is difficult to have information about how the ideas and initiatives of stakeholders were respected.

Table 12.5 (De)centralisation of RDTI policy compering S3 processes and previous RIS experience – overview of selected dimensions

Dimensions	Bulgaria	Czech Republic	Hungary	Poland	Romania	Slovakia
Policy process	More centralised	More centralised	More centralised	Still decentralised	More centralised	More centralised
Process leaders or managers	Appointed at national level	Appointed at national level with two regional exceptions	Appointed at national level with contribution of regional agencies	Appointed at national and regional level	Appointed at national level with one regional exception	Appointed at national level with one regional exception
The level of formalisation	Mandate and responsibility of Ministry of Economy	Mandate and responsibility of Deputy Prime Minister	Mandate of National RTDI Office and regional agencies	Mandate and responsibility of Minister of Economy and Marshals	Mandate and responsibility of ministry and regional agencies	Mandate and responsibility of ministry, no clear obligation for regions
Public institutional capacities at regional level	Still weak, at national level process happened due to support of external institution	Still weak with some regional exceptions, the supportive role of S3 managers and facilitators financed by government	The role of regional agencies weaker and their future uncertain. This does not let for keeping and improving their capacities	Still different quality depending on regions, processes often commissioned partially or fully to externals	Still different depending on the regional agencies, some processes done with support of externals	Still weak at regional level besides the one capital region
Deepening and widening participation	Efforts to vary and balance pool of stakeholders	Idem	Idem	Idem	Idem	Idem

Dimensions	Bulgaria	Czech Republic	Hungary	Poland	Romania	Slovakia
Civil society	Strong focus on attracting enterprises	Idem	Idem	Idem	Idem	Idem
Selection of stakeholders	N/A	N/A	Relevant stakeholders identified by regional agencies	Calls for expressing interests	Relevant stakeholders identified and addressed	Relevant and key stakeholders identified
Action and style of process management	Top-down driven	Mainly top-down driven with two exceptions at regional level	Dominance of top-down with some significant bottom-up contribution	The mix of top-down and bottom-up	Rather top-down than bottom-up	Rather top-down than bottom-up with one exception
Recognizable influence	Feedback and discussions during meetings & focus groups	Proposition and discussions in various forms e.g.: round-table meetings, regional coordination platforms	Active engagement of stakeholders during the regional events, working groups; national body including stakeholders	Feedback, interviews and discussions in working groups; partnerships	Consultations, common elaborations & feedbacks in meetings and debates	Working groups, strong impact of the representatives from capital region, week influence of BERD performers

Source: Author's elaboration based on ERAWATCH and RIO Country Reports.

9 Conclusions and policy implications

The EU Cohesion Policy aims to address both countries and their regions. By promoting the concept of regional innovation strategies and imposing the smart specialisation concept, the EU wants to address the RTDI issues at the lowest, but still relevant level. The second effort is to gather around the process local actors. They can be considered as stakeholders who can contribute or can have an interest in developing their economic system in order to increase its innovativeness. Failure to sustain power/authority at the regional level caused horizontal decentralisation of the process at the national level. The existence of regional level agencies was used to facilitate the process at the national level as in Hungary and in the Czech Republic, Romania and Slovakia. Often leading regions supported national authorities in carrying out this process. This shows the potential hidden in these communities.

The tendency for centralisation in the majority of countries in question was compensated for by the efforts to increase participation of stakeholders. This might simply reflect the fear of not meeting the *ex-ante* requirement, but there is visible progress in the numbers of participants and variety of ways they were involved. From this perspective the decentralisation of RTDI policy has progressed. The challenge might be the sustainability of these involvements in continuous EDP and the selection of those which are the most important for innovation development.

These studies have not brought many insights to the methods employed to select, attract and reach agreements in this process so there might be room for deeper exploration. Further research can examine the implementation phase of these strategies in the regional (de)centralisation context. Finally, more detailed studies on the comparison of the (de)centralised approaches in these countries and their final result would be welcome.

It will be difficult for the EU and its Cohesion Policy to change power decentralisation patterns in the Member States. The S3 exercise shows that there might be a problem in addressing regional issues at national level and counting on the regional structures to carry out this kind of exercise.

Notes

1 See for example Myant, M. and Drahokoupil, J., 2010. *Transition economies: Political economy in Russia, Eastern Europe and Central Asia*, New York: Wiley.
2 For a comprehensive typological study on decentralisation see: Dubois, Hans F. W. and Fattore, Giovanni, 2009. Definitions and Typologies in Public Administration Research: The Case of Decentralization, *International Journal of Public Administration*, 32(8), pp. 704–727.
3 Mitchell and others' elaboration is adopted for the purpose of public policy from business perspective.
4 These two cases were chosen as they met ex-ante conditionality requirements for formal EC approval on the days of working on this chapter.
5 On the days of writing this chapter, the set-up of one group was pending.
6 Some of the individuals can be counted twice because they are representing different stakeholders' profiles – research institutions, 220; business, 206; business chamber, 21; business support institution, 40; NGO, 10.

7 There are 19 chairs and 33 vice-chairs (at least one chair and one vice-chair per group).
8 For example a new proposal for innovative maritime technologies was supported by 62 enterprises, 21 research institutions and 15 social-economic chambers.

References

Ackermann, F. and Eden, C., 2011. Strategic Management of Stakeholders: Theory and Practice. *Long Range Planning*, 44, pp. 179–196.

Baláž, V., 2009. *ERAWATCH Country Report 2009. Analysis of Policy Mixes to Foster R&D Investment and to Contribute to the ERA. Slovakia*. Seville: EE, JRC-IPTS, DG RTD.

Baláž, V., 2013. *ERAWATCH Country Reports 2011: Slovakia*. Seville: EC JRC-IPTS.

Baláž, V., 2014. *ERAWATCH Country Reports 2013: Slovak Republic*. Seville: EC JRC-IPTS.

Baláž, V., 2015. *RIO Country Report Slovak Republic 2014*. Seville: EC JRC-IPTS.

Bardhan, P., 2002. Decentralization of Governance and Development. *Journal of Economic Perspectives*, 16(4), pp. 185–205.

Brady, N., 2002. *Striking a Balance: Centralised and Decentralised Decisions in Government,* s.l.: New Zealand Treasury.

Bryson, J. M., 2007. What to do When Stakeholders Matter. Stakeholder Identification and Analysis Techniques. *Public Management Review*, 6(1), pp. 21–53.

Burby, R. J., 2003. Making Plans that Matter: Citizen Involvement and Government Action. *Journal of the American Planning Association*, 69(1), pp. 33–49.

Carayannis, E. G. and Rakhmatullin, R., 2014. The Quadruple/Quintuple Innovation Helixes and Smart Specialisation Strategies for Sustainable and Inclusive Growth in Europe and Beyond. In: *Open Innovation Yearbook 2014*. s.l.: s.n., pp. 42–60, Luxembourg: EC.

Chase, L. C., Schusler, T. M. and Decker, D. J., 2000. Innovations in Stakeholder Involvement: What's the Next Step? *Wildlife Society Bulletin*, 28(1), pp. 208–217.

Chioncel, M., 2009. *ERAWATCH Country Report 2009: Analysis of Policy Mixes to foster R&D investment and to contribute to the ERA. Romania*. Seville: EC, JRC-IPTS, DG RTD.

Chobanova, R., 2014. *ERAWATCH Country Reports 2012: Bulgaria*. Seville: EC JRC-IPTS.

Damianova, Z. and Stefanov, R., 2009. *ERAWATCH Country Report 2008. An Assessment of Research System and Policies. Bulgaria*. Seville: EC, JRC-IPTS, DGR.

Damianova, Z., Galev, T., Georgieva, T., Mineva, D. and Stefanov R., 2010. *ERAWATCH Country Report 2010: Bulgaria*. Seville: EC, JRC-IPTS, DG RTD.

Dőry, T., 2015. *RIO Country Report Hungary 2014*. Seville: EC JRC-IPTS.

Dőry, T. and Havas, A., 2014. *ERAWATCH Country Reports 2012: Hungary,* Seville: EC JRC-IPTS.

Dubois, H. F. W. and Fattore, G., 2009. Definitions and Typologies in Public Administration Research: The Case of Decentralization. *International Journal of Public Administration*, 32(8), pp. 704–727.

EC, D. R., 2006. *Innovative Strategies and Actions: Results from 15 Years of Regional Experimentation*. Brussels: EC DG Regio.

Edelenbos, J. and Klijn, E.-H., 2005. Managing Stakeholder Involvement in Decision Making: A Comparative Analysis of Six Interactive Processes in the Netherlands. *Journal of Public Administration Research and Theory*, 16(3), pp. 417–446.

Elżanowski, M., Maciołek, M. and Przybysz, P., 1990. Region jako instytucja prawnoustrojowa. *Państwo i Prawo*, 8, pp. 59–63.

EU, 2013. *Regulation (EU) No 1303/2013*. s.l.: Official Journal of the European Union.

Foray, D., Goddard, J., Beldarrain, X. G., Landabaso, M., McCann, Ph., Morgan, K., Nauwelaers, C., and Ortega-Argilés, R., 2012. *Guide to Research and Innovation Strategies for Smart Specialisation (RIS 3)*. s.l.: JRC.

Foray, D. and Goenaga, X., 2013. *The Goals of Smart Specialisation*. Seville: JRC.

Getimis, P., 2003. Improving European Union Regional Policy by Learning from the Past in View of Enlargement. *European Planning Studies*, 11(1), pp. 77–87.

Gheorghiu, R., 2014. *ERAWATCH Country Reports 2013: Romania*. Seville: EC JRC-IPTS.

Gheorghiu, R., 2015. *RIO Country Report Romania 2014*. Seville: EC JRC-IPTS.

Grävingholt, J., Doerr, B., Meissner, K., Pletziger, S., von Rümker, J. and Weikert, J., 2006. *Strengthening Participation through Decentralisation: Findings on Local Economic Development in Kyrgyzstan*. Bonn: German Development Institute.

Guimón, J., 2013. *Smart Decentralization of Innovation Policies*. s.l.: World Bank and OECD.

Hebakova, L. and Kostic, M., 2009. *ERAWATCH Country Report 2008. An Assessment of Research System and Policies. Czech Republic*. Seville: EC, JRC-IPTS, DGR.

Hooghe, L., Marks, G. and Schakel, A., 2009. *The Rise of Regional Authority. A Comparative Study of 42 Democracies (1590–2006)*. Amsterdam: s.n.

Izsak, K., 2012. *Regionalisation of Research and Innovation Policies in Europe*.Belgium: Technopolis Group.

Karo, E. and Kattel, R., 2015. Economic Development and Evolving State Capacities in Central and Eastern Europe: Can 'Smart Specialization' Make a Difference? *Journal of Economic Policy Reform*, 18(2), pp. 172–187.

Klepka, M., 2005. *Raport z inwentaryzacji Regionalnych Strategii Innowacji (RIS) w Polsce*. Warszawa: Krajowy Punkt Kontaktowy Programów Badawczych UE.

Koschatzky, K., 2005. The Regionalization of Innovation Policy: New Options for Regional Change? In: G. Fuchs and P. Shapira, eds. *Rethinking Regional Innovation and Change: Path Dependency or Regional Breakthrough*. Boston: Springer Science + Business Media, Inc., pp. 291–311.

Kroll, H., 2015. Efforts to Implement Smart Specialization in Practice: Leading Unlike Horses to the Water. *European Planning Studies*, 23(10), pp. 2079–2098.

Kyriakou, D. and Periáñez-Forte, I., 2016. *Entrepreneurial Discovery Processes*. s.l.: EC, JRC-IPTS.

Lépineux, F., 2005. Stakeholder Theory, Society and Social Cohesion. *Corporate Governance: The International Journal of Business in Society*, 5(2), pp. 99–110.

Manor, J., 1999. *The Political Economy of Democratic Decentralisation*. Washington, DC: World Bank.

Mercado, A., 2012. Social Inclusion or Social Illusion: The Challenges of Social Inclusion, Social Participation and Social Cohesion in Venezuelan S&T Policy. *Science and Public Policy*, 39(5), pp. 592–601.

Meske, W., 1998. *Institutional Transformation of S&T Systems in the European Economies in Transition: Comparative Analysis*. Leibniz: WZB Discussion Paper.

MG, 2013. *Strategia Innowacyjności i Efektywności Gospodarki. Dynamiczna Polska*. Warsaw: MG.

Mieszkowski, K. and Kardas, M., 2015. Facilitating an Entrepreneurial Discovery Process for Smart Specialisation: The Case of Poland. *Journal of the Knowledge Economy*, 6(2), pp. 357–384.

Mineva, S. D. and Stefanov, R., 2013. *ERAWATCH Country Reports 2011: Bulgaria.* Seville: EC JRC-IPTS.

Mitchell, R. K., Agle, B. R. and Wood, D. J., 1997. Toward a Theory of Stakeholder Identification and Salience: Defining the Principle of Who and What Really Counts. *The Academy of Management Review*, 22(4), pp. 853–886.

Müller, U. and Haisch, T., 2009. *From Subsidiarity to Success: The Impact of Decentralisation on Economic Growth, Summary and Conclusions.* BAK Basel Economics.

Myant, M. and Drahokoupil, J., 2010. *Transition Economies: Political Economy in Russia, Eastern Europe and Central Asia.* New York: Wiley.

OECD, 2011. *OECD Reviews of Regional Innovation: Regions and Innovation Policy.* Paris: OECD.

Oldřich, H., Pavel, G. and Jiří, N., 2011. Regional Innovation Strategies in the Czech Republic. *Journal of Competitiveness*, 2, pp. 11–19.

Panth, S., 2011. *Meaningful Citizen Participation in Decentralization and Local Governance.* [Online] Available at: http://blogs.worldbank.org/publicsphere/meaningful-citizen-participation-decentralization-and-local-governance [Accessed 15/07/2015].

Phillips, R., 2003. Stakeholder Legitimacy. *Business Ethics Quarterly*, 13(1), pp. 25–41.

Pollitt, C., Birchall, J. and Putman, K., 1998. *Decentralising Public Service Management.* London: Palgrave Macmillan.

Ranga, M., 2011. *ERAWATCH Country Report 2010: Romania.* Seville: EC, JRC-IPTS, DG RTD.

Ranga, M., 2013. *ERAWATCH Country Repots 2011: Romania.* Seville: EC JRC-IPTS.

Rodríguez-Pose, A., di. Cataldo, M. and Rainoldi, A., 2014. *The Role of Government Institutions for Smart Specialisation and Regional Development.* Seville: JRC-IPTS.

S3 Platform, 2015. *Benchmarking Regional Structure.* Seville: s.n.

Sandu, S., Zaman, G., Gheorghiu, R. and Modoran, C., 2009. *ERAWATCH Country Report 2008. An Assessment of Research System and Policies: Romania.* Seville: EC, JRC-IPTS, DGR.

Sejm, 1998. *Ustawa z dnia 5 czerwca 1998 r. o samorządzie województwa.* Warsaw: Dz.U.

Sejm, 2006. *Ustawa z dnia 6 grudnia 2006 r. o zasadach prowadzenia polityki rozwoju.* Warsaw: Dz.U.

Srholec, M., 2014. *ERAWATCH Country Reports 2013: Czech Republic.* Seville: EC JRC-IPTS.

Srholec, M., 2015. *RIO Country Report Czech Republic 2014.* Luxembourg: EC JRC-IPTS.

Todeva, E., 2015. *RIO Country Report Bulgaria 2014.* Seville: EC JRC-IPTS.

UNDP, 2004. *Decentralised Governance for Development: A Combined Practice Note on Decentralisation, Local Governance and Urban/Rural Development.* s.l.: s.n.

White, S., 2011. *Government Decentralization in the 21st Cenury.* Washington, DC: Center for Strategic and international Studies.

World Bank, 2015. [Online] Available at: http://www1.worldbank.org/publicsector/decentralization/political.htm [Accessed 15/07/2015].

Yang, K., 2005. Public Administrators' Trust in Citizens: A Missing Link in Citizen Involvement Efforts. *Public Administration Review*, 65(3), pp. 273–285.

Żurek, M., 2013. Próba klasyfikacji i typologii podejścia Multi-level Governance. In: J. Ruszkowski and L. Wojnicz, eds. *Multi-level Governance w Unii Europejskiej.* Szczecin-Warszawa: Instytut Politologii i Europeistyki Uniwersytetu Szczecińskiego, Instytut Europeistyki Uniwersytetu Warszawskiego, pp. 87–106.

Conclusion

There is an old quip that philosophy is like looking for a black cat in a dark room; capturing the essence of the entrepreneurial discovery process in smart specialisation approaches is similarly straightforward – only you don't know a priori what the cat or the room look like. Quips notwithstanding, this book is aimed at drawing a picture of what to expect, what to pursue, and what to avoid on the entrepreneurial discovery process (EDP) journey.

This is timely, due to the growing popularity of smart specialisation in diverse circles, as well as to the fact that its initial formulation left considerable latitude for policy makers to interpret the specific content and implications of its prescriptions in any particular set of circumstances. This is in principle good news since the generic approach has a strong potential to transform regional innovation policy making it more effective and efficient relative to the more traditional 'regional strategies'. However fast growing popularity and high flexibility entail also great risks: the language of entrepreneurial discovery and smart specialisation becomes commonplace in the EU cohesion policy, but what we see being implemented in practice is often the rhetoric not the substance. The risk is that smart specialisation may be implemented in a way that turns it into a top-down planning procedure, because of a misunderstanding of the importance of the entrepreneurial discovery process.

There is hence a need to anchor the EDP operationally at the centre of smart specialisation strategies (the S3 process), and, in turn, anchor the S3 process on a profound, no-stone-left-unturned EDP.

The latter can be facilitated by a) supporting cross-sectoral and inter-institutional connections and collaborations in order to facilitate new knowledge combination and integration, as well as mobilising potential initiators/coordinators of collective projects of ED; b) deploying ED infrastructures under the form of platforms of tools and services to support interdisciplinary and intersectoral explorations and exploitations of new opportunities; c) generating the proper incentives to encourage and support risky collaborative projects exploring a new domain of opportunities and structuring these incentives in such a way that information spillovers (about the discovery) are maximized; d) identifying and assessing the most promising projects in order to prioritise them and support the early growth of the new activities.

A regional strategy that is characterized by the centrality of ED as a mechanism to generate the knowledge-input to set priorities provides great opportunities for regional policy to develop and cultivate new features such as embeddedness (i.e. an ability to develop and maintain a high intensity of interactions and communications with the private sector and other local stakeholders), an experimentalist culture and a dynamic and long-term vision.

The aforementioned risk of reversing the key bottom-up feature of the smart specialisation process, most clearly manifested in the EDP, towards a top-down corruption of its essence should be taken seriously. As Chapter 2 on exit and voice argues, one must guard against top-down research-plan-ning-driven approaches (as opposed to the place-based, regional economic transformation of S3) which can be detrimental to the EDP and the smart specialisation process. Similarly one must guard against the other two great pitfalls facing the EDP implementation process. The first is the risk of further entrenchment of incumbent firms, where the voiceless (e.g. the firms that are yet to emerge) remain disenfranchised; the second involves the difficulties/ risks (e.g. free-riding) when organising/promoting collective action involving firms that are in principle competitors. We propose arguments and steps to address and help mitigate those risks.

Moreover, there is a complex relationship between the EDP and the insti-tutional context within which it occurs. Four central conclusions emerge from this exercise. First, entrepreneurial actors, policy makers and society more broadly all assume roles within the entrepreneurial discovery process and no single actor's role is more important than another's. Second, there are a range of methods through which policy makers may engage local stake-holders, but it is essential, irrespective of method, that a sound relationship is developed between the two parties to permit meaningful interaction and the sharing of insights and knowledge. Third, the institutional dimension of EDP cannot be overlooked as the institutional context influences the viability and outcomes of EDP. Fourth, and finally, EDP can, and in fact must, occur in both strong and weak institutional contexts, although external intervention will likely be necessary in adverse institutional environments to overcome the constraints and barriers that weaker institutions impose.

At the core of this institutional context is the public sector whose ability to innovate, and to foster innovation, will be tested, but also forged through quite demanding EDP. This moreover will be taking place in a political culture becoming increasingly contradictory: while it extols public sector experimenta-tion when it leads to successful innovation, it berates public sector managers if they make a mistake. In other words the public sector is enjoined to innovate, so long as it does not lead to mistakes or failures, outcomes that tend to trigger public sector crises and political scandals. To redress this, national govern-ments will need to deal frankly with three taboo issues that have stymied public sector innovation – namely feedback, failure and learning.

If the deep cultural barriers to public sector innovation can be tackled in a more open and honest fashion – and feedback, failure and learning are simply three of the most egregious examples – then public bodies will be better equipped to promote innovation in and through the public sector.

Public sector institutions must engage fruitfully with private sector entities in order for the EDP to be productive; both sides must adapt to the requirements of the process. Steps which can facilitate this adaptation involve focusing on common challenges/interests, beyond proprietary knowledge areas; de-stigmatising and extracting value out of failure, through appropriate knowledge management systems; pursuing priorities that are matched by powerful spillover mechanisms; promoting cross-border partnerships; targeting public procurement to foster innovation; developing tailor-made performance metrics, to encourage innovation and discourage short-termism; creating fora where opinions expressed can stay confidential; and encouraging institutional and resource-assignment flexibility.

A set of key institutions, which in many ways combine both public and private sector characteristics, includes research performing institutions such as Research and Technology Organisations (RTOs). These institutions have a policy role and have capabilities to identify industry needs and technological opportunities as a key input into the EDP. Second, being increasingly international organisations, they can collect information on international R&I markets and facilitate access to global knowledge for regional firms through their networks and research collaborations. Third, they often have a central role in the development of particular cluster groupings through their specialization around core technologies, and as such can be a central player in the development of such technology and business clusters.

Much of the success of a continuous EDP depends on monitoring. Monitoring provides the necessary information to analyse the constituents and causal relationships defining the strategy, and in this connotation it is essential for the realization of strategy outcomes. It can also have an emergent advocacy function towards stakeholders and the broader community of citizens and organizations which constitute the ultimate recipients of the policy strategy. Both these functions are important for the sustainability of the policy process.

A cyclical view of the policy process is the most meaningful way to conceive policy making in a world characterized by fundamental uncertainty about the future, and it is even more necessary when policies explicitly aim at pursuing innovation in the current state of affairs. Stakeholder involvement in strategy design and implementation and hence in strategy monitoring is necessary in order to close potential implementation and legitimacy gaps and it is instrumental for achieving an effective and sustainable policy cycle. In the context of smart specialisation, this implies that the entrepreneurial discovery process through which tacit knowledge about the states of the world is gathered, compared, integrated and distilled into decisions needs to be a permanent and recursive process that goes hand in hand with policy implementation and not just a phase of strategy design.

Finally, the sections on case studies, covering regions with very different geographic and economic characteristics, provide a wealth of information on

the intricacies of specific cases, demonstrating the wisdom of insisting, as the
S3 approach does, that there can be no one-size-fits-all policy. The variety of
responses and interactions with local contexts, administration practices, etc.
also suggests that no a priori plan survives intact its contact with real conditions in the field (to paraphrase Moltke's famous dictum, often attributed
to Eisenhower). The key to success is adaptability, feedback, and making
the best use of what is available, instead of insisting on ideal-type responses/
resources that are rarely, if ever, available.

Index

Page numbers in *italic* indicate tables. Page numbers in **bold** indicate figures.